Playground

A Childhood Lost Inside
the Playboy Mansion

Playground

JENNIFER SAGINOR

HarperEntertainment
An Imprint of HarperCollinsPublishers

While this is a true account of my life and times growing up in and around the Playboy Mansion, I have decided to change the names of all of my cohorts from that time, with the exception of Hugh Hefner and the other celebrities who traveled in the same circles. If any of my fictional names are also the names of actual individuals, it is merely coincidental.

HarperCollins books may be purchased for educational, business, or sales promotional use. For information please write: Special Markets Department, HarperCollins Publishers, 10 East 53rd Street, New York, NY 10022.

FIRST EDITION

Designed by Jeffrey Pennington

Printed on acid-free paper

Library of Congress Cataloging-in-Publication Data

Saginor, Jennifer.
    Playground : a childhood lost inside the Playboy Mansion / by Jennifer Saginor.— 1st ed.
        p.   cm.
    ISBN 0-06-076156-3 (hc : alk. paper)
    1. Saginor, Jennifer.   2. Playboy Enterprises—Biography.   3. Children of divorced parents—Psychology—Biography.   4. Girls—Conduct of life.   I. Title.

HQ777.5.S24 2005
306.89'092—dc22
[B]   2004059947

05 06 07 08 09 WBC /RRD 10 9 8 7 6 5 4 3 2 1

In loving memory of Ashley Boyer,
who inspired me to speak the truth

Acknowledgments

Jennifer Joel—my agent who has supported me since day one and persistently found a way to make this book see the light of day.

Josh Behar—my fabulous editor. Thank you for always seeing beyond the bullshit. You never once doubted me or anything you read, even if we had to delete it.

Beth Silfin—my attorney at HarperCollins. I truly appreciate all the time you invested in making this book happen.

Seale Ballenger—publicist extraordinaire. He is always one step ahead of me, providing as much compassion as expertise.

The Poker Boys—how would I survive without you? A special thanks to Asher and Kenny.

To my friends—you know who you are. Thank you all for your help along the way. I am sure you are sick of hearing about this book. We can talk about something else now.

To my family—hopefully we can close this chapter and begin a new one . . . that is, if we are still on speaking terms.

In the journey to unravel our past we are confronted by our demons. In order to avoid our demons we create distractions. It's in these distractions we will find our own personal playground.

—JS

One

*I*t's 1975. I'm six when I see sex for the first time.

After school, I wait alone by the fence. Most of the other kids have gone home. I push my Coke-bottle-thick glasses up my small nose as my green eyes squint against the sun. I pull my long brown hair back into a ponytail.

Dad's housekeeper, Carmela, a Hispanic woman with broken English, blares the horn of Dad's champagne Rolls-Royce convertible from across the street. She picks me up today because Dad is too busy.

Carmela cooks, cleans, and drives, but mostly she is my friend.

"*Jennifer!*" she hollers.

I rush to the car and duck inside.

"Where's your sister?" she asks.

"She's at Mom's. She stayed home sick," I tell her.

Carmela drives the car carefully to my father's five-bedroom, six-bathroom estate in the heart of Beverly Hills. Pulling into the circular driveway, the automatic gate opens. Water trickles down a large Mediterranean-style fountain.

Inside the foyer, a huge staircase parts to the left and right, dividing the room. The walls display the works of Alberto Vargas: nude women with perky breasts and thin legs, and nude women clad in black fishnet and holding whips posing next to white dogs. Dad's favorite is titled *Temptation*.

Arcade games and pinball machines line the living room walls and an air hockey table sits in the center. In the corner is an old-style jukebox. I punch in Linda Ronstadt and Kenny Rogers since my father's always telling me how lucky I am to know them.

I throw my Hello Kitty purse on the leather sofa and play a quick game of pinball. After beating my highest score, I go into the kitchen for a grilled cheese sandwich.

Carmela tells me now there's a note from my father at the top of the staircase in the pair of oversize porcelain breasts designed to hold mail. The note is placed between the breasts and reads, "I'm up at the Mansion. Have Carmela drop you off if you're bored."

I crumple the note, flicking it at the enormous Andy Warhol portrait displaying six different angles of my father's face on the wall.

I tear my eyes away from his multiple faces and ask Carmela to take me to Dad.

As we're driving down Sunset Boulevard my curiosity gets the best of me and I ask, "What's the Mansion?"

"You know, Jennifer, I am just supposed to drive you, you should ask your father," Carmela rambles.

We pull up to a gigantic barred black gate. I start to get a sick feeling in my stomach. We look around for a few minutes until we hear a voice coming from a large rock next to Carmela's window. If you look closely, you can see a small round speaker inside the rock.

"Carmela Delatora. I have Jennifer Saginor," she announces and the enormous gates open.

We drive up a long driveway and I notice at least five gardeners working on the cliff-like lawn. A castle comes into view and I instantly feel like Alice in Wonderland, diving into the Great Unknown. My nerves take over again as we near the massive gray stone mansion before us. I tell Carmela I've changed my mind and to please take me home. She assures me that my father is waiting inside as she pulls around the circular driveway. I ask her to come in, but she says that it would not be right.

Reluctantly, I slip out of the car and begin the journey of my life.

I enter a grand marble foyer to find men lined up in funny black penguin suits. The men smile at me creepily; they already know my name. One of them escorts me through an enormous living room with the biggest television screen I've ever seen. It's like a movie theater, but with soft plush couches, a fireplace, a grand piano, and as much free popcorn as you want. Lounging girls in short shorts, poufy hair, and Heaven T-shirts stare at me as I pass.

The butler opens the doors to a smoky room where five men glance up for a split second. They're playing cards. There's a built-in backgammon table that is surrounded by a comfy couch and leather chairs. My father's eyes instantly light up at the sight of me as he proudly introduces me to the men one by one. They nod, distractedly, and wave hello. Dad motions for me to say hello to Hef, the handsome, kind-looking man dressed casually in a silk robe.

"Hello, darling." Hef smiles graciously, as if he's known me my whole life. "It's a pleasure to finally meet you. Doc, you have such an adorable daughter, are you sure you're related?"

"Why, thanks, Hef. Your girls aren't so bad themselves."

Dad excuses himself and leads me through the screening room, where four young blondes jump up to kiss him and wrap their skinny arms around him.

Dad is a powerfully built man in his forties, with broad shoulders, an athletic body, manicured hands, and a handsome face—a face people turn to look at. He's a doctor, but he looks more like a movie star playing the part of one.

He's the kind of guy everyone wants to know.

My father, a bookworm from Ohio, graduated at the top of his Dartmouth class Phi Beta Kappa, and from Harvard Medical School. He then moved to Los Angeles and opened a private medical practice in Beverly Hills. He soon became a renowned Hollywood fitness internist during a time when various weight-loss regimens, including the Beverly Hills diet, a pineapple and grapefruit diet, the cabbage soup diet, amphetamines, and unidentified vitamin shots, were beginning to peak in popularity.

As far as his rich and famous Los Angeles patients were concerned, he was not just a world-class doctor but also a true genius. He regularly prescribed the appetite suppressants they so coveted. Pill popping was trendy and purses had become portable pharmacies. Everyone knew if you were famous and in real or imaginary pain, prescriptions were a phone call away. Though concerned for their reputations and restricted by a code of ethics, doctors made names for themselves by providing legal ways for their clients to get high. And my dad was the biggest name in Beverly Hills. Before long, my father was referred to as "Dr. Feel Good." All this in addition to his regular practice as an internist.

The legitimate part of his practice skyrocketed when Suzanne Pleshette wrote a heartfelt poem that she dedicated to him and read aloud on *The Tonight Show*. This poem announced to the world how her diagnostician saved her life.

Shortly thereafter, the Hollywood invitations began to pour in.

My parents were treated with celebrity status at movie premieres, nightclubs, and art openings. There was a two-month waiting list to book an appointment. His office was always full of rock stars, professional athletes, Playmates, models, and actresses sucking on sugar-free lollipops with hopes of transforming themselves into perfection.

One of the Playmates teases his sandy-blond hair and then looks down at me. "Who's this pretty young thing?" she asks in a high-pitched voice.

"Have you met my daughter?" Dad asks.

The girl giggles, bends over, and shakes my hand. I stare at her big boobs as my father pulls me into the marble foyer now packed with bright, smiling faces. We climb the staircase as he leads me down the upstairs hallway. A tall glass cabinet filled with naked figurines in weird positions catches my eye.

Hundreds of framed photographs line the hallway. My father points out Farrah Fawcett, Vanna White, Dorothy Stratten, Kenny Rogers, Dolly Parton, James Caan, Aaron Spelling, Jimmy Connors, Sammy Davis Jr., and Frank Sinatra, who he says are all patients.

We stop in front of a closed door.

"Number two is my room. If you need anything, the butlers will get it for you."

Dad opens the door. The room is massive. There's a king-size bed to the left and windows overlooking the garden to the right. An armoire with a large television is in front of the bed along with a wooden chest of drawers. I take a few steps into the room and run past the closets to the back where there's a marble bathroom with two toilets!

"Use the phone to order anything you want. I have to get back to the game," Dad instructs, hugging me good-bye.

When he's gone, I open the door and walk slowly down the hallway, making my way back down the grand staircase. I wander through a circus of strangers. Everyone looks past me. I open a small stained-glass door with an iron knob, which leads to the backyard.

A butler in a black suit startles me as I step into the outdoors.

"Your father asked me to show you the pool," he says, peering down at me.

"How do you know who I am?"

"I just do." He smiles.

The butler escorts me down a cobblestone pathway, through the backyard and into a rock-lined corridor with tons of changing rooms. He hands me a robe and towel along with a plastic container filled with bathing suits.

"Is there one for me?"

"Of course. Mr. Hefner is very accommodating to his friends and family," the butler informs me.

I select a slightly oversize orange polka-dot bikini, and the butler guides me into one of the changing rooms. He closes the door as he leaves.

I look around the changing room noticing the open shower and plants covering the glass window. Different-colored robes and matching towels line the closets. One of the shelves has an enormous supply of Listerine, Q-tips, Dove soap, Lubriderm lotion, Vaseline, aspirin, toothbrushes, and boxes of Trojans stacked neatly on shelves.

After changing, I open the door to find the butler waiting for me outside.

"Ready?" he asks and we walk past an outdoor bar and over to a bigger section of the pool.

"You don't have to watch me," I tell him.

"That's all right, I don't mind." He smiles as I get in and swim under the water, away from him.

There is a mountain in the center of the pool that creates a U shape, so I follow it around the bend. Beyond the ripples from the waterfall, I notice a strange, spooky black hole that looks like it could suck me in if I'm not careful. I swim over to take a closer look; it appears to be some sort of tunnel.

"Stay away from the tunnel!" the butler shouts as I come up for air.

"Why?"

"It's for adults," he says sternly, so I swim over to the step in the shallow end.

"I'm thirsty. Can I have something to drink?"

"What would you like?"

"Juice, please."

"Do you mind stepping out of the pool while I'm gone?"

"Sure," I say, trying to be the picture of sweetness.

When the butler is out of sight, I dive back in and swim underwater toward the tunnel. As the black hole comes into view, goose bumps prickle up and down my arms and legs. I circle around it for a few seconds. The water seems different here: it's darker and there's a strong current swirling around the rocks.

Closing my eyes, I envision a mystical passage into a foreign land.

I plunge in, holding my breath.

Underwater, panic sets in immediately as my hands feel along the endless, rock-lined passage. I try to turn around, but the water is rushing too quickly and I become disoriented, my lungs aching for breath. I push myself forward, willing myself to the end, hoping desperately that there is an end.

I push against the tunnel with my feet, forcing myself upward. Finally, I surface. I look around frantically while taking huge gulps of air.

I'm in a large dark cave. There is only candlelight. The Beatles' "Lucy in the Sky with Diamonds" plays softly. There are several couches lining the interior of the cave, but I can't see well, so I swim over to one of the bigger pools, paddling with all my might to hold myself up. I lean against a jet, and finally it registers—I'm in a gigantic Jacuzzi!

I hear moaning sounds over the gurgles of water. I peek around to locate where the noise is coming from. My eyes squint as they begin to investigate.

Something moves on one of the couches. The something becomes clearer and I see that it is a naked man. There is another figure too. A naked lady is sitting on top of him and she's bouncing up and down. Her boobs are flying everywhere. I know that I'm not supposed to be seeing this. Later I learn it was John Belushi screwing one of the Playmates.

I am no longer six. I have grown to full maturity in a matter of seconds.

The lady moans.

I sneeze.

"Hey! What are you doing in here?" the guy yells, as he continues bucking under the moaning girl.

Terrified, I take a deep breath, dive into the pool, beneath a waterfall, and swim frantically out of the Jacuzzi. I come up for air and open my eyes. The butler's face stares back at me.

"I was playing hide-and-seek and got lost," I say quickly.

I climb out and race past him, wiggling my way into the changing rooms. I'm so completely shocked that I throw on my clothes, barely drying myself. I sneak back down the hallway made of rocks, coming to a halt as the couple from the cave heads my way.

They're coming after me.

I duck down another outdoor hallway, running toward a small white door. I throw myself through the door and am bombarded by flapping wings. I hit the floor as screeching noises thunder overhead.

It feels like an hour of being surrounded by shrieks and cries before I realize I'm in a huge birdhouse.

I dart outside again. It's getting dark and I don't know which way to go. I'm too terrified to go back to the Mansion because now it looks like a haunted house. I stop to catch my breath when a man with a walkie-talkie appears out of nowhere. My stomach drops as I skitter down a pathway lined with tall trees and thick grass. I hide behind a large shrub.

Another man is walking down the path toward my hiding place. There is a small house on the grounds, much smaller and safer looking than the haunted Mansion, so I make a run for it. The lights are on inside and I race up the steps to the front door. It's unlocked. I turn the handle and peer cautiously into the dimly lit room. The room's interior looks like a warm, cozy lodge decorated with high beamed ceilings, rustic wood paneling, and green plaid carpet. An old-fashioned piano plays eerily by itself in the corner. Objects of Pop Art fill the corners: oversize bottles of Pepsi and Coke, and cans of Campbell's soup. Images of icons of the forties and fifties like Judy Garland, Elizabeth Taylor, Liza Minnelli, and Marilyn Monroe line the walls. The room has all my favorite pinball machines.

I have found the coolest, most secret arcade.

I grab handfuls of red and yellow gumballs from bowls on the tables in the middle of the room, and stuff them into my pockets. There's a picture of Hef surrounded by girls on one of the pinball machines.

I see shadows flickering in a blue-painted room. I dash across the arcade, through a mirrored door, and almost trip as I sink into carpet three inches deep. There are mirrors on every wall, even on the ceiling. I lock the door, noticing a box of Kleenex, pads of paper with bunny ears on them, and a sea of cushions on the floor.

Sinking back into the carpet, I flip the television on and see naked people rolling around on the screen! I spin around, wondering if anyone is watching. The images remind me of the man and lady in the Jacuzzi. The bottom of the screen reads, You are watching the Playboy Channel.

I'm afraid and curious at the same time. Someone pounds on the door.

"Jennifer!" Dad raises his voice.

I shut off the television and immediately begin taking hoards of gumballs out of my pockets, shoving them underneath the pillows.

"Hang on, I'm trying to open the door," my voice quivers.

Please, God, don't let him be mad at me. I promise I'll never go into that cave again. He continues banging on the door as I frantically try to unlock it. The door finally opens and my father hovers over me!

"Don't ever lock this door again!" he shouts.

We ride home in silence. My heart races. Am I in trouble? What if Dad knows I saw those people?

Dad pops in a cassette of the Eagles. I catch him stealing glances at me, but I don't turn my head. He begins to sing along to the words and eventually I begin to relax.

Two

It's Thursday, Dad's day with us, and I can't wait to jump in his pool. The school bell rings and I race through the hallway and run outside to wait for Carmela to pick me up.

I see Dad's Rolls-Royce parked across the street with Christopher Cross blaring from his tape deck. My sister, Savannah, waves me over.

Savannah is about two and half years younger than I am. She's a cute little girl with golden blond hair, big blue eyes, and a smile that illuminates a room. She's a typical girl, one who likes to wear dainty sundresses and tie yellow bows in her hair. Her favorite thing to do is put on her ballerina leotard and dance around the house. She is happy but also emotionally fragile and quick to cry.

She slides into the backseat of the car as I hop into the front seat, taking my position next to my father.

"I need to make a quick stop at the Mansion," Dad tells us.

"We want go to McDonald's," I whine.

"Don't bug me," he snaps back and my stomach tightens. He's been snapping at me more and more recently. We pull up to those huge iron gates. The rock speaks again and I'm fearful of what this visit will bring.

We head up the long driveway as gardeners spritz the exotic flowers that dot the lawn. The castle comes into view.

"Are we at Disneyland?" Savannah asks.

"It's more like a haunted house," I mumble.

"Why would you tell your sister that?" Dad rasps at me harshly as he hurries us out of the car and into the front door.

Savannah stares at the butlers in the funny black suits. One of them offers to take Dad's briefcase.

"Good afternoon. Should I put this in your room?" the butler asks my father.

"Yes, thank you," he responds.

I don't say anything, but still wonder why my father has a room here when this isn't his house. We follow him upstairs, passing the glass cabinet filled with naked figurines. My sister doesn't even notice. We go inside Room Two and Savannah's eyes open wide. I grab her hand, leading her into the spacious bathroom.

"Wow! There are two toilets!"

"And a Jacuzzi!" I say.

We run our fingers across the smooth marble edge. We peek inside the shower, which is stocked with shampoo, conditioner, and Jergens body lotion.

"You kids can watch television. Jennifer knows what to do if you want anything to eat," Dad shouts before he disappears down the long hallway.

Savannah and I immediately run back into the bedroom and snoop around.

"Look at this." Savannah points to a picture of us on the dresser.

I nod, inquisitively opening drawers and cabinets. I find my father's T-shirts, shorts, and swimming goggles, holding them up for her to see.

"What are these doing here?" Savannah shrugs.

"Hey, want to see the pool?" I ask.

As much as I want to forget what I saw near the pool, I can't get it out of my head. Something inside wants me to show my sister, even though I know it will scare her too.

We walk along the pathway to the forest and keep looking over our shoulders because it feels like we are being watched. Nearby, a monkey screeches. We jump and huddle close together.

"What's that?" my sister asks, slightly shaken.

"It's just the monkey cages," I explain, pretending I've seen them before. "Do you want to go down there?"

We turn off the main pathway and weave our way through a forest of trees and branches. Savannah clings on to me for dear life. I play it off like I know where I'm going. We walk cautiously down the steps as dozens of small monkeys screech at the top of their lungs and jump on the fence in front of us. Scared to death, Savannah and I grab each other, holler, and make a run for it. Savannah trips over a bucket of fruit and begins to cry. My heart breaks when she cries.

"Don't cry. Maybe they're just hungry," I say, trying to comfort her.

I dash back to the bucket to find peanuts and grapes inside.

"They haven't eaten yet. That's why they're screaming. Let's feed them!" I holler.

I wipe the tears off her soft, rosy cheeks. She nods and we grab a few grapes, approaching the cage once again. The monkeys make noise as they gather around, accepting our offerings willfully and playfully. Happy smiles sweep over our faces as they devour the pail of food. We throw kisses to them and continue roaming.

Turning another corner, we discover a group of blonde tan girls in bikinis playing volleyball. My sister laughs because one of the girls isn't wearing a top and her boobs bounce, practically hitting her in the face.

"Look at all the booby ladies!" she says.

We giggle, noticing my father, Hef, and a few other men surrounded by more topless women by the pool.

"Ew! Gross!"

Savannah and I nudge each other.

"Why are they naked?" Savannah asks.

"I don't know. Let's spy on them."

We sneak through the bushes, whispering into pretend walkie-talkies, ending up near the fishpond, where Savannah opens the wooden food basket, drawing all the fish over to us. The giant koi make loud splashing noises and we try to calm them down, but it's too late. Dad spots us and I freeze momentarily because I'm not sure whether we're supposed to be out here. He then waves us over. He's in a tight blue Speedo bathing suit, sitting with a group of men smoking cigars and playing backgammon as girls fawn all over them.

"Hi, girls!"

I stare at my father, surprised by his cheerfulness as he introduces us to the ladies whose names all sound the same. Hef hugs us both and we feel special.

"Hello, darlings," he says, his warm voice already familiar to me.

His cheek is soft when I kiss him, and it is no wonder why all the girls like him so much. Hef's gentleness is comforting.

Out of the corner of my eye, I see an annoying lady nudge Dad.

"Do you think I need to lose weight?" she asks.

"You could drop a few pounds," Dad answers and she slaps him playfully.

"And about these things," he squeezes her breasts, "they could definitely be bigger."

Dad chuckles as he reaches for something in his black medical bag.

I overhear two Playmates whisper to each other.

"He's Hef's doctor," one Playmate informs the other.

"What about me? Am I fat?" another one whines to my father.

"Why don't we go upstairs and I can take a look," Dad says, giggling like a boy.

"Do I look fat?" Savannah blurts out.

"Sugarplum, we won't know for a few more years, but you can come see me whenever you want, just like the Playmates do."

"What's a Playmate?" Savannah asks.

"They're models," Dad whispers back.

"Why are they naked?"

"Because they're proud of their bodies," he explains firmly, as his eyebrows lower and his facial expression hardens.

Clouds pass over us briefly.

"We got to feed the monkeys," I tell Hef, who smiles instantly, giving me attention. "They came over to us, and we even pet one."

"They must like you. They hide whenever your father goes anywhere near them," Hef chuckles with ease.

"Little fuckers," Dad laughs.

"I want to feed the monkeys!" some blonde shouts.

"I've got a hungry monkey for you," a hairy tan guy with a mustache offers.

"Spoken from the mouth of a true smut star!" Dad laughs.

"At least I'm paid well for my time," the guy responds.

Dad lifts the thinnest blonde in the air like a child. "Let's go, sweetheart."

My face turns beet red as I watch him and the bimbo walk off. I'm not sure if I'm mad because he is taking her to see the monkeys or that he didn't take us.

A tall, conservative, aloof-looking woman approaches, smiling at us in a parental way like she knows us. Her name is Crawford. The girls are overly friendly to her. Crawford bends down and whispers something into Hef's ear and I try to overhear what she says.

"I am being summoned; excuse me. I will return shortly," Hef announces.

He smiles warmly at Savannah and me before he leaves.

The sun is going down and the Playmates are getting cold. Savannah and I are wrapped in towels. Dad still hasn't returned from feeding the monkeys and the girls ask if we're staying for the party.

"It's movie night," one of them hoots.

"We didn't bring any clothes," I say, looking down at my dirty T-shirt and shorts.

"Don't worry, we'll doll you up!" the Playmates shout and they grab their sunglasses, chattering to one another as we follow behind, seemingly forgotten.

"Living at the Mansion has been so incredible. My friends back home still don't know what to make of all it," one of them boasts.

"Someone told me if I fucked the Doc I could be a centerfold."

"Or at least get free prescriptions."

"Fuck 'em; take them for all they're worth," one girl whispers to another. This was clearly their attitude.

"Gold digger," another says.

"Her conscious lies somewhere between Gucci and Prada."

The girls slap each other high-five.

These girls are from outer space. Savannah and I glance at each other and they must pick up our vibe because they finally ask, "Wait, who's your father?"

"The Doc," we tell them.

"Wait, who's your dad?" another dingbat asks, like she didn't hear us the first time.

"Oh my God! Oh my God! That's your father? I love him! I didn't know he had kids! He put me on my diet!"

"So your Dad and Hef are really good friends, huh?" asks one of the Playmates.

I'm not sure if she means to sound stupid or if she just is. Either way, I decide not to respond.

"We went to a party with him the other night. What's it like being his daughter?" a Playmate asks and we shrug.

We enter a small house through the kitchen door. It reminds

me of *Little House on the Prairie* because there's lots of wood and everything seems old-fashioned. The living room has exercise equipment and the girls jump on as one of them grabs my sister's arm.

"Let's find you something to wear!"

My sister's eyes perk up. The girls blast Donna Summer and dance around, grabbing bottles of Pepsi out of the fridge.

"I'll be right back," I tell Savannah, but she doesn't hear me. She's too busy playing with her new gold hoop earrings.

As I wander the grounds, I realize this has turned into more than just a quick visit. I pass the tennis court and outdoor bar with white tables and yellow umbrellas. I turn right down a long grass-lined pathway leading me back to the castle. Entering the large front door, I try to recall which way to go. I turn left, noticing a small door, so I peek inside. It's a phone room.

I pick up one of the phones. "Security," a man's voice says on the other end.

I hang up instantly.

On the table is a black matchbox with white rabbit ears, so I stick it in my pocket and leave, startled by a butler when I exit.

"Are you looking for your father?"

"Yes," I answer, fearful he knows I took the matches.

"He is in the library."

I smile and walk slowly past the screening room, where a pretty young girl with hazel eyes sits on the couch staring into space. I look at her, but she doesn't flinch. What is she staring at? I push my way through a purple velvet curtain and find myself in a room feeling around for a doorknob. I push on it hesitantly and am bombarded with loud men shouting.

"Park Avenue!"

"Madison Avenue! Hand it over, baby!"

"Jail time for you, sucker!" another guy yells.

I feel small, embarrassed. Hef acknowledges me first.

"Well, look who we have here. Hello, darling," Hef says, welcoming me in his usual charming way.

I kiss him on the cheek again as if he's my second dad and then make my way over to my father. I sit on his lap, feeling special because I'm the only girl in the room. I recognize one of the Playmates on a cover of a magazine as I pet a small black poodle, which I'm told lives upstairs with one of Hef's friends.

I wonder why so many people live here, but I never ask.

"Have you seen Vanessa lately? Man, she has a phenomenal rack," the guy with a mustache blurts out.

"Great work. Who'd you refer her to?" a tall guy with broad shoulders asks as he nudges my father.

"I have my sources," Dad laughs.

"She looks like that stripper—you know, the one from last weekend," the man with the poodle says.

"Which one, the blonde, the blonde, or the other blonde?" They laugh.

I slip out of the library and trace my steps back to the prairie house to check on Savannah.

When I enter the room, she's been done up in a flapper outfit.

"Why are you wearing that?" I ask.

Savannah ignores me because she's too busy parading around, showing off her sparkling Bulova jewels and feathered Lacroix scarf.

I weave my way through the fashion frenzy, wandering cautiously down a small hallway of bedrooms. I peek my head into the crack of a doorway, spying on one of the girls as she leans over and sniffs white powder off the dresser. She holds the side of her nose after she lifts up and exhales, "Ah." She pushes a tiny straw into her other nostril, leans down, and sniffs harder this time. It appears painful as she lifts up and shakes her head a bit. I jerk my head back, hiding the instant she turns in my direction.

In another room, a girl poses naked in front of the mirror holding several skimpy outfits up to herself. She clasps a choker around her neck and traces the edge of her fingers down her stomach, touching herself. I stumble back, startled by a woman towering over me in the hallway.

"Your turn to dress up," she smiles.

By now, a dinner party is under way in the main house. We enter the foyer as guests in colorful outfits greet us, dancing to the hustle. We move to the dining room, where a huge buffet is spread out. My father and Hef sit at the head of an oval mahogany table. They seem to be deep in conversation. Dad's face is glowing. It's like no one else is even around. He doesn't notice us until the Playmates scream for his attention, showing off our new outfits. I tap Dad on the shoulder and both of them break their conversation and acknowledge me.

"Hello again, darling. Are you enjoying yourself?" Hef asks.

"The ladies wanted us to wear their clothes, but I didn't want to get too dressy," I tell him.

"In my home, you can wear whatever you're comfortable in," Hef responds warmly.

I grin like I just got all Os for "Outstanding" on my report card.

My sister twirls past us in her oversize dainty blouse and sparkling jewelry. Suddenly, I don't feel as special anymore.

The rest of the ladies come running over. Dad, Hef, and the men greet them with hugs and kisses.

"Don't they look incredible?" one of the Playmates shouts.

"Anything for fashion," another girls says.

"You can dress me any day," the big-shouldered guy jumps in.

"Or undress me," jokes the guy with the mustache.

"Or we can just play doctor," Dad comments with a devilish grin.

"Maybe I'll do fashion part-time," the Playmate giggles.

"You're hired, little one. Do you want to move in?" Dad jokes.

"Depends on the size of the house," the Playmate responds, as if she's been asked this question before.

Dad squeezes her like she's his daughter, but then kisses her hungrily on the lips.

"The movie is about to begin," a butler announces.

The screening room is filling up fast so Savannah and I race in, jumping on the big velvet cushions on the floor in front of the couches and rows of chairs. Bowls of M&M's and popcorn are everywhere. A cloud of smoke fills the room. Hef sits on the first couch along with my father and a few Playmates who mold themselves in between. A butler comes up to me and asks if I want something to eat.

"Sure," I say, wondering how he knew I was hungry.

I notice Crawford whispering to Hef again. There are lots of secrets here.

It's late when we pull up to Mom's house and kiss Dad good night.

I help Savannah out of the backseat of the car as the front door to Mom's house flies open. She's yelling as she runs toward Dad's Rolls, furious about the late hour on a school night.

My father turns to me. "Don't worry about that bitch," Dad says to me before he drives off.

Savannah and I walk into Mom's house while she continues to chase after Dad's car, still screaming something about the time.

My mother was born and raised in Beverly Hills and was crowned Homecoming Queen at Hamilton High School. She looks like a model, but still has that girl-next-door quality about her with dazzling green eyes, long, slender legs, and silky brown hair that falls just below her shoulders.

She graduated from UCLA, and although her parents had instilled a strong work ethic in her, what they truly wanted was for her to get married to someone respectable and prominent. At twenty-two, she made them proud by marrying a well-known doctor with a very large home in Beverly Hills.

They seemed like a perfect match. They were adored by everyone and soon their calendars were filled with colorful pool parties, round-robin tennis matches, and Sunday brunches at Nate 'n' Al's. They were the charmed newlyweds of Beverly Hills, but it didn't stop there. In the eyes of Mom and her parents, not only had she married successfully but her lifestyle had surpassed their wildest dreams.

Life turned sour when Dad started inviting striking young girls to play tennis in the backyard while Mom helped serve lunch by the pool.

"They're patients. I'm networking. You're being jealous again. You need to see someone for that," Dad began to say.

Mom continued watching Dad flirt incessantly with the pretty girls and in the process made my mother feel stupid and crazy for suspecting anything out of the ordinary. Despite his best efforts to convince her she was the insecure one, instinct warned her this picture wasn't right.

Dad claimed to work late shifts at Cedar-Sinai Hospital and eventually Mom decided to follow him. She drove a block or so behind him and watched as he pulled into another woman's driveway. It was a house call all right, only the blonde she spotted him with was in perfect condition.

When my father returned home that night, my mother tore downstairs to confront him. She accused him of having an affair. I spied on them through the crack in the den door and saw Dad sitting calmly and nonchalantly, with a large black gun on his lap, denying her accusations, turning the conversation around to make her feel guilty for not trusting him.

"I am not having an affair. You're creating this within yourself. You've somehow construed this in your demented mind," he said.

Their argument continued for what seemed like hours until my mother screamed, "I can't even talk to you!" and stormed out. This was the first of many fights between them.

Months later, Mom finally endured enough and although she was afraid to leave him, something inside told her it was the right thing to do.

Mom and Dad separated, and Dad moved out of the house.

One night soon after, while my mother was at dinner, my father and grandfather snuck in the house to take furniture. They moved large, expensive pieces out the front door and were halfway done when my mother returned home. Tempers flared. There was yelling, screaming, and banging. I made myself small as I witnessed the bitter, ugly blowout from the staircase above. My sister was in bed sleeping in her floral wallpapered room beside mine.

"First you cheat on me with some hooker and then you steal my furniture? What is wrong with you?" Mom screamed, throwing old vintage bottles of wine against the wall.

I watched silently as my father's face crumbled and then turned away from the shattering glass.

"What the hell do you think you're doing with my wine?" Dad yelled as he grabbed her by the shoulders.

Traces of red wine dripped down the wall like blood in a horror movie. What I saw became blurry as loud-pitched noises like fingernails screeching down a chalkboard overcame me. My entire world was caving in.

My parents divorced and in the settlement, my father reclaimed the house on Camden and paid my mother to move into a home in West L.A. She obtained custody of my sister and me while Dad's visiting days became Thursdays and every other weekend. Though many afternoons when Mom was working and Dad was busy playing backgammon with Hef by the pool, Carmela would pick us up from school and take us to the Mansion to be with Dad, even though we knew we weren't really going to be with him.

When my parents were together, I had ice cream with my father downstairs in the kitchen every night. I must've been three or four at the time. I don't remember whether he came into my bedroom and woke me or if I heard him and then got out of bed. Each night it was the same: Jamoca Almond Fudge and a tirade of accusations against my mother, who was fast asleep.

His harsh words about my mother resonated into a sort of early brainwashing.

Each night he made it clear that our discussions were private, not to be repeated to anyone. The more he spoke, the more I realized I could not. Any thoughts I had about what he was saying, any opinion I held, froze in my mind and then melted away as quickly as the chocolate on my tongue.

The mean words he said about my mother floated like butterflies around his head as I squinted away their meaning, concentrating only on our intimacy, his love, his availability, his trust in me. Ice cream was one of the first of my father's many enticements to pull me away from my mother.

It's a quiet afternoon in my mother's house. Her home chills me: its perfect order, regimented knickknacks, and white carpet are invitations to disaster. Only Savannah feels at home here. I am careful to avoid contact with any of the antique furniture and crystal vases filled with white silk roses as she and I slide across the hardwood floors in our socks.

I ask Savannah if she wants to play doctor. She wants to have a tea party instead. We settle on dress up. I grab a bunch of tissues and push them up my shirt.

"I'll be the girl. You are the boy," I suggest.

"I want to be the girl," Savannah whines.

"Fine," I grab the tissues and stick them down my pants.

Savannah and I pile pillows in a big circle forming a makeshift Jacuzzi. My pants are down while I adjust the balled-up tissue in my underwear. Savannah has paper boobs the size of footballs, which she fluffs with her hands.

Meanwhile, Mom returns home from her long day at school where she's enrolled in a graduate psychology program, trying to earn her doctorate.

When she was married, Dad didn't want her to work, but now that they're divorced, he only gives her enough money to support us.

Later I'll learn that she was frustrated because she was struggling to get her Ph.D. and work while her friends lunched at the country club, safely entrenched in their marriages to millionaires.

While rummaging through our laundry, Mom finds the Playboy matches I took from the phone room at the Mansion. She examines the black matchbook closely and shrieks when she sees H.M.H. along with the white bunny ears on it. Savannah and I hear Mom's high-pitched screeching and share petrified glances as we hustle to clean the room. I have an anxious feeling in my stomach, the kind I usually get when there's trouble.

We're panicking, scrambling to put the pillows back, tossing them onto the couch, picking up piles of tissues off the carpet, yanking them out of our shirts and pants.

Mom storms in as I'm pulling up my pants, the matchbook clutched in her hand as she waves it in the air.

"Would you please tell me what the hell this was doing in your pocket?"

Mom looks down at us playing dress up, my pants still only halfway up. Savannah has mounds of tissues hanging out of her T-shirt. Mom's horrified. Her eyes say it all.

My sister and I are now crammed into Mom's red Datsun as we speed over to Dad's house. I can't breathe. I'm in trouble and I don't know why. Savannah is crying. A horrible pain boils in the pit of my stomach.

We pull into Dad's horseshoe driveway. My mother gets out of the car and runs over to the front door. She bangs on it with all her might until a young blonde I recognize from the Mansion steps onto the upstairs balcony. She waves to Savannah and me, her blonde hair swaying gently in the breeze. My mother pounds even harder. Dad finally answers the door wearing a blue terrycloth robe.

"What are you doing here?" he shouts.

My mother holds up the black matchbook with the white bunny ears.

"I do not want my daughters around this sort of filth! Do you hear me? I will not sit around and watch you poison them!" she yells with determination on her face.

"Thanks for dropping by, dear."

Dad begins to shut the door between them.

"Look at yourself! It's three in the afternoon!" my mother screams, pointing upstairs. "And what's that? Your flavor of the week? Great role model!"

Dad opens the door again; his voice is stern as he shoves her away from the house.

"If you ever fucking come here again I'm calling the cops!"

"Don't touch me!" Mom squirms out of his grasp. "I'll take you to court if I have to!"

Mom turns to us.

"Do you see how crazy your father is?" she asks.

Dad looks over at us with suspicious eyes, and my stomach aches and lurches. I don't know where my loyalties are supposed to lie—I am torn. Mom jumps back into the car and we speed out of there.

At school, my behavior begins to deteriorate. First grade becomes a battleground. I no longer fit in. I have become isolated and re-served. I stop socializing with the other kids my age. I don't trust anyone; my moods are unpredictable and my temper is erratic. Not only am I furious at my parents, I am pissed off at the world.

It's early in the morning when a short, fat boy in the front row sticks his tongue out at me. Blood rushes to my head as the kid continues making funny faces. After a few minutes, I get up, walk slowly over to his chair, raise my hand high over my head, and punch him in the face. The teacher hauls me into the principal's office.

"She's a problem child," I overhear someone say.

I sit in the corner of the room as teachers whisper among themselves.

"I heard her parents are separated."

"Divorced."

"She could be mentally challenged."

"Attention Deficit Disorder?"

"It's more like Attention Seeking Disorder."

My thick glasses fog up as I hold back tears. I don't want them to see me cry.

They send me to Dr. Parker, a well-known child psychiatrist with tiny spectacles and an irritating, pseudo-Zen, condescending voice.

"Let's pretend this is your house. And let's say this is you," Dr. Parker picks up a tiny figurine of a girl and places it inside a large pink dollhouse.

I ignore him and stare intently at the clock, watching the seconds go by. He places more figurines representing my "family unit" inside the dollhouse.

"Tell me what you are feeling, Jennifer," he repeats over and over until I can't take it anymore. My emotions overcome me and my hands move wildly as if on their own accord. I slam the dollhouse onto the floor and shatter it into tiny pieces.

I hurry out of his office at once.

I am branded a difficult child. A troublemaker. Detention, Saturday school, and the principal's office become routine stops.

All I can do is think of ways to hide, break free from rules, and escape the mundaneness of everyday life.

Three

*I*t's 1977. By the time I'm eight years old, going to Hef's is like going to our secret uncle's house. Ever since Mom insisted we stop going to the Mansion, the bargain became simple: we lie to her, our visits to Wonderland will continue; tell her the truth, our fun will end.

Hef's palace has become our own private playground. We have free rein of the house. The butlers know us, security guards know us, and even the Playmates call us by name.

My sister and I find a hidden rock staircase to a grassy mini-garden above the pool, where we take turns jumping off the top of the waterfall. Dad and the guys smoke cigars and play backgammon while the girls lounge beside them listening to KC and the Sunshine Band. We swim over to them, laughing at the topless girls spritzing themselves with bottled water.

"Looks like we're shooting the opening scene to one of Rick's movies," says Dad, referring to a girl rubbing oil on Rick's hairy chest.

"What role do you have, honey?" Rick asks the girl.

"I'm the fluffer, can't you tell?" The girl flips her permed brown hair.

"Why don't you come over here and fluff this?" Dad cradles his stethoscope.

"There's the image for the day," says a quiet man with white hair while he puts his book down.

I think his name is Ted.

"Little tease." Dad shakes his head.

"You should know, Doc. All the hot babes in and out of your office for physicals everyday," Duke exclaims.

"What about you . . . tit soup? It's like a casting call inside your surgery room," Dad chortles back at Duke.

"It's hard enough keeping up with all your girlfriends you send in," Duke laughs quietly.

"Something tells me there's enough silicone to go around," Dad retorts.

"Plastic tits for everyone!" Duke shouts for joy.

I glance down self-consciously at my flat chest, wondering if I am next.

In the pool, Savannah attempts to pull down my bathing suit bottoms, catching the attention of the guys and the fluffer.

"That's it. Now you're gonna get it!" I say.

I dive under the water and pull her bottoms off. The Playmates help Savannah because she starts to cry and act likes a baby. I feel bad for making Savannah cry, so I swim over to her.

"Let's play pinball! I'll let you go first!"

Savannah's frown instantly turns to a smile as we get out of the pool and wrap towels around ourselves. We slip into the back door of the kitchen pantry, where six different kinds of homemade cookies are separated into jars on the counter. Grabbing handfuls of double-chocolate chip, we race out to the game room. My mission in life is to have my name on Hef's champion pinball plaque. We sit for hours trying to beat the highest score. Savannah and I take a break, and I pick up the phone and dial the kitchen to order food.

"Can we have two hamburgers, two chocolate shakes, and two orders of fries, please?" I ask the butler.

Minutes later, trays of food are delivered. In the carpet room, I push on a wood cabinet that opens into a mini refrigerator filled with Pepsi bottles. I pull two out and give one to Savannah.

"Savannah, do you want to see something funny?"

I click the TV on and the sex channel appears. A naked man and two women are having sex in an outdoor Jacuzzi at a motel. Savannah stares at the screen in total shock.

"Who is that?"

"People," I laugh, sinking three inches into the carpet.

I push one of the corner mirrors in slightly and a secret cabinet opens. It's filled with bags of gumballs, M&M's, peanuts, and bottles of Pepsi. Savannah's mouth drops. We grab all the yellow gumballs out of the bag.

"Wait! There are secret hidden cameras behind the walls!" I say.

We stop scrounging. Savannah has a petrified expression on her face as she empties her pockets of yellow gumballs.

"I'm just kidding," I giggle, but I wonder if there really are hidden cameras in the walls.

During the day, we're outside lounging by the pool at the Mansion when Dorothy Stratten shouts, "Crank it up!" as Sister Sledge's "We Are Family" comes on the radio. Another Playmate leaps up, flapping her pastel-colored wraparound skirt with fringes. Chinese jacks are tossed against a rock as Savannah and I scream: "Beauty pageant!" And the contest is on!

Playmate number two pops on her black hat, modeling her

new fluorescent green bikini with gold chains, while Savannah and I flash her a "9." Playmate number three struts down the pathway wearing nothing but a speckled headband, bangle bracelets, and big hoop earrings. Polaroid pictures are snapped.

It's fun playing games with them because no one treats us like we're younger—it's like we're all the same age, even though I know that we're not.

All the girls chime in singing and dancing, and it's difficult to keep score. The pageant quickly turns into a silly dance party by the pool. The Playmates take our hands and show us intricate dance steps that we attempt awkwardly with our sandaled feet.

After a while, we all order club sandwiches, barbequed potato chips, and Pepsi from one of the butlers. As we eat, I ponder all the mean things that both my mother and the kids at school say about the Playmates. Kids at school say they're prostitutes and stupid. Mom says they're worse than that.

The Playmate in the fluorescent green bikini helps French braid Savannah's long blond hair. Savannah giggles, loving the attention.

One of the Playmates looks at me and smiles.

I smile back, confused and slightly guilty.

As time passes, nudity doesn't bother us as much. After we swim, we use the changing rooms near the sauna. The rock-lined showers have no curtain or door separating the shower from the rest of the bathroom. My father takes off his bathing suit, never caring that anyone, including his daughters, sees him naked. He even lets us shower with him.

I try to be careful not to look at Dad's penis, but it's difficult to avoid.

Dad says there's nothing wrong with nudity and thinks that people who have problems with it are not only insecure but ignorant as well.

He tells us that certain cultures view nudity as artistic expression. He says it's very natural and people have to let go of their inhibitions and recognize that it's just a form of self-expression. Savannah and I act like nothing's wrong, but we never tell Mom.

It's 1980. I'm eleven years old and school no longer interests me. My life is divided between going to the Mansion and bragging about it to friends at school.

Every morning I stand in a circle of girls in front of El Rodeo Elementary.

"People drink and smoke around me, and no one cares. I hear swear words and see topless women. I'm number four on the pinball plaque, and order anything I want to my room," I boast.

"Have you seen anyone naked?"

"Of course," I respond, as if I'm the Queen Bee of sex.

I've become popular overnight. I've switched from coke-bottle-thick glasses to contact lenses as new friends surround me. I sport a new perm and parachute pants with lots of zippers. I've adopted the Izod signature look and wear colored tuna clips in my hair. Aviator Ray-Bans have become my trademark. All my friends want to come with me to the Mansion but their parents won't let them. Their parents give them the same reasons my mother gave me.

"They're close-minded and don't have a clue. They don't even know Hef." I defend him as if he were my own father. Sometimes I sneak a friend or two up there, but they have to promise not to say anything to their parents.

Slumber parties with my girlfriends at school have become really huge. After being MIA for a while, I tell them I will definitely be at Amber's sleepover that Friday night.

Come Friday, four of us lie around upstairs in Amber's room surrounded by junk food and Queen, Michael Jackson, and Bee

Gees records. The conversation shifts from boys in our grade to the Mansion in a matter of seconds.

"Why does your father take you up there so much?" asks Sonya, flipping her permed hair.

"Do you think your dad sleeps with all those Playmates?" Michelle blurts out in a snotty tone.

My face turns bright red.

"I don't know, but Hef has a huge game room with three pinball machines, a jukebox, a pool table, and foosball!"

Everyone is silenced, clearly impressed.

Later that night, I glance around Amber's bedroom at my friends, who are fast asleep. The television is on downstairs, so I make my way there, sneaking a peek at Amber's mother and father in the den.

"I feel sorry for that girl. Sweet kid. Too bad her father's such a wacko," her mother says.

"Her father lives at the Mansion. I mean who in their right mind brings an eleven-year-old up there?" Amber's father asks, shaking his head. "She's going to be one fucked-up girl when she's older," he affirms.

I am stung, unable to move. It's at this moment that I realize how different my life is from that of all my friends. A part of me can see it clearly, though another part of me knows I will forget this by dawn.

Sixth grade bores me. There is no way it can compete with the magical kingdom filling my head—that perfect place, free of rules and monotony. I fidget in my seat until we are finally let go. I don't want to go home to my mother, to her cold stares and lists of chores.

I walk next door to my father's office, which is on the twenty-second floor of the Century City Medical Building. The reception room is packed with fitness freaks obsessed with losing weight. You never know which celebrity is going to pop his head through the door. The countertops are lined with greeting cards and head-shots from only the most famous.

Buzzed through by reception, I reach Dad's office and stop to stare at a life-size portrait of a little girl in a light blue bathing suit. She stands beside a large tree, holding a gardenia in her small hands. Her blue eyes look sad. I stare at the girl, completely captivated.

I don't let myself see that she resembles me. The gardenia she holds is the same flower my father sends me for special occasions: birthdays, Easter, Valentine's Day. Like this girl, I am caught, for-ever a child, suspended in a frame of his design. I only recognize that the picture saddens me. Like living in his love, seeing this like-ness chokes me to the point where I cannot breathe.

Dad hurries in.

"Hi, honey. Good to see you."

His phone buzzes as he searches for something in his office.

"Where did it go?" he asks himself, shuffling things around.

"Ah," he sighs, picking up a wrapped gift with a pretty pink bow. "I got a little something for you."

Dad hands me a white box.

"Hef 's on line two," his secretary screams over the intercom.

"Open it," Dad mouths, excited, as he picks up the phone.

I tear open the wrapping paper to find a new Wilson tennis racket!

"I'll be right there," Dad says into the receiver before hanging up.

"Wow. Thanks, Dad. I love it!"

He is pleased by my reaction. "I have to go to the Mansion. Do you want to come along for the ride?"

"Sure." I shrug.

Twenty minutes later, we arrive at the iron gates.

Dad hops out of the car and carries his medical bag inside. A butler greets us at the door as Dad hurries upstairs while I make a mad dash for the game room. I cut through the tree-lined pathway, wondering if anyone has beaten my highest score.

After hours of Space Invaders and Andy Gibb on repeat, I head back into the house and enter the Med Room, a breakfast nook with a glass table, chairs, and a stone fountain gurgling in the corner. It's bright and comfortable. When I enter, I find an older man sitting with a young girl. I sit down at the end of the table.

"You're Doc's daughter, right?" the man asks.

He gives me the creeps.

"Right." I smirk back, hoping he will recognize my disinterest and leave me alone.

"Have you met my daughter, Sofia?" he asks.

"No." I move to shake the shy girl's hand. She seems a few years older than me. I grab a pad of paper and doodle, pretending not to notice how affectionate they seem. I try to inch my chair away from them, but it doesn't help. I'm incredibly uncomfortable, although I'm not quite sure why.

Dad comes down the main staircase and joins us in the Med Room a few minutes later. He shakes hands with the guy and says hello to the girl. He sits down beside me, ordering a sandwich and a bowl of soup from a butler.

"How was everything?" I ask.

"Fine. Routine," Dad answers discreetly, as always.

I peer over stunned by what I see next. The "shy" girl stands up and kisses her father good-bye. Their mouths are slightly open as they kiss softly on the lips.

After she leaves, I whisper, "That's his *daughter*," into my father's ear, horrified. "Did you see how they kissed?"

Dad nods nonchalantly. "That's what people do when they love each other." His eyes peer right through me. My body goes numb. He does not comprehend where he ends and I begin. I try to think of something to say, but I cannot. I look away from him quickly, knowing I saw something gross.

Soon, I care less and less about roller-skating rinks, spin the bottle, or boys my own age, all of which seem elementary to me. My father, without being conscious of it, causes a tug-of-war between the kid I am and the adult he wants me to be. He wants me to tag along as his partner in crime and is threatened by anyone with the power to divert my attention or love.

"Why do you need to sleep at other kids' houses when you have everything you need at my house? It doesn't make any sense," he repeats over and over.

"That's what we do. We have sleepovers," I try to explain, but he doesn't get it.

His love and devotion are intoxicating. We become so attached that leaving each other seems as final as death. Before long, I start to second-guess why I'd want to sleep anywhere else or even be with anyone else.

We're at our usual corner booth at Hamburger Hamlet in Century City, eating burgers, shakes, and fries.

"The Village People are performing at the Mansion," my father mentions, nonchalantly, between bites.

I drop the fries that were headed to my mouth. Ketchup splatters all over my white Esprit shorts. I don't notice.

"Are you serious? They're my favorite group!" I scream frantically.

"I would invite you," he eyeballs me, "but it's a pajama party for adults and I certainly don't want your mother yelling at me again."

"You always want me to go with you everywhere, and now you're saying I can't?"

"Hey, I'm okay with it; it's your mother who has the problem," he reiterates smoothly.

I switch gears, instantly understanding the complex dynamic at hand.

"It's probably because she's jealous," I say, knowing it's what he wants to hear.

"I hate to say it, but I think you're right," he smiles.

I envision myself jumping up and down onstage with the Village People: *Let's hear it for "Y.M.C.A."!*

"You know she acts like she cares about you, but she doesn't care about anyone but herself," he says about my mother.

"Oh, I know," I say, while trying to figure out what I'll wear to the event.

"Well, I suppose what Mom doesn't know won't hurt her," he says.

We exchange smiles.

Another image of me onstage with the Village People flashes through my brain. Dancing with them, flailing my arms in the air, motioning the letters to "Y.M.C.A."

"So, it's settled then," says Dad.

From under the table, he pulls out an autographed album of the Village People with my name on it.

"Wow! Thanks, Dad. I can't believe you got it signed and everything!"

We hug, having, once again, successfully tiptoed through the land mines of our relationship.

The day of the concert, the commotion on the front lawn is enough to drive anyone wild—balloons, colorful umbrellas, a popcorn trolley, and endless pretty girls in bikinis. A roller disco party is under way as I spy on everyone, watching Vanna White and Dorothy Stratten from the bushes above the tennis court.

After a while, I retreat into the game room, grab a few gumballs, play a quick game of Frogger, and then head into the bathroom. Next to the sink is a small, weird-looking cigarette, which has a strong odor. I light a match, stick it between my lips, inhale, and start to cough incessantly. I quickly twist open the window, worried that someone will smell the smoke.

I know I have done something wrong as I look into the mirror and see my guilty reflection. My eyes find their way down to my feet. The marble is miles from the bottom of my soles. I reach for the door handle but it won't open. I twist and turn the knob, unsure of which way will free me from this bathroom that has now become a looming cellar. Panic sets in and I'm scared I will never get out. I blink my eyes a few times and try to focus. It feels like forever since I've been in here. I yank on the handle, turning the lock back and forth with all my might. It finally unlocks and I step out, exasperated, wiping sweat off my forehead. In my mind, I can picture the main house, but somehow it seems so far away. I give up on the idea of finding my way there and fall backward onto the couch in the game room, feeling a rush of fresh air in my lungs with considerable relief. I grab handfuls of M&M's from bowls on the coffee table, ignoring other bowls filled with white pills. I collapse back onto the couch, melting into the soft leather seats and feel myself slowly begin to drift away.

That night I'm in my usual secret spot above the banister, spying on guests in pajamas and lingerie as they mingle down below. Everyone looks past me. There are lots of people rushing around, constantly moving, dancing, and posing. Everyone sparkles. Along the perimeter of the room, Playmates and guests pose like Grecian statues in bugle-beaded, jeweled gowns with avant-garde paisley and spiraling designs swirling over mile-high shoulder pads.

A couple makes out in the corner. Two pretty girls dressed as bunnies hold hands and kiss.

The lights go down and a spotlight brightens the stage as the Village People step up, one by one, looking just like the major rock stars they are. Everyone cheers as *"Y.M.C.A."* kicks off the night. I dance alone, upstairs, shifting my hands to make the letters. Wild energy courses through the colorful party and part of me wishes I were older so I could be downstairs with everyone else. There isn't a sad face in the crowd.

Women shine in their Nolan Miller, cream-colored satin suits with plunging necklines. Their ears are weighed down by dramatic clip earrings with clusters of brilliant rhinestones. There is so much dazzle that it looks as if everything was on fire. The brilliance surrounds me and lifts me up to a place of music and light.

On days when Savannah decides to stay at Mom's I occupy myself by playing hide-and-seek inside the Mansion. Dorothy Stratten and I split up in the foyer. Dorothy closes her eyes while I make a mad dash past the screening room and into the library. I look around, deciding to hide underneath the bar. I open one of the cabinets under the bar and crawl in. But before I have time to shut the door, one of the butlers sees me. I hold my finger over my lips and then duck inside as Dorothy is quickly approaching.

"Have you seen Jennifer?" she asks.

"Let's see, that would be who?" he says, jovially.

"Can't say I have for sure," he says, leaving. I feel around in the darkness accidentally squeezing something rubbery. It squeaks and Dorothy busts open the cabinet door to find me holding a large rubber boob! We laugh and split up again. I count to ten before I hunt her down. I run upstairs and wave to my favorite security guard, asking him if he's seen her.

"No." He shakes his head as I pop my head into Dad's room. I open a big wooden armoire. No sign of her, but I do find a funny looking plastic hotdog. I turn it all around, unsure of what it is. I grab it and run out, bumping into a security guard on my way out.

"Is everything all right?" he asks.

"Fine," I say, as my face turns bright red.

"What do you have there?" he asks and I shrug. The security guard takes the hotdog away from me and says, "Little girls shouldn't be playing with this."

Next stop, room five. I enter, calling out Dorothy's name. I open the closet door, shouting, "I got you!" I find nothing but extra robes on hangers. I look under the bed. Still nothing. I stare at the closed bathroom door. I make my way to the door, careful not to make any noise. I turn the knob and yell, "Found you!" A naked woman screeches as a man rolls off her in the tub. I freeze momentarily, and then spin around and peel outta there!

I return downstairs, where I find Dorothy outside lounging on a chair by the pool. She smiles brightly telling me I won, even though I know I really didn't. I ask if she wants to play again, but she tells me she has a photo shoot in half an hour and reassures me that we will play again soon.

We're at Mom's house when we receive the news. The phone is handed to me and on the other line is Dad who sounds unbelievably down.

"I won't be able to see you girls this weekend. Something came up," he tells us.

"What?"

"I didn't want to get into it over the phone, but Dorothy Stratten was killed."

You can hear his frustration, his devastation.

"What happened?"

"It's a tragedy," he explains in a low, hushed voice. "Her estranged husband murdered her and then took his own life."

"Why would he do that?"

"It's a long story. It's just a shame. Really sad."

"I'm sorry."

"Me too. She was a special lady. I'll call you later; I just wanted to tell you it's going to be a hectic weekend," Dad says.

"Okay. Bye, Dad. Love you."

We hang up and I stand there for a minute thinking about Dorothy. I felt suddenly more alone than ever. Years later, the repercussions of losing someone I am close to begin to sink in. I realize the people who mean the most to me are taken away the fastest. I cling on tighter to those I am attached too; never wanting to let go.

My sadness is wrapped around a sort of disbelief that she is actually gone. This surreal world and all that occurs begins to not feel real after awhile.

It was only last weekend we saw her laying by the pool with friends.

Four

*I*t's 1981. I am twelve when Dad moves into the Mansion full-time for over a year. And though he eventually moves back to his house, he continues to keep his room at the Mansion through the rest of the eighties.

He starts dating Pamela, a natural redhead with fair, silky white skin, freckles, and hazel eyes. She is a genuinely nice, warm-hearted television actress who comes from a family of entertainers. She is really kind and seems to care about us. Pamela has her own house but spends most nights at Dad's.

Pamela is different from the girls we're used to seeing Dad with—for one thing, she doesn't like going to the Mansion. She says she wants a normal life. She tucks us in at night and tells us bedtime stories about a Pink Land where kids run wild in fields of pink flowers and everyone is always happy. She cooks us dinner and makes us eat all our vegetables. Even Dad becomes more like a dad when she is around—he's calmer, he asks about our homework, he even acts kind of goofy, sometimes. At times, I start to feel like his house is a real home.

Out of nowhere Dad tells me he is going to remodel his house.

"Where will you stay?" I ask.

"My room at the Mansion until the house is done," Dad says matter-of-factly as if we should know better, and I can tell Pamela is hurt.

"Don't be ridiculous, Richard; you can stay with me." Pamela offers a cute, small smile.

"I don't want to inconvenience anyone," Dad answers.

"You're not. Don't be silly; I'd love to have you," Pamela insists.

"I'm up there all the time. I already have my own room. Plus, the kids will need a place to stay when they visit me," Dad says, oblivious to Pamela's look of disbelief.

Our faces light up.

"Will we get our own room too?" we ask.

"Of course," Dad smiles.

"You're unbelievable," says Pamela, shaking her head before leaving the room.

Dad shouts after Pamela as if she were Mom. "What do you want me to do, rent a house? Would that make you feel better?"

The following day, Savannah and I race into Mom's house thrilled about having our own room up at Hef's.

"We're gonna live at the Mansion! We're gonna live at the Mansion!" we chant without thinking of the consequences. Though we know how she feels about the Mansion, we are hoping our enthusiasm will change her mind.

"What's going on?" she asks.

"Dad's house is going to be remodeled for a year. Dad's going to live at Hef's and said we could have our own room there too!" blurts Savannah.

Hopeful, we look at Mom,

"Please, Mom? It's really fun up there. There's so much to do. There's Frogger and monkeys and a waterfall. We never see anything bad. I swear," I say.

"Please?" Savannah begs.

"I've been there before and have seen many inappropriate things for children."

"It's changed!"

"The answer is no."

Mom sees the childish excitement in our eyes—the whole world will fall apart if she denies us. She softens for a moment.

"Can't you at least come and see for yourself? We can show you around."

"We can show you the monkeys!" says Savannah, tugging on Mom's hand.

"Please?"

"Okay. I'll take a look around."

Mom shakes her head like she's disappointed in herself for giving in.

"Yippee!" we shout, dancing around.

"But if I find anything inappropriate, that's it. Understand?"

Savannah and I nod at each other as we continue to cheer.

The next Friday, movie night, Savannah and I give Mom the full tour of the Mansion before guests arrive. We lead Mom around by the hand, showing off the mansion like it's ours.

We stroll by the animals, the pool, and the birds. Savannah distracts Mom in the changing room while I check out the grotto to make sure no one's there, signaling to my sister that the coast is clear. Mom enters the steamy grotto, spinning her head around in every direction, scrutinizing the steamy space, immediately questioning all the open bottles of baby oil by the cushions.

"Mom, it's for tanning!"

I quickly pull her back out into the daylight.

We take her inside to the library, where she eyeballs a set of porcelain boobs and *Playboy* magazines on display. Mom's eyes lower in disgust as she lifts her nose to the indecent material.

"Don't worry. We never come in here. This is where the guys play cards—I mean, Monopoly," I say.

At this point, Mom seems okay, not entirely convinced, but Savannah and I are still hopeful.

"You should see upstairs!" I yell.

We smile when butlers pass and Mom's head turns as they refer to us by name.

We walk up the grand staircase and Mom comments on the oversize pair of brass breasts hanging on the wall.

"Mom, some really famous guy did that, Picasso or something."

Mom shakes her head as we hang a left, past Hef's bedroom. We are halfway down the hall when she stops to examine the glass cabinet filled with naked figurines. I cringe, fearful of her reaction, motioning to Savannah to yank Mom by the arm immediately.

"Mom, over here!" she screams and Mom glances away just in time. We continue walking, pointing to room number two.

"That's Dad's room!"

We head down the long corridor lined with framed pictures of celebrities. Mom stops to stare at a picture of Warren Beatty.

"I didn't know he came up here."

"All the time," I brag, as if we're old-timers.

"Oh, Tony Bennett. Look at Clint Eastwood!" Mom stares at their photos.

Savannah and I cross our fingers.

"I love Tony Curtis!" Mom rattles off.

"Cheryl Tiegs, Farrah Fawcett?"

"See Mom, women come here too!"

"Mick Jagger, Al Pacino, Jack Nicholson . . ."

"This place isn't as bad as you think," I say.

Mom turns and looks at me sharply, as we turn another corner lined with more pictures along the hallway and stop at room six.

I enter first, Mom follows, then Savannah. Mom scans the room like a hawk, opening the wood cabinets and drawers. She practically sniffs the place as I quickly cover a few *Playboy* magazines with my backpack. Mom walks around as I push an ashtray underneath the bed, panicking because the butlers must've cleaned the room and put everything back that I hid! Mom reaches for the wooden box filled with cigarettes as I step on Savannah's foot, hard.

"Ouch!" Savannah cries at the top of her lungs.

Mom swings around to comfort her as I leap for the wooden box, shoving it behind a chair.

"I'm sorry," I mouth to Savannah.

My heart pounds as Mom moves to the window and gasps.

"What on earth! Who are those women?" Mom shrieks, referring to the topless Playmates basking out by the pool.

"Booby ladies!" Savannah shouts for joy.

I cringe, grabbing my head with my hands.

"Oh, they're nothing," I say casually, hoping she won't notice that they're naked.

"Nothing? They aren't wearing any clothes!" Mom shouts.

"I mean, they're nobodies!"

"Nobodies?"

"I don't know who they are!"

"I know exactly who and what they are!" Mom yells.

"In some countries nudity is considered art!"

"Whoever told you that is probably a sex maniac!" she screams.

Mom is pissed. We're now walking briskly back down the hallway.

"I will not have my daughters around naked women! It creates a negative message and one day you will thank me!"

A couple in terrycloth bathrobes exits the bedroom beside us and Mom glares at them scornfully, ushering us away.

"That's it! I've seen enough!" Mom assures us.

The celebrity pictures on the walls blur together as we pass.

We're a few feet from the glass cabinet filled with naked figurines in sexual positions and I try to divert her attention away from it, but it's too late. She presses her face against the glass and peers inside. Her expression is one of sheer horror.

"What the hell is this?" she shrieks.

We're dead. Game over. I can hear *Donkey Kong* fall down to his cage as Mom drags us out of there in a hurry.

My mother files a court order restraining my father from taking us to the Mansion. The court order states that Savannah and I are not allowed anywhere near the property.

"Your father will be in serious violation of the law if he does not comply with this." Mom waves the piece of paper forcefully. "We know how well your father listens, so I am warning you girls. This is serious. I know you think I'm being mean, but I'm not. This is for your own good, trust me. No female with any self-respect goes up there."

Savannah and I pretend to understand, but we don't. We nod in agreement and promise never to go up there again.

As expected, Dad ignores the court order, and rents a beach house in Malibu so Mom won't suspect where we sleep when it's his days and weekends with us. We spend most of our time racing back and forth from Malibu to the Mansion. Dad is always in a rush.

Savannah and I continue to share room six at the Mansion. Clothes are thrown everywhere. At night, Dad is busy playing Monopoly with the guys, while we order trays of food in bed, never caring if we spill or get crumbs anywhere. The butlers deliver our feast and clean the trays in the morning. We have pillow fights, hang up on security, chew lots of bubble gum, and stay up late watching the Playboy Channel, even though we know Mom will kill us if she finds out.

In the morning, Savannah and I race downstairs to help the butlers pack our lunches. Excited about the vast selection, we choose peanut butter and jelly sandwiches, fruit rolls, homemade cookies, and bottles of Pepsi, along with copious amounts of gumballs.

Dad is usually too tired to drive us to school, so Hef's limo drops us off while we blast Diana Ross, feeling like big-time movie stars as we near the front of El Rodeo. The fun ends when we spot all the nosy parents dropping their kids off. We make funny faces at them through the tinted windows, knowing they will definitely tell Mom if they see us. We duck, asking the driver to drop us off down the block, and walk the rest of the way.

After school, Hef's driver picks us up because Dad is busy playing backgammon. Back at the Mansion, the thought of doing our homework never crosses our minds. It is not enforced or talked about because here we are not children—we are treated as adults. While most kids are in ballet, gymnastics, Girl Scouts, or engaging in after-school activities, our main desire is to find out who's playing in Hef's pool. We don't need to play with Barbie dolls because there are live ones walking around everywhere.

We race up to our room, throw our books down, change into swimsuits, and head down to the kitchen, grabbing handfuls of cookies on our way out to the pool. Savannah and I wave to Dad and the others as we climb the hidden staircase to the grassy land above the waterfall and take turns jumping off.

This place has become our sacred retreat, our home away from home, a magical passage into fantasyland where we can forget all about our problems and become lost in our adventures.

Nights are far from quiet as my sister and I roam the halls of the Mansion like Eloise at the Plaza, spying on everyone from behind the wooden banister. Down below, strobe lights twirl; another disco party is in full swing. Everyone looks so different at night.

They look like the people on *Dynasty:* glittering, untouchable, heavily made-up, and perfectly at ease.

I recognize designer outfits from the pages of my mother's fashion magazines. A black Givenchy jersey gown drapes a petite woman with brunette hair piled on top of her head. The dress falls open to the small of her back, nearly exposing the crevice that lies millimeters below.

My father and Tony Curtis schmooze bubblegum blondes and big-hair brunettes. Vanna White, in a lavish sequin-encrusted Halston gown, is surrounded by a herd of men. She always radiates warmth and a genuine smile. She is very approachable and friendly to everyone.

Across the way, Hef and a small group of people come up the stairs and go into his bedroom, closing the door behind them. I feel slightly left out, but Savannah is content watching the beautiful people and admiring the glamorous outfits the women wear: long fur scarves, turquoise glitter, huge shoulder pads under ruffled silk shirts, tight jeans, tall leather boots, spiked heels, and bright makeup.

By this time, Mom and Dad split custody over the summer, so during Dad's half, Savannah and I spend most of our time by Hef's pool, lying on rafts, tossing beach balls, and jumping through gigantic plastic tubes in the water. Savannah and I set up a small Kool-Aid stand with little cups while the Playmates play topless volleyball in the pool.

"What are you girls doing?" one of Hef's friends asks.

"Making Kool-Aid. Want some?"

"Why thank you, girls; how lovely of you. How are you both today?" the nice white-haired man asks.

"Fine, thank you. How come we always see you reading so much?" I ask, noticing a book in his hand.

"I'm a writer, so I enjoy experiencing the world even if I

haven't seen it all myself," he explains as we peer at him quizzically. "Imagine taking a vacation to an unknown place all in three hundred small pages," he chuckles, waving the book in his hand.

"We love vacations," we tell him.

"The key is to never stop learning." He smiles as he walks away.

"What kind of service is this?" Dad waves his arm, cigar in hand, waiting for his Kool-Aid to be delivered. He wears a tight Speedo and sits next to Hef, who's in silk pajamas, smoking a pipe. Savannah and I bring a cup of Kool-Aid to them.

"Thank you, my angels," Hef smiles kindly.

"Thanks, girls." Dad puffs on his cigar as proud smiles sweep across our faces.

"Do refills come with these?" Dad asks.

"Of course, but only for a tip," we say, smiling back.

"I taught my girls well," Dad gloats as we race back to our stand to make more Kool-Aid. After mixing up a fresh batch, we see Dad lift his cup high into the air. We rush the pitcher back over to him and refill his punch, pouring Dad's glass first.

"Out of breath, kid?" Duke chuckles. "We might have to put you on an exercise program. You can follow Hef's latest health kick: three blondes, two brunettes, and one redhead."

"Doctor's orders!" Dad chortles.

We all laugh.

It's morning, and Savannah and I are the first ones up.

We roll out of bed, open our door, and walk quietly down the hallway. I notice new photographs of my father, Savannah, and me along the wall. A warm sensation travels through me. This really is like our home.

Clicking noises catch my attention so I tiptoe slowly toward the sounds. Savannah follows carefully, putting her feet exactly where mine were.

Over the clicking we hear a man's voice.

"That's it, shake it out, move it all around," he says.

Through the partially opened door we see a tan, thin blonde lying on a bed while men in blue jeans and T-shirts move; light stands in a circle around her.

She kneels on the bed, squeezing her breasts together, her mouth slightly open.

The man holding the camera clicks every few seconds as bulbs flash.

"You're doing perfect. Give me that 'Fuck me' pose. Every man in America is going to love you for this," the photographer says.

Savannah is in awe at what she sees as a glamorous photo shoot. Her eyes sparkle at the sight of the lucky blonde getting all the attention.

The Playmate pulls her skimpy, black lace lingerie down with one finger as I accidentally lose my grip on the door panel and crash to the floor.

"Who's that?" the photographer yells.

Jumping up, Savannah and I race down the hallway as one of the men rushes out.

We take a sharp left down the back staircase and out the side door and lean against the wall sighing heavily.

"Maybe I'll be a model one day," Savannah says with a dreamy expression.

Not me, I think, worried that my sister wants the wrong kind of attention.

As the summer continues, Dad's mood swings begin to become erratic. He is more abrupt and short with us than ever before. His tone takes on a new meaning as it leaves us feeling stupid and worthless. His temper flares from nowhere and we can't figure out why. It doesn't seem to matter whether we misspell a word, forget to do something, or don't do something and say we did. We don't know why he gets so mad; we know he doesn't mean it. He just can't control his temper.

Savannah and I are jumping up and down on the bed, singing along to Sugarhill Gang when Dad enters our room, his eyes zeroing in on the wet bathing suits and clothes littering the floor. The record scratches to a screeching halt as our smiles fade to frowns.

"Who left this crap lying around?" he demands, sick and tired of our sloppiness.

"We didn't mean to leave it here," I explain, defending us.

"Then why is it here?" he questions, his eyes making us feel even more stupid.

"We must've forgotten it after we changed," I mumble, watching as he paces, wiping his nose, furious as he cogitates about how to deal with his idiot children.

"That's right! You forgot. You two don't have jack shit to do around here! I gave you a very simple task! Maybe you can try picking up your crap for a change!" he shouts.

Savannah and I glance at each other, frightened by his mean tone.

"You girls have everything you could possibly want. Most kids are envious of your lifestyle! But I can take it away if you're not happy!" he screams violently. His tone makes us weak.

"You don't need to get so mad," I say, hesitantly, knowing he could ask us calmly or perhaps remind us not to leave our things lying around, but that never happens.

"Don't tell me how to act! Do you hear me?"

Dad shakes his head violently as he stalks through the room.

"Where did you learn your manners? Your mother?"

Our faces burn with shame from constantly swallowing critical comments about Mom. We try to block them out, but sometimes they sink in and we wonder if they are true.

"Is somebody going to answer me?" he rages, and Savannah begins to cry.

The more she cries, the more he screams.

"And what's that smell?" he sniffs, leaning toward Savannah, who visually disintegrates and breaks down.

Her cry terrifies me; it shatters my heart into tiny pieces.

"You stink! Go wash under your arms! How many times have I told you to wash under your fucking arms? Jesus! Didn't your mother teach you how to clean yourself?"

I want to stick up for her but I am afraid. I can't stop him. We remain silent, lost in shame.

Dad leaves, slamming the door behind him.

I try to comfort Savannah. I want her to be okay, but she isn't. Sobs rack her small body while my thin arms wrap around her.

Terror and self-loathing begin to build in each of us. Savannah and I become uncomfortable with our own development as we learn to dislike our bodies.

For years and years we will look into mirrors and see ourselves as not good enough, not pretty enough, not thin enough. We will see fat even when there is none. We will feel dirty when we are clean and want to jump out of our skin, escaping our imagined flaws and imperfections.

I wore many hats as a child with my father. My role was never clearly defined. I was either his daughter, his running mate, or the son he never had. I don't expect anyone to understand it really. It's rather complex. In other words, he socialized me, trained me, programmed me to disrespect women and treat them with little regard. Women were viewed as lesser people and for years I believed them. The admiration I had for the men I was surrounded by began with my seeking their approval and identifying as one of them. Soon, my respect and admiration turned to disgust and disappointment.

Yet, regardless of who he was dating or screwing at the time, my father always put me first. He kicked girls out of his house at the drop of a hat. I knew all their secrets and it was clear I was his favorite.

Meanwhile, my sister's role was always consistent. She was

treated like a weekend pet. He was always trying to train her in a derogatory way. My father knew she favored my mother so he went out of his way to berate her and treat her like a typical girl, like a hooker with no respect. He humiliated her regularly. I tried to stand up for her as best I could, careful not to set off his temper even more. But my efforts were useless. Perhaps I lowered my head in shame one too many times, deep down grateful I was the one not getting yelled at. I may never forgive myself for not protecting my younger sister from the madness of a man we both loved and knew was volatile.

The saddest thing is, all she ever wanted was his love and attention.

Years later, my sister and I will drift apart. We won't speak and if we do our language is superficial, our relationship competitive. I will continue to stay angry at my parents and push love away while my sister will search for it in all the wrong places.

I hold Savannah close to me, smelling the sweet chlorine scent in her hair.

Regret grips my heart and starts to squeeze for not saving my younger sister.

When we hit puberty, our development becomes even more important to Dad. Savannah and I try to present ourselves in ways that will gain his approval. Though his temperamental outbursts become more frequent, we manage to bury them, reminding ourselves that he only wants to be proud of us. Dad is very eager to present his daughters as glam and sexy. We are a reflection of him. He wants others to stop and look at us, knowing that we are his daughters, polished and sophisticated. If we were top students in our class, most parents would be happy. This is not the case with him. We learn that our bodies must be perfect in order to gain his approval. We are on display, constantly critiqued and scrutinized like the Barbie dolls we never had but over the years morphed into.

We learn that big boobs, tight asses, and flat stomachs define the norm in Dad's world. Hearing his analysis and critique of each girl he meets shows us that women are valued by their appearance. The better you look, the further you can go.

My mother contributes to this in her own way. She's a psychologist who specializes in eating disorders and depression. She watches me from afar, never truly understanding that I may eventually struggle with the same issues her patients do. I never feel a sense of being taken care of by her. Instead, she will acknowledge me inasmuch as I make myself the child who pleases her. Her approval is gained through a facade of plastic image or accomplishing goals she deems worthy or important.

I awake to the sound of birds chirping outside the window. Sunshine gleams over the backyard as I get out of bed before my sister wakes up. I run out to the game room, tiptoe into the carpet room, and lock the door behind me. I turn on the television and The Playboy Channel washes over the screen. I lie on my back, half watching TV, but more interested in the mirror on the ceiling.

The light from the television flickers across my clothes and face, giving my skin a ghostly appearance. I run my hands over my face and chest.

In this place, in this magical castle, I want to be safe and I am, most of the time. The memory of my father's vicious attack the night before pushes its way into my consciousness and I shudder.

Panic from the memory builds, seizes my lungs with hot hands, and I want to disappear. I want to escape. I want to forget it like the other memories of his anger.

My small hands find their way down my white Fila tennis shorts, searching for comfort and forgetfulness.

My visits to the carpet room become more frequent.

The summer takes a turn when Dad hires Cindy, a twenty-year-old babysitter (so he says) with feathered blond hair. Cindy watches us while Carmela oversees construction on Dad's house. According to Dad, Cindy is both well traveled and culturally liberated, but Savannah and I know she is just an airhead.

At the beach house, "Centerfold" by the J. Geils Band blasts across the deck as Cindy prances around in a skimpy polka-dot bikini. Savannah and I spy on her as she refills Dad's cocktail.

"Total Valley girl."

"Orange County. She is so cheese. Did you see her matching pinstriped miniskirt and tank top?"

"Blue eye shadow?"

"Flat-ironed rooster bangs?"

"Sassoon jeans."

"Ooh la la!"

"Check out the Members Only jacket she borrowed from Dad. What a poser."

We chew on Pop Rocks while we rag on Dad's latest addition. I have become as highly critical of women as he is.

Savannah and I duck underneath the deck and race into the ocean before they notice us.

The sun is going down. Dad flips through the newspaper on a beach chair while Cindy's at the market.

"Where's Pamela? How come she's never around?" I ask Dad with Savannah at my side.

"She's been busy lately. She has a new TV show, and she's jealous of the girls at the Mansion. But I'm seeing her tomorrow," he mentions nonchalantly.

"Why is Cindy always with us?"

"Cindy's here to do errands, make life easier, take care of your needs and my needs," Dad laughs to himself.

"We miss Pamela. Cindy's so Valley."

"To the max," Savannah says and we giggle.

"What's wrong with you girls? Cindy's great." He shakes his head. "You're both spoiled."

Savannah and I continue to make Valley remarks as we run into the house and head straight for the fridge, which is stocked with oranges, pasta salad, and club sandwiches from the deli down the street.

That night, I walk in on Cindy and Dad in bed together. Dad scrambles to play it off, jumping up as Cindy rolls over.

"I insisted Cindy spend the night since it's so late and potentially dangerous to drive home," Dad explains.

I look at him in disbelief. I can't believe he thinks I'm stupid enough to buy that excuse.

"Do you need anything?" Dad asks warmly.

"No, I just wanted to say good night," I add before closing the bedroom door.

I run back to my room to tell Savannah.

As the weekend comes to an end, Pamela drops by the beach house to say hello. While Dad's busy talking to one of the neighbors, I take Pamela into my bedroom, shut the door, and sit her down.

"I don't know if I should say anything, I mean, you probably already know, but I just thought I'd tell you . . ."

"What is it, honey? You can tell me anything, of course," Pamela offers warmly.

"I don't want you to say anything to Dad 'cause he might get mad at me."

"Sweetie, you can tell me anything, you know that. What we discuss is between us. I won't say anything if you don't want me to," Pamela says and I believe her.

There's a pause as she waits for me to continue.

"Well, you know Cindy sleeps here, right? I mean, she was in Dad's room last night watching TV and she sleeps at Hef's all the time, and I don't understand because she's just supposed to be driving us around," I spit out.

The room is silent and I can tell by Pamela's horrified expression that my life is about to end.

We are at the Mansion when Dad corners me in my room, slamming the door shut behind him.

I can see the pool through the window where Playmates slip and slide across a greased blue pole suspended over the water. My father stands in front of the window and sunlight shines behind him, darkening his features, his body.

"How dare you go behind my back! Pamela told me you told her I was having an affair with Cindy!"

Terrified, I swallow his verbal attack, melting into the ground, wanting to erase myself.

My father circles me like a lion. I stare out the window again, avoiding his glare, and watch topless girls splash into the pool.

"I'm sorry, Daddy, please don't be mad. It was a mistake." I tremble, hiding behind a well of tears.

"There are no mistakes!" he screams, pointing his finger in my face.

I wish I were dead.

"Did you really think Pamela wasn't going to say anything to me? She is a lying, manipulating, self-centered bitch. The only reason I was with her was to make you happy!"

My heart falls out of my chest. Is he right? Is this all my fault? My head swims.

Outside, half-naked girls climb out of the pool, grabbing brightly colored cotton towels and laughing.

Inside, my father continues his diatribe. His words swirl around my head and push into my eardrums like cold small knives.

"You're just like your mother!"

I can hear what he's saying to me. His words are clear and uncompromising. By betraying him I am relegated to the lowest rank. I am my mother, a whining girlfriend, a useless whore, and as replaceable as the girls by the pool.

He grabs a book off the shelf and hands it to me.

"I want you to stay in this room and memorize the definition of loyalty and under no circumstances will you come out until you can recite exactly what loyalty means! Do I make myself clear? Loyalty!" Dad yells into my ears and then storms out.

Hands shaking, I look up the meaning of loyalty in Webster's dictionary: the quality or state or an instance of being loyal; faithfulness or faithful adherence to a person, government, cause, or duty. The lesson had been delivered. A lesson reinforced often during my childhood: faithful adherence to a person, my father, no matter what.

As a child it never occurs to me that he might be disloyal.

I collapse onto the bed and sob because I thought Pamela loved me, but she betrayed me. She was not loyal.

I wake up unsure of where I am. I look over and see the alarm clock and wooden box of cigarettes on the dresser. I'm still in room six at the Mansion.

There's a knock on the door, so I hide underneath the sheets, not wanting to wake up. The knocking continues. I throw the sheets back, get out of bed, and open the door. My father is there holding two tennis rackets, a smile splitting his face.

"I thought we could play some tennis," he says.

"I'm not up yet," I answer, still groggy.

"Well, get those lazy buns up. It's gorgeous out," he says energetically. "I'll even give you a couple games to start."

"I don't need a couple games to beat you," I say, still mad at him for last night and unsure of what to expect.

"You're right. Just do me a favor and don't embarrass me too much," he giggles.

I start to give in, my face hinting at a smile.

"I'll meet you out there in five but you better hurry before I get too warmed up," he chuckles.

I close the door and throw on a plaid tennis skirt, a white Polo collared shirt, and red visor, knowing this outfit will definitely gain Dad's approval.

I jet down the pathway to the tennis courts, where we rally back and forth.

"Listen, about Pamela, the truth is I'm actually relieved. I've been trying to get rid of that cunt and she never took a hint. Sometimes there are women who are such a pain in the ass you can't get rid of them; no matter how hard you try, they just won't leave. You have to understand one thing: I date a lot of women and some of them may send you messages just so they can get to me. Pamela has major problems, so please just do me a favor and let me handle my own personal business."

"Okay, Dad."

"We have to stick together," he emphasizes.

I slam a straight shot down the line, leaving him in the dust.

Summer is over and my sister retreats into my mother's arms. Savannah is terrified by my father's temper and finds safety by Mom's side. My father views her fear as an act of disloyalty and continues to abrade her whenever given the opportunity. Meanwhile, he spoils me, making me feel special and important, like one of the guys.

The relationship between Mom and me becomes more antagonistic. She overhears from some of the parents around Beverly Hills that Savannah and I have been living at the Mansion. When we deny it, Mom doesn't believe us.

We're in the kitchen as Mom paces back and forth. She's furious.

"Why do you kids lie to me?" she asks. "Is this where you've been all summer? At the Mansion?"

"No," we lie.

"Sneaking behind my back?" she yells.

"We've been at Dad's beach house," I tell her.

"Your father is completely out of line, putting you kids in the middle! Damn him!" she yells. "You're both grounded!"

Savannah and I retreat into our bedrooms and sit in silence, afraid Dad will get mad if he finds out. I call him to give him the heads-up and let him know what Mom is up to.

"Good work, Jennifer. You are a loyal daughter," he praises me, telling me not to worry because his lawyer will take care of everything.

Mom visits her attorney, explaining how Dad is ignoring the court order that clearly states that we are not allowed on the Mansion premises. He is taking us there against her will. The lawyer insists little can be done unless there is proof of us on the property. There is no proof. No one will come forward and she is not allowed on the grounds.

We are silent as Mom returns home depressed and tries to appeal to my father, calling him while we listen quietly from the den.

I can tell from her face that he's mocking her from the other end of the phone line, denying taking us to the Mansion, trying to convince her that she is paranoid. His words, his wealth, and his power are very intimidating. I imagine Mom hears Dad's satisfaction in slowly stealing her children away.

Instead of trying to understand Mom's hopeless attempts to keep us from the Mansion, I rebel against her. I listen to the part of myself that doesn't want my magical kingdom to be taken away.

Months pass. Savannah is reluctant to see my father at all. Although I want to be with my sister, I find myself bored and isolated at Mom's.

Mom is so exhausted when she returns home from work that after she's done tending to my sister's needs there is little room left for me. When she sees me, something in her blood runs cold and the way she speaks to me makes me feel sick and sad; not for what she says but for the way she says it. She and I are always fighting. We argue about how she talks to me, doesn't talk to me, small things, big things. There is no middle ground, no matter how hard we try. There is a huge void inside me, a void that is full when I am around Dad and all the excitement that comes with him.

Savannah stays home with Mom while I spend all my free time with my father.

I love being Daddy's Little Girl, his favorite.

Five

After the remodeling, Dad's house becomes a mini Mansion. It's 1983, and by now I'm in my early teens. Dad and I still have our rooms at the Mansion. However, Hef's leftovers seem to migrate over every weekend. You can feel sex in the air—it's everywhere. He loves the high-life filled with gorgeous people and perfect bodies. No in-betweens. Many of the women are models who want to be Playmates as they busy themselves poolside by posing and kissing ass.

People come in and out of Dad's newly remodeled house in a hysterical frenzy. Everyone's in a good mood. The stereo blasts constantly and the fridge is always stocked with food and drinks. Nude magazines are piled over every surface in the house.

Dad drops thousands of dollars on the women he dates. He pays for their maintenance. Most of the girls have either white bandages covering their nose or chin, or tight wraps around their breasts. Our guest bathrooms are stocked with glass containers of damp gauze pads, iodine, hydrogen peroxide, tape, and six-inch Q-tips.

Our home is now a hospital specializing in Playmate potential.

Carmela is run ragged serving cocktails to Dad's topless girlfriends by the pool.

Dad struts around naked.

It's the times. It's just the way things are.

Dad looks like a king on a throne as he lies back on a lounge chair, a cigar in his mouth.

He leans in and whispers, "Check out her bikini."

My head turns. Dad has taught me well: I can differentiate between girls who are really attractive and those who are just okay. I know exactly what to look for: tight ass, flat stomach, light eyes, full lips, soft skin, and tan but not overbaked. As for breasts, I've become an expert: too big, big enough, too small, saggy, firm, perky, soft.

Critiquing girls with Dad is so much fun.

"She's really pretty, don't you think?" I comment.

"A little cottage cheese on the thighs," he replies.

The girls jump up and down to "It's Raining Men" while Dad prances around pushing them into the pool without regard. Dad elbows me when one of the girls' tops flies off. I laugh, finally knowing what it's like to be the son he never had.

One of the girls stops him.

"What's up, sexy Daddy?" she asks. "It's my birthday. Aren't you going to take me shopping for my birthday?" She pulls playfully at the strings of her bikini.

"Of course I am," he says. "As long as you're going to shake that sexy ass for me."

Dad smiles and pulls me aside.

"Jen, I have something for you. Come with me upstairs."

I follow him to his room, passing more girls along the way.

"Where are you going?" Dad asks some blonde who appears ready to leave.

"I have to go to work," she explains.

"No, stay with me," he whines.

"Sweetie, you know I'd love to stay but I have to go shake my ass and make two grand. Unless you can pay me?"

"Never mind, go to work." Dad waves her off and mumbles "stripper" as we walk down the hallway.

He makes a quick stop in his bathroom. I stand there and watch as he points his penis down and urine shoots into the toilet. When he is done, he shakes it, walks into his bedroom, and reaches for something underneath his bed.

He hands me a gift-wrapped box.

"I had this made for you and I forgot all about it until just now. I hope you like it."

I open the box to find a Michael Jackson–style red leather jacket with suede fringes on the ends.

"Thanks, Dad. I've been wanting this jacket!"

I hug him as one of the hookers walks in, slightly surprised to see him naked and hugging me.

"What are you doing?" she asks.

"I'm giving my daughter a gift. Is that all right with you, dear?" he snaps. "She's off the payroll."

"Oh, I just wanted to give you a little something, if you know what I mean. I miss it," the girl whines, bending at the waist, shooting him a "fuck me" pose.

"Can't you see I'm having a moment with my daughter?" he says.

"Well, I'll be down the hall whenever you're ready, Daddy."

The girl bats her lashes and walks out.

At night, Dad asks one of his girlfriends to check in on me. He likes to make sure I'm okay. He knows I get lonely.

It's late when one of the girls knocks on my door, comes in, and lies down on the bed.

"What are you doing?" I ask her. She smiles at me.

She stares at me with luminous eyes that make me feel uncomfortable, like she's flirting with me, though part of me enjoys the attention.

"My dad is probably wondering where you are."

"He won't miss me. He wanted me to check on you," she assures me, caressing my arm.

Startled by her touch, I jump up.

"Well, you checked on me. Thanks," I pull back. "I'm fine, really."

"You sure are jumpy."

She pushes her curly brown hair behind her ears flirtatiously.

"Just tired," I mumble, wanting her to leave.

"Okay," she sighs, getting up slowly.

I tell her to close the door on the way out.

In the late '70s, I tag along with my father when he plays poker at Pips, an exclusive, private cigar bar at the Rodeo Collection. At the poker tables, I help set up the chips and race for new decks of cards on every occasion. I learn to quickly read the players' facial expressions, their gestures, and body language. Some of the men keep a steady face, raising, bluffing with no pairs while others throw in chips, betting loudly, trying to win the pot with nothing while others ask for a new stack before the round is over knowing they have the winning hand.

The dynamic with my father shifts regularly. I'm never quite sure why or when to expect the sudden change. Dad sends me flowers on Valentine's Day, we go to fancy restaurants, screenings, plays, travel to Europe, Hawaii and Morocco, just the two of us.

In Rome, we share the same bed and sometimes at night, I give him a massage before we go to sleep. My fingers press hard on his strong shoulder muscles and after a few minutes, I have to stop because my hands are sore. He says my massages are better than anyone else's. In the morning, he takes pictures of me asleep in the bed.

We spend our first day in Venice on a gondola moving slowly through the canals. The sun sets, reflecting shades of yellow off the uneven cobblestone streets.

"I can't wait to come here with someone one day," I tell him.

"*Someone?*" he answers in a bitter tone and I swallow hard, instantly aware that I said something wrong.

"I'm not good enough?" he barks.

"No. I just meant . . ."

"What exactly do you mean? Please tell me, because obviously I'm a little confused," his temper explodes.

"I meant with someone . . ." I stop, unable to complete my thought, quaking because I have offended him.

"Last time I checked, I was somebody! I don't know many fathers who would take their ungrateful daughters on trips like this! Do you?" he asks, threateningly.

"No." I shake my head, afraid to speak because I know his temper. The gondola moves slowly underneath a bridge and out of the sunlight.

A dark shadow sweeps across my father's face as he continues to abrade me. The rest of the day is a blur. He comes around at dinner when I begin talking negatively about my mother.

After two weeks of traveling through Venice and Rome, I write Dad a thank-you card while staying at the Ritz in Paris. I stand in front of him in my favorite red dress, awaiting his approval. I am shocked and then petrified when his mouth turns from a smile to a snarl.

"What the hell does this mean?" he screams.

He hovers over me, screaming louder than before.

"Do you want me dead? Is that it?"

"What? Of course not!" I shake my head wildly, trying to figure out what I did to make him so mad. I tremble as he continues to yell while waving the card I gave him in the air.

"Dead Dad!" he screams, handing it to me.

I look at it, my hands shaking uncontrollably. There it is on the opening line: "Dead Dad" instead of "Dear Dad." How could I be so stupid? How could I make such a careless mistake?

"You must want me dead!" he rages as thoughts of his death cross my mind. I am instantly guilt-ridden for even thinking these thoughts. He points his finger in my face. He looks like he's going to beat me up.

"I didn't mean it," I sob, trying to prove how much I love him.

I betrayed him. I swear to him that I will never do it again. I play whatever mind games I have to in order to return to our usual state of denial where we pretend nothing happened.

By that night, the storm has cleared and all the forgotten chaos has dissipated. He finally finds it in his heart to forgive me.

Six

By 1984 I'm a freshman at Beverly Hills High School.

After school, I take tennis lessons at Dad's house. I do anything to avoid home and the constant fighting with my mother. I hate it there.

One night, Dad decides to take me to Helena's, a well-known nightclub for celebrities. People stand in line for hours to get in, but it wasn't a problem for Dad and me. He hires a limo, and as we walk onto the red carpet we are instantly greeted by the doorman and owner, who lift up the velvet rope and let us enter without a second thought. I hear others in line whisper, wondering who we are and why we we're so important. I walk in on my father's arm with my head held high, feeling as though I am his equal. I am no longer a child.

I return to Mom's house at twelve-thirty in the morning

piss-drunk, reeking of alcohol. Mom storms down the hallway to greet me. A quiver of worry runs through me. If she had known what I was doing or whom I was with tonight I would be grounded for life.

"Where have you been? Are you drunk? Your curfew is midnight!" she yells, her eyes speak volumes.

"Midnight? Everyone else is allowed to stay out until at least one," I contest.

"You're not everyone!" Mom declares with conviction.

"Dad doesn't care what time I get home. He lets me do whatever I want," I scream.

"I don't care what your father does! As far as I'm concerned, he is not a parent! And as long as you're living under my roof you will listen to my rules, not your father's!" She paces back and forth. "Your father isn't normal," she mutters under her breath, not comprehending the enormity of what she is saying. Neither of us does.

"At least he isn't mean!" I shout.

Mom grounds me. I run back to my room, slam the door shut, and pick up the phone to call my father.

"Playboy Mansion," the other line answers.

"It's Jennifer; can I speak with my father?"

"Hello, Jennifer. One moment, please," the voice on the other end says.

A few seconds pass.

"Hello?" Dad answers cheerfully and I start to cry. "Jennifer?" his voice drops, immediately concerned. "Is everything all right? What's the matter?" he asks, but I am too choked up to talk.

"Nothing," I finally get out.

"It doesn't sound like nothing," he says as I take breaks for a moment to cry.

I miss him with a sudden and irresistible force. In a subtle, unforeseen way I was addicted to him, conveniently forgetting the bad times. Despite my near paralysis I manage to say, "Mom grounded me."

"She's a cold, selfish bitch," he says, welcoming every opportunity to criticize her. I somehow ignore what I don't want to admit. I don't let myself see that vilifying my mother has anything to do with his own personal agenda or his attempts to capture me out of spite for her. I hear him puffing on a cigar.

"I can't even talk to her," I sob.

"How can you? She's jealous and resents you because we're close and she can't have me," he says. "Do you want to come up here? I can send someone to pick you up. I'm in the middle of Monopoly," he says.

"I can't, remember? I'm grounded."

"That's a joke," he laughs. "I'm going to have a talk with her in the morning. You know how to reach me if you need anything."

"Thanks, Dad."

"I love you."

"I love you too."

We hang up and I lie on the bed, staring up at the ceiling listening to Pat Benatar for hours.

The next morning, while Savannah and Mom are out shopping, I call a cab and run away to Dad's house, where I know I can find exactly what I am looking for: freedom. We don't fight over things like rules, curfews, or partying. His parenting ethics belong to the school of breaking rules and having fun. I'm not sure he knows how to be a parent. I never question his ethics because they were all I knew. Being part of a real family is the furthest thing from my mind or anything I know. I arrive at his house and Carmela lets me in.

"What's the matter with you?" she asks, looking at my red, flushed face.

"Nothing. Mom and I had a fight," I exhale, out of breath.

"Your father is outside." Carmela hollers to let him know I'm there, and I join Dad by the pool and tell him I've run away.

"It's about time," he responds nonchalantly, applying tanning oil, as if it's no big deal.

"I can't even talk to her," I tell him.

"That's the one thing about you and me. We might get angry, but we always talk things out," he says. "Unlike your sister, who runs back to your mother like a fucking baby."

We nod our heads in agreement, understanding each other. When my father is with me, he sees nothing but me.

"Your mother always thinks I'm doing things behind her back, but it's not the case. I just want you kids to enjoy the opportunities I never had growing up," he explains.

I am completely enchanted as I see a softer side of him, and won't allow myself to recall his demeaning ways.

"What should I do?" I ask.

"Do you want to live with me?" he asks enthusiastically. "You know, there's always a room for you here at the house. I'd love to see you more often. I miss you when you're not around. I'll give you a key, a bank account, a credit card, and let you do whatever you want. No curfews—just make sure you don't get thrown out of school or get caught ditching," he laughs. "You can come and go as you please; you know I only want to make you happy. Besides, why would you want to live with that bitch anyway?"

I am conflicted because on one hand I don't want to disappoint him. I want to flee and run away, but my gut tells me I'm too young to be put in this awkward position. I allow his power and persuasive ways to influence me and make the final decision.

Dad says that he is the only one in the world who understands me. He promises me that life with him would be far better than the one I have now, and I believe him.

The clouds pass as Carmela brings a tray of fresh iced tea out to the pool.

There is something about millions of "fuck you" money and the freedom it buys that is hard to pass up.

Once my decision is made, I walk around Mom's house on

eggshells. She has no idea what I'm thinking and I'm too scared to tell her. I keep putting off the inevitable confrontation. But she can tell I'm slipping away. She senses I'm distancing myself from her, we're both so guarded, so closed off from each other, that we can't even talk about it. I feel like she doesn't really care about me and that she considers herself supremely unappreciated.

I'm in my bedroom listening to Prince's "When Doves Cry," when Mom storms in without warning. She glares at me as if I'm a stranger.

"Your father called and told me you want to move in with him. Is this true?" she asks, furious.

"Well, I know he wants me to live with him." I don't look at her.

"Do you want to live with your father?"

She stares into my room with no emotion. Her eyes are empty mirrors; they reflect nothing. She won't look me in the face anymore. Maybe she's too afraid of what she will see. Maybe she's afraid of what she won't see.

"Well, we just don't get along and when I'm with Dad I never seem to have any problems," I say, trying to sound sure of myself. She seems resigned to losing me. I secretly want her to demand that I stay, to prove that she loves and wants me.

"Do you want to live with your father?" she asks again in a tone as icy as the look she gives me.

Her words fade in and out like radio static. My mother's expression has changed to one that betrays the kind of fury and powerlessness I associate with war victims or people who have lost everything.

"We just don't get along," I reply with conviction.

Mom knows the problem runs far deeper. She knows from experience that there is a powerful energy drawing me toward my father. It is the same seductive force that pulled her toward him years ago. Something in her eyes tells me this is not an unfamiliar story to her. She should be warning me of his temper, the verbal abuse, the reasons she left him, what she has been through and is frightened by. But she seems too exhausted to face reality. She chooses instead to act as though my desire to live with him is about his money, an excuse that she can live with—that I have chosen luxury over her.

I am fifteen when I completely move out of my mother's house and into my father's.

A decision I will always question.

A decision that will be a determining factor in my life, and I will always wonder what would have been in store for me had I stayed. I learned too late that to leave is not the same as being left, but for some reason it feels the same.

Our lives are about to change forever.

I'm in my bedroom at Mom's packing my last bag when Savannah comes in. It's quiet when she enters and I'm sad as I hand her my sticker collection and stack of Judy Blume books.

"I don't see why you have to go." She sits down on the bed.

"I can't take it anymore. All the rules and curfews make me sick."

Tears stream down her cheeks. I stop packing and sit beside her on the bed.

"It's nothing you did—don't ever think that." I wrap my arms around her. "Don't cry. We'll still see each other."

"No we won't." Her tears fall even harder.

"I'm only going to be a few miles away."

"It's not the same."

"I want us to be together, but if I stay, Mom and I will kill each other."

"I don't know why it has to be this way," Savannah sniffles.

"You can call me anytime."

"I'll miss you." She looks up at me.

"I'll miss you too."

We sit there for a while and hold each other, crying in each other's arms.

Dad's horn blares outside and we slowly pull apart. I wipe the tears off Savannah's face. She helps me carry my suitcases to the front door.

"We'll talk soon, okay?" I say.

I kiss her soft, rosy cheeks and we hug, not wanting to let go.

Dad waves to us from the car. Savannah stays standing in the doorway while I walk down the brick pathway to his Rolls-Royce.

I am finally breaking free from the confines of reality and entering a fantasyland of enchanted fables. I will no longer be treated like a child.

I throw my suitcases into the backseat and hop inside. My insides shrivel up as I wave good-bye to Savannah, who stands motionless in the doorway where I left her.

Seven

My bedroom at Dad's is stocked with all the latest high-tech electronics. It is as immaculate as a palace. There are no traces of a child living here, unlike my room at Mom's, where I was free to hang posters of my favorite rock stars on the walls. A big-screen television stands beside a brand-new Sony stereo system with huge speakers. My king-size bed is perfectly displayed, suited to fit a princess. The gold-plate canopy is elevated from the rest of the room with sheer white linen sheets draping over the frame. Pink satin sheets with lace trim are tucked under a Victorianesque comforter. The bathroom is decorated with Italian flowered tile, with a grandiose marble shower and a Jacuzzi bathtub to match.

The walk-in closet is even more impressive. Dad sent his personal assistant to shop Rodeo. When I arrive, my closet is filled with the latest fashions fresh off the Milan runway. There is everything ranging from Sergio Valente jeans to Versace sequined and rhine-stone tops, leather jackets in every possible silhouette imaginable, and an array of designer stilettos to snakeskin boots.

Karate, tennis, and a personal masseuse once a week all become routine occurrences. Everything is at my disposal. I can drop thousands a week shopping for outfits I will wear only once.

I begin to associate materialism with love, or what I now consider love.

Despite the fabulous lifestyle, my life becomes cold and lonely. Lonely because my father is never home. I sit in his huge house with everything I've ever wanted except love and attention. Loneliness is the catalyst that pushes me to delve into the seductions of drugs and escapism. Dad tells me to join him at the Mansion every day. He doesn't understand why I wouldn't want to sleep in my old room there.

By the end of my first week at Dad's, he tells me he's taking my mother to court.

"I will not pay her child support when you're not even there! Because you are mine and you live here now. Do you understand? I own you."

Instinct warns me to agree with him even if I don't understand why he's so angry. He is good at making me believe white is black and black is white. I try not to think about the many faces he wears as resentments resurface and I continue to bury them.

"Are we clear?" he commands, towering over me. I feel a tremor run through me as I begin to question if all his seductions and enticements were worth it.

"Yes." I nod.

"Personally, I think she should pay me child support," he chuckles to himself.

I smile and pretend to grasp what he is saying as I turn around and walk back down the hallway to my room.

Hours later, I'm playing Nintendo when I hear faint sounds of someone knocking on the front door. I hear Dad yelling, so I get up and quietly open my bedroom door. He screams over his balcony.

I take small steps down the hallway, leaning my head toward his bedroom, eager to hear what he's saying.

"She isn't home. Don't come here again! You're trespassing! I'll call the cops if I see you anywhere near this house again!" he shouts.

I peer out the window just beyond the staircase to see he's yelling at my mother, who's standing in the driveway.

I shiver, wanting urgently to run to her, to tell her I've made a terrible mistake. I miss her and Savannah and want to go home. But I am too afraid to move, to speak, to admit that I need the one person my father despises the most.

"Don't bother calling her; she doesn't want to talk to you!" he shouts, slamming his balcony door shut. The sound makes me jump. I have never felt so helpless or vulnerable. I feel completely and utterly alone, as if everything I had trusted had been taken from me. Immobilized by fear, I stand there for a moment unsure of what to do, though the thought of him finding me eavesdropping makes me run back to my room and close the door. I collapse onto the floor as silent tears course down my cheeks.

Dad and I are driving down Wilshire Boulevard in his Rolls as he sings along to Linda Ronstadt's "Hurt So Bad." His mood is cheerful.

"I finally gave that bitch what she deserves!" he shouts with vigor.

"What?" I ask naively.

"You are solely mine. The judge awarded me legal custody of you and your mother has legal custody of Savannah."

"Why?" I ask, unsure of what he's talking about.

"Why? No mother loses custody of her child in the state of California! I humiliated her in front of the entire community! My greatest revenge is taking away what every woman fears losing: her children!" His deep voice fills the car. I realize this has all been a game to him. I am the prize he has won. I feel sick. I never meant for it to go this far. What alarms me most is how angry he is at her, how angry I am supposed to be, if I know what's good for me. I wasn't sure what had happened to make him so upset. Was he mad at me or my mother, or did he simply want revenge so badly that he didn't comprehend how much his temper would hurt me? I knew in my heart that I loved him, and that in itself is unnerving because it left me vulnerable to him.

The bargain is simple. Hate my mother, and I am treated like a queen; defend her, and I am verbally berated for what feels like an eternity. Hidden beneath the spell of my own denial, I continue to believe that he loves me and wants only the very best for his little girl.

My relationship with my mother continues to crumble beneath my father's vicious attacks. In this split, each parent gives up one child. The trauma of losing my mother and sister leaves permanent gaping holes in my heart. An impenetrable barrier comes down between Savannah and me: she's on my mother's side, and I'm on my father's. I lost her the day I lost my mother.

Years later, I will learn that even my mother's lawyer pulled her aside and said, "Off the record, it's too late for Jennifer. If she wants to live with her father, there's nothing you can do about it. If I were you, I would protect your other daughter from him." And that's exactly what she did.

I practice not hurting. I learn to feel nothing at all.

I've slept in my new bedroom for two weeks and still feel like a stranger in this house. Dad is out every night and I hate to be alone. I start to have trouble sleeping. Close to midnight, I snoop in his bathroom and find every kind of prescription pill imaginable. Opening his cabinets and drawers, I am careful with the bottles because I know he has them positioned precisely, though seemingly haphazardly, in a certain order. Some bottles lie on their side, slanted to the left, upside down, while others sit upright, tilted to the right.

Like a good physician, Dad keeps everything on hand: Valium, Percocet, Halcyon, Xanax, Demerol, even Quaaludes. There's one bottle for each of his girlfriends. Unlike the girls themselves, the bottles are all unique.

I've heard about them. I know what they're for.

I steal handfuls of pills: Xanax so I can sleep without nightmares and Halcyon to forget that I can't sleep at all.

I shut the cabinet doors and hurry back down the hallway to my bedroom. I pop a few Xanax and get back into bed.

After school, I sit at the desk in the den with my books and homework scattered in front of me. Carmela brings me a tray of fruit as I watch *Santa Barbara* and pop a Xanax.

My high school tutor arrives and I sit with her in the den showing her my homework. We begin an English assignment until I retreat upstairs to take a few more Xanax from my father's medicine cabinet. When I return, my tutor intermittently listens to the dramas in my life as she continues to write my papers. When she is done, I thank her profusely and tell her to send us the bill. She leaves, and Carmela yells from the kitchen that my friend Liz is on the phone.

Liz invites herself over and brings Hunter with her. Liz is fun, tomboyish, and easygoing. She likes to mix up her punk look with splashes of high fashion. Today Liz wears pink Doc Martens boots with a pair of shiny black leggings and an Yves St. Laurent blouse she's tied in a knot above her belly button.

Hunter is a strikingly blond, blue-eyed teenage actress. She's much more feminine and loves candy wrapper dresses and strappy Candies in an array of sorbet colors.

We sneak outside and smoke a fatty on the tennis court.

"Is your dad ever home?" Hunter asks. Liz hands me the joint.

"Dude, we could have some killer parties here." Liz exhales as I take another hit.

"Totally. Major ragers." Hunter looks around the spacious backyard.

I agree, coughing.

"Killer bud, huh?" Liz asks and I nod, turning purple.

"My neighbor down the block grows the best chronic. He's always giving me free shit. He deals," Liz explains.

The French doors open and out comes my father, shirtless and wearing white tennis shorts.

"Oh shit!"

We panic and scramble to hide the bud.

Hunter flips her hair with her hands. Liz squeezes Visine drops into her eyes. I hyperventilate, trying to get the pot smell off my breath. We pretend to laugh, looking and pointing at nothing in the trees as he waltzes over.

"Hi, girls."

"Hi, Dad. This is Liz and Hunter, friends from school."

"Pleasure to meet you," Dad says and extends his hand confidently.

I can tell by the look in his eyes that he likes Hunter.

"What are you girls doing?" he asks.

"Just hanging out," I answer, annoyed by his apparent attraction to her.

"Are you an actress?" Dad asks.

"Yes," Hunter smiles.

"Do you have an agent?" he asks.

"I'm meeting with a few different people," she answers.

"You should give me your head shots. I'll send them over to Aaron Spelling—he's a personal friend," Dad brags, looking her up and down.

I'm dying of embarrassment. Why doesn't he just ask if he can fuck her?

Dad smiles at Hunter one last time.

"Call me at the office. Jennifer has the number."

Invisible fumes shoot from my ears as I pull my friends into the house and away from the lecher.

After they leave, I bump into my father in the upstairs hallway. I decide not to bring up the fact that he humiliated me in front of them and that, by lunch tomorrow, everyone will know he's a total perv.

Instead, I ask if I can have people over Friday night, knowing he probably won't be home anyway. He tells me he's going to Vegas, but says Carmela will be around if I need her.

His confidence in my ability to handle myself makes me forgive him for his inappropriate behavior. I second-guess myself, thinking I blew the whole thing with Hunter out of proportion.

At school the next day, Liz, Hunter, and I high-five each other in the halls as we pass out flyers. It's all about Friday night.

We hire two bartenders and a DJ and borrow a couple off-duty security guards from the Mansion. I wrap a few strands of sparkling lights in the trees and sprinkle fake snow on the tennis court. "I Want a New Drug" by Huey Lewis and the News screams through the outdoor speakers.

I greet guests at the front door in a silver bobbed wig and pass out vodka-infused Jell-O shots. Hundreds of people stroll in, decked out disco-style.

Girls in black off-the-shoulder leotards and short-shorts strut in, their faces and necks coated with glitter. Guys wearing layered Izod shirts, ribbed tank tops, and ripped Levi's slap each other high-five.

A large group comes through the door at once. As I place a Jell-O shot into someone's hand, I recognize a bracelet and instantly pull back. It's my sister.

"Savannah? I'm so glad you came!"

I hand the plate of Jell-O shots to Hunter. Savannah and I embrace. We walk into the study.

"Rad party. Is Dad here?" she asks.

"Yeah, right. He's gone for the weekend and I'm in charge of regulating recklessness. Be careful, there're tons of older guys here."

"Don't worry, I can handle myself." Savannah smiles.

She appears remarkably poised while sitting on the brown leather chair. She easily looks like she could be in high school. I hear a glass break in the other room.

"I have to go play hostess. We'll catch up later?"

An hour later, amid the dense mass of bodies, I notice Savannah with a cocktail in her hand talking to a junior. As I pass her, I take the cocktail away. "You'll handle yourself a lot better without this," I whisper.

Liz grabs me, pulling me into a clandestine meeting in the pantry. Michelle, Sonya, Hunter, Liz, Amber, and I gather around as Quaaludes are dispersed and water bottles are passed around.

Liz pulls me aside ten minutes later suggesting we pop another. The effects of the first pill haven't kicked in, so we figure, Why not?

Ten minutes later, we do it again.

One more Quaalude and I'm out. There are no nightmares, no worries, and no memories whatsoever.

When I wake up the next morning at ten, I'm surprised to find a random guy passed out in bed next to me. Replaying the night, I vaguely recall flirting with a senior on the baseball team at Harvard High. There's soreness in between my legs that I've never felt before. Throwing the covers back, I stumble out of bed and step on a rubber.

Images of him penetrating me flash through my mind. I remember the pressure of his body, the tightness between my thighs, and gritting my teeth. I didn't want him to know it was my first time.

For a split second I am bummed that I have lost my virginity to a random guy I don't know. But I rationalize it, telling myself that I was bound to lose it eventually.

I slip on a robe and stare at the stranger in my bed.

I have to get this guy out of here.

"Hey, buddy, get up. It's time for you to go," I say, echoing a phrase I've heard my father use.

He doesn't flinch.

"Excuse me, whatever your name is! You're going to have to leave now."

The guy scratches his head, barely conscious.

Downstairs, I hear Carmela shriek at the top of her lungs. She must've just arrived. Her footsteps pound in my head as she approaches my bedroom. She stands in the doorway in a state of shock.

"Jennifer, your father would be furious if he saw this mess! I have to clean or we both going to be in big trouble," she rambles.

I nod at her, excusing myself momentarily so I can go puke in the toilet.

My parties become a huge hit, their reputation traveling to all the private and public high schools: Uni, Harvard, Westlake, Marymount, and Brentwood.

Most of the kids who come graduated Beverly years ago. I am suddenly in "the know," the bad girl with the attitude and wild reputation. Invites to all the lavish parties, club openings, and hottest restaurants are all at my fingertips. I no longer need to approach anyone, return phone calls, or even smile. As a sophomore, I am beyond It girl status. I am an L.A. socialite and have become an infamous high school legend.

At one point, I'm chilling on the third-floor patio with my Ray-Bans, Gloria Vanderbilt jeans, Keds, and a string of green, black, and pink plastic bracelets up and down my arms. Kids try to schmooze me, dropping hints about parties they'll never get invited to.

"There's a huge bash in Aspen this weekend. It's definitely the place to be," says a guy while passing a dime bag to a friend.

"If Jennifer's going to be there, then definitely," says a guy with spiked red hair, loud enough for me to hear.

I walk down the steps, blowing smoke in their faces. "Little children," I say, flicking my Marlboro Light at the guy with red hair. "You have no idea what these parties are about. Nothing's happening in Aspen. Robert Downey Jr. and I are kicking it here this weekend," I say with a smile, fucking with them.

Eight

Life becomes more exciting when I get my driver's permit and Dad buys me a red Mercedes convertible to practice with. He doesn't mind that I'm only fifteen; in fact, he think's it's ridiculous that I have to wait, especially since I'm such a good driver.

After school, friends jump in and we cruise the front of Beverly High singing along to the Go-Gos' "Our Lips Are Sealed." I get a huge adrenaline rush while shifting the gears of my new car. Most of my same clique of friends from elementary school are glammed out in culottes, crop tops, and scrunch boots. We paint our faces with Chanel makeup, hold cigarettes between our fingers, and perch our arms out the windows.

At Pastels for blended daiquiris, the maitre d' greets us warmly and escorts us to our usual patio table.

"Hello, Ms. Saginor; so nice to see you again. You just missed your father. Should we put this on his house account?"

"That would be great, Alfredo," I say, giving him a peck on the cheek.

After Pastels, we hit the Polo Lounge for more blended daiquiris and then whiz over to Bistro Gardens for chopped salads and a refill on the patio.

"It's almost seven; I have to get going," Hunter says.

"Dude, you are not going home yet," I say, exhaling smoke.

"I have to. My mother will kill me if I'm not home for dinner."

"Me too," Liz confesses. "We eat at seven-thirty."

"You guys are not bailing? That is so lame. Just chill, have another drink. Call your parents, and tell them you're going to be late."

I motion to the waiter to bring us another round.

"All right, one more." Hunter sits back down.

"I wish I didn't have to go home," Amber sighs.

"You're so lucky your parents don't care about dinner," Sonya says enviously. If only she knew how dark and lonely my life has become.

I chug the last few sips of my cocktail as new ones arrive.

We stumble out of Bistro Garden seeing double of everything. We hug each other, blow air kisses, and say our good-byes for the night.

Later that night, Carmela serves me dinner. I sit alone in the living room, remembering dinner at my mother's house and Savannah kicking me under the table while she giggled.

"Have dinner with me," I say softly. "I'm not even hungry."

"I have so much work to do before I leave. You know how your father wants everything just right," Carmela insists.

My tutor arrives an hour later and Carmela carries a plate of beautifully garnished desserts into the den for us to nibble on. The tutor works on my homework until I get bored watching her, and I head upstairs to make a few phone calls. When my work is completed, my tutor leaves and my father's house becomes very quiet. I hate the silence.

I take a second look at the note my father leaves me every day in the upstairs hallway.

"I'm at the Mansion," it reads. "Come up if you want."

Gin night, Monopoly, movie night, fight night, Sunday backgammon, or any other night, I know where to find him. Maybe if Dad and Hef were lovers I would understand why he devotes so much time to him.

I can't sit still. My ADD is in high gear and my anxiety shakes me from my daiquiri coma. I'm wired, scattered. I debate watching TV, reading, writing, and taking a walk. I organize and reorganize candles, picture frames, and magazines.

I flip through the pages of my algebra book. Anything to keep me occupied in this huge and lonely house. Bored, I slip off my chair, walk back into the hallway, and stare at Dad's note. Since high school, I've kept my Mansion visits to weekends only. Mom always said, "No parties on a school night." But she's not around to tell me what to do anymore.

Ten minutes later, I stroll into Hef's foyer dressed sloppily in Sergio Valente jeans, checked Vans, and a pink Camp Beverly Hills T-shirt. The guys are in the library playing Monopoly while a group of Playmates with size-zero waistlines lounge in the med room, picking at pineapple salads.

Everyone turns to examine me as I kiss my favorites, hugging others left and right. Tobey, a super-cool, down-to-earth actress with straight blond hair, blue eyes, and a sweet Southern accent, grabs my hand.

"Hey, girl; good to see you," Tobey says warmly.

I hug Austin, an outgoing brunette, who will eventually open a nightclub.

"I saw Nicolette Sheridan at some party in the Hills last night," Tobey mentions.

"You just wish you were her," Austin smirks.

"You're right. She always dates the hottest guys."

Morgan, a genuinely nice makeup artist and photographer, plops down next to us.

"I saw Charlie Sheen at the Roxy. Weren't you dating him?" Morgan asks.

"We've fucked, but we're not dating," Tobey answers.

Her voice trails off as Dolph Lundgren and Grace Jones walk down the staircase and into the foyer. Grace looks amazing in Azzedine Alaïa black body-conscious Lycra pants and Charles Jennifer pumps with wraparound leather wings winding up her ankles. Her chunky gold Egyptian-style necklace looks like it could stop bullets.

Kendall, Hef's nineteen-year-old girlfriend, pops up behind them, licking her lips naughtily.

Kendall is tan with wavy dark brown hair and enticing green eyes. Her skimpy lavender outfit clings to the toned curves of her perfect body.

For some reasons, Kendall annoys the shit out of me. She's got this fake laugh that makes me want to bash her in the face. There's something about the way she stares at me that gives me the creeps. Plus, I've heard she's into girls, which *really* grosses me out.

I have to give her credit though; she always manages to get what she wants. The Playmates jump up from the table when Kendall enters the room. Her presence changes the energy, makes it vital, edgy and electric.

She is dressed so sparingly her nakedness and body exude sexuality in a perverse and almost intoxicating way. She is a magnet for attention and no one seems to give it to her. Disingenuous laughs and compliments fly out of everyone's mouth except mine. The playmates kiss her ass, though I'm not certain why. The phoniness in the air has skyrocketed to such a degree I feel uncomfortable in my own skin, let alone seat.

I look away from her whenever she peers in my direction. We glance at each other with mutual loathing.

Duran Duran's "Hungry Like the Wolf" plays while Natasha, a

Swedish coke whore and Kendall's newest best friend, sprays Afrin in her nose.

"Damage control," Natasha shrugs, offering it to me.

"I've sworn off all nose sprays," I tell her.

I gaze out the window at the flamingos, but am interrupted when Dad, Hef, and the other guys come in.

"Hi, my sweet daddy. I love you," says Kendall, fawning over Hef.

"How's Baby-boo?" Hef asks sweetly.

They sound like third-graders. Dad waltzes in wearing an Izod shirt from Rudnick's with his collar turned up.

"Hi, sweetheart," he says.

Anticipating a warm welcome, I turn to him, but quickly realize he's not talking to me when he grabs a Playmate and kisses her hungrily on the lips, petting another one on the head like a dog. Slouching in my seat, I stare from my father to Kendall and wonder why I'm not at home doing homework. In fact, I'm not sure if he even notices me at all.

"Hi, dear. You staying?" Dad asks.

"I just wanted to stop by and say hi," I tell him.

"And here I thought you came to see me," Kendall mumbles.

I ignore her, sighing audibly.

"How was school?" Dad asks.

"Boring," I say with a shrug. "I have to do my homework."

"You can do it in the library or go upstairs to your room," Dad offers, urging me to stay.

"I don't think I can concentrate here," I tell him.

I am holding on to every last bit of self-discipline.

"Homework? Fuck homework," some guy says.

What the hell does he know, I think to myself. He's a fucking porn star.

"You're in a pool of distractions, kid. It's up to you to figure out which direction to take," Ted whispers.

"Oh, will you stop with all that philosophical jargon! You're gonna taint the girl's mind for Christ's sake," Duke shouts.

"Movie time," Hef announces.

All the girls file into the screening room to watch an old Spencer Tracy movie. Dad slaps one of the many blondes on the ass.

"I'm out," I say, throwing him an air kiss.

" 'Bye, dear. Call if you need anything."

I have a bottle of Xanax waiting for me at home. I won't need a thing.

I hug him good-bye.

The next day I flake on tennis practice, go home, and flip through television channels, stopping on *General Hospital*.

I call Liz.

"What's up? Wanna smoke a fatty?"

"I can't. I'm babysitting my sister," she answers.

"We can smoke your sister out too," I say.

"She's nine."

"Nothing like starting young."

We dial Hunter on the party line.

"Cocktails at the Polo Lounge?" we ask her.

"I'm rehearsing lines for a play," Hunter whines.

"Scorpion bowl at Trader Vic's?"

"I wish. Did you see Greg totally checking me out in third period?"

"Shut up!"

"I swear."

"He's so hot, I'm spazzing out."

"Let's celebrate!"

"Do you think he'll call tonight?" Hunter asks.

"Who?" I ask, taking off my double-striped socks and pink leg warmers.

"Greg!"

"I don't know," I say, annoyed that we're obviously not going out for drinks.

"I'm in the middle of making macaroni and cheese," Liz shouts, "I've got to bolt!"

"Later."

We click off and I tell myself I should stay home and study for the math quiz in the morning. I turn on the radio, grab a joint from my jewelry box, light it, and blow smoke out the window into the dark backyard.

Laura Branigan's "Self Control" comes on the radio as I squeeze my head in my hands, resisting the temptation to go up to the Mansion.

After school the following day I'm hanging with Amber, Hunter, Sonya, Liz, and Michelle. We're in Amber's kitchen munching on Twinkies and Ding-Dongs while Michelle and Hunter are in the den doing the worm to the B52s' "Rock Lobster."

Amber takes off her cardigan sweater, leaving her white button-down hanging out as she picks up the phone and calls Dean, a stud at Beverly High.

Dean has plans with Brian, so Amber motions for me to pick up the other line.

"Put Brian on," says Amber. "Jennifer wants to say hi."

I wave frantically, mouthing, "No!"

I run an oversize turquoise plastic comb through the top of my teased hair.

"You guys should come over," says Amber.

"What are you doing?" Brian asks.

"Nothing. That's why you should come over," she repeats.

Amber hangs up the phone, smiling, giving us the thumbs-up. She wraps a side ponytail into her hair with a pastel blue mesh tie. Sonya cranks up "Girls Just Want to Have Fun" as they dance around and primp, waiting for the guys to arrive.

Michelle puts in hoop earrings and a sweatshirt with the neck ripped out while Hunter changes into an off-the-shoulder shirt kept together by safety pins.

Glancing at my Swatch watch, I pick up the phone and call my father at the Mansion. A butler transfers me to a phone by the pool, where Dad's playing backgammon with the guys.

"Hi, dear; you okay?" he asks, sounding concerned.

"Yeah, I'm okay."

"You don't sound okay," he says.

"I'm at Amber's."

"Well, why don't you call me back when you can talk," he says empathetically.

I don't respond.

"Or come up if you want. I'll be here," he says warmly.

"I can't," I answer, conflicted.

"Tell them you have to meet me," Dad suggests, picking up on my desire to leave. "Hope to see you soon. Love you," he says, sincerely.

"Me too."

We hang up and I look around at my friends spraying Rave into their hair.

"I have to go," I tell them.

"What do you mean? You can't leave. Dean and Brian are on their way over," Amber whines, slipping on a new pair of striped Vans.

"I forgot about this thing. I told my Dad I was going to meet him," I say, grabbing my Louis Vuitton clutch.

"Come on," sighs Hunter.

"We just got here," Michelle adds.

"We haven't even watched *Fast Times at Ridgemont High* or *Sixteen Candles*," Sonya says as she adjusts the roach clip and feathers attached to her belt loop.

"Hit me later," I say, bailing out the front door. Cruising down Sunset Boulevard, I blast Bananarama's "Cruel Summer," apply bronze lipstick, adjust my Ray-Bans, and think about how boring high school kids are compared to Hef's A-list crowd.

High school becomes something of an afterthought. I begin ditching school every day at noon. I show up long enough to make an appearance but excuse myself to the nurse's office or hand over one of many forged notes that I keep at my disposal. My time, empty of adolescent concerns, is spent hanging out at the Mansion. Going to Hef's is like a drug. It seeps into my system, pumps through my veins, until it is part of me. Like any drug, the first time you take it, there's a rush. After a while, you can't stop thinking about it, you want it, you crave it, and then you need it. You don't know why, you just do.

Waltzing into the Mansion's foyer in my Jordache pinstripe jeans tucked into my Peter Pan boots, I join the Playmates in the med room. They're sporting the neon *Flashdance* look: Spandex, nylon jumpers, leg warmers, Reebok high-tops, bandanas, and ponytails on the side of their heads.

"I'm dying over this workout," Morgan sighs, out of breath.

"It was so major," boasts Charlie, an energetic, upbeat Playmate.

"Where did you work out?" I ask.

"Here. In the gym," Charlie answers.

I look at her blankly, trying to recall exercise before I picked up smoking.

"It was awesome. You should come tomorrow," Tobey offers.

"For sure," I answer casually as Crawford, Hef's right-hand assistant, enters and whispers into my ear.

"Go say hi to your father," she advises, as if she is my mother.

"I will, in a sec," I smile obediently.

"While you're at it, take Louie outside," Crawford says, referring to the little black poodle.

"I'll go. I want some fresh air anyway," says Charlie.

Kendall glances at me for a split second and looks away. By avoiding eye contact, we acknowledge our unspoken dislike for each other.

The girls order tuna sandwiches, sliced cantaloupe and yogurt, and wheat germ health shakes. Kendall combs through magazines, pointing out sexy guys and girls.

"She's so hot. I love girls with toned arms," Kendall says sensuously and I turn red, embarrassed.

Through the window, I see my father and Hef by the pool.

"So, what have you been up to?" Austin asks while flipping through *Vogue*.

"Nothing really. I'm just sick and tired of school, which is kind of a bummer considering I'm only a freshman."

"Ahh, you're just a baby . . . ," says Kendall, jumping into the conversation.

"So are you," I shoot back.

"Yeah, but I feel old," she laughs.

"Not enough pampering?" I joke, sliding a magazine featuring "The Recent Rise of Plastic Surgery" in her direction.

Neither one of us blinks.

"You've got balls." Kendall lowers her shades as a butler comes by and offers the girls more Chardonnay.

Morgan pushes her crystal glass away.

"No thanks; I gave up drinking for a while."

"You're serious?" Tobey asks and Morgan nods yes proudly.

"How do you do it?"

"I just don't think about it. After a while it becomes habit."

"Are you speaking abstractly or specifically?" Austin asks.

"Specifically. It's like when you quit doing coke. The first year is tough but then you're over it. Anyone can pull a vial out right in front of you and you don't even flinch."

"You're full of shit. I quit coke two years ago and when people are doing it around me, I want to lick the countertops after they leave the room," Natasha jumps in.

We all look at one another.

"It was a defining moment," Natasha exhales and we all burst out laughing.

"You should work out with us tomorrow," Charlie says, as she turns to me. "Wait, is tomorrow Friday or Saturday? I can't remember."

"Girl, you need a hobby," Austin shouts, throwing a napkin at her playfully.

I start to spend all my free time at the Mansion. I am accepted and welcome into the circle of Playmates as "one of the girls." Tobey draws a picture of us and titles it "Our Gang." She hands the picture to me, and for the first time I feel like I am part of something, a group, a family.

The school bell rings for nutrition class, and I hop into my car and take off.

I arrive at the Mansion just in time to work out with the Playmates. We're in the Playmate of the Month's house listening to Culture Club's "Karma Chameleon" in the gym when Kendall whines, "Do you think I'm too flabby?"

"You're a size zero," smirks Tobey.

"A walking public service announcement for anorexia," I mumble under my breath.

Kendall sighs, picks up the phone, and dials the kitchen.

"Hi, it's Kendall. Can you bring juice out here? I don't know— orange, carrot, beet, maybe blended—you decide." She hangs up, fans herself, and lifts the weights again. "Do I have bags under my eyes?" Kendall asks and I debate leaving.

"Are you guys going to Helena's tonight?" Tobey asks.

"I'm totally beat from last night. I was at the Florentine Gardens and ended up at Peanuts. It was so random," Kendall brags.

"Hi? Lesbian haven," Charlie laughs.

"Loved it," Kendall giggles.

"I'm so over the club scene. I had to wait in the most bogus line at some underground bar—and I was on the guest list. Can you believe it?" Charlie chimes in.

"Tell the doorman we're friends—he'll take care of you," Kendall says.

"Kendall's known throughout the underground. She's even known in parking lots," Natasha blurts out as Tobey rips the sleeves off her Heaven T-shirt.

"Very Kristy McNichol," Austin comments, referring to Tobey's ripped sleeves.

"I think I'm in love," Kendall says, looking at her arms. "Let's get out of here," says Kendall. "I swear the goddamned walls are caving in on me! I am fantastically bored."

The girls look at her quizzically.

"Where do you want to go?" Austin asks.

"Madrid," says Kendall, "Cyprus, Ireland, India, Paris! Let's take a cruise through the Mediterranean!"

"La Scala?" asks Morgan, referring to a restaurant in Beverly Hills.

"Chopped salad?"

"Let's take the limo!" Kendall offers.

"Fab idea!"

"I'll tell Daddy." Kendall gets up, smiling at me. "Come on, we'll go together."

Kendall grabs for my hand, but I resist taking it.

"I don't bite, you know." Kendall stares at me, holding her gaze a few seconds too long.

"I know."

"You don't like me, do you?"

Kendall looks me up and down as we breeze through the backyard.

"You're okay," I answer, taken off guard.

I allow our eyes to meet, but then quickly look away.

My father, Hef, and the other guys are playing backgammon by the pool. Kendall caresses Hef while I say hi to Dad.

"Boo-boo, we were thinking about taking the limo and running into Beverly Hills to grab some lunch," Kendall whispers to Hef in a baby voice.

"There's nothing you want here?" Hef asks endearingly.

"We thought it would be fun to get out with just the girls," Kendall responds sweetly.

"I guess coming back after lunch is better than not coming back at all," Dad jokes.

"You would know. That's why you give 'em a shot before they know what hit them!" Duke chuckles.

"Desperate times call for desperate measures," Dad responds.

"We're going to leave you guys to wallow in your misery," Kendall laughs. "Love you, Boo." Kendall kisses Hef on the lips.

" 'Bye, Dad." I kiss him good-bye, like I too just got permission to leave.

We make our way through the backyard. Kendall takes my hand in hers while we walk. I feel her delicate palm cradled in my own and my heartbeat races while the world around me moves in slow motion. There is a fine line between my disgust and my desire to be included, to be cared for. Kendall's acceptance of me washes warmly through my veins. It is nice to finally feel wanted.

Before we reach the girls in the foyer, Kendall and I lock eyes one last time. Her eyes are seductive and inviting. They catch me off guard. No one has ever looked at me like that.

We all pile into Hef's limo and head toward Beverly Hills. Kendall pops open a bottle of champagne. We drink straight from the bottle. She turns up the volume and sings along to Styx's "The Best of Times."

I search my reflection in the tinted window, suddenly unable to recognize the girl I see there.

People stare as our black limo pulls up in front of La Scala. Kendall is out first, the rest of the entourage follows. Heads turn at the six glam divas strutting up the stairs. Kendall has a jeweled Maud Frizon calfskin bag slung over her shoulder and strides confidently in strappy Claude Montana spike-heel shoes.

We enter the restaurant with rock-star confidence and order a round of Bloody Marys. Seated immediately at a corner booth, we review the menu, compare mental calories, and decide not to eat.

Kendall examines my bracelets, picking through the rainbow of colors.

"I like the sparkly ones," she says.

My arm tingles.

"I could use a lift." Kendall looks at us with void eyes. "My connection is all tapped out. Does anyone know anybody?"

"I've never done it, but it's all over high school. I can make a phone call," I say.

"Right on!" Kendall shouts, ordering us another round.

"To good times." Morgan raises her glass.

Kendall scoots her chair closer to mine, kicks off her three-inch heels, and stretches her tanned legs under the table.

"You are so adorable," she says, and I can't help but notice how striking she is.

I don't respond. I am embarrassed but flattered. I want to continue hating her, but it's becoming more and more difficult.

When I finish my Bloody Mary, Kendall motions to the waiter, who quickly brings me another. The chopped salads everyone craved earlier have been forgotten as drinks flow around the table. The girls cast their eyes around the restaurant like star fuckers scanning for somebody famous.

"Can you be any less discreet?" I ask.

"Discreet is what you say when you sneak into the Beverly Hills Hotel and have kinky sex with your married orthodontist," Natasha says.

"Or when you indulge in a passionate midday orgy," Kendall smiles.

"Don't mind her. She's just frustrated that everyone wants her and she can't do a damn thing about it because she has a boyfriend," Tobey laughs.

"It's not cheating if it's with a girl," Kendall jokes, but it doesn't feel like a joke as she reaches under the table and places her hand on my thigh. She allows her fingers to brush across my skin, arousing a side of me I never knew existed. I am deeply distracted for reasons I don't yet understand. The growing tension is almost unbearable. I feel dizzy, drugged. I can barely breathe. I look away first, afraid someone will see she has teased my fear and confusion to the surface. Though part of me doesn't want her to stop. I am aware how calm I feel at the first sign of anyone's loving touch.

Three hours later, the shameless gossip reception comes to an end and we stumble out of La Scala. Making a swift escape, we pile into the limo and head back to the Mansion.

The following day, I pop my head into the med room but find no one there. One of the butlers tells me Kendall is in the bathhouse. I walk past the pool, waving to Hef and my father, who are too involved in backgammon to notice me. I pass the guest bathrooms and head for the tanning bed where Kendall lies naked. Her body is flawless. There are no tan lines. Even her boobs are brown. There isn't a single inch of fat anywhere.

I turn to leave when she lifts the small tanning goggles off her eyes.

"Hey," Kendall says sweetly.

"Hey, where is everyone?"

"Charlie had an appointment, so they came earlier to work out." She wipes sweat off her flat, toned stomach.

The fact that she's naked and touching herself makes me uncomfortable.

I reach into my backpack and pull out a small vial of coke.

"Here you go," I mumble uncomfortably. "I picked this up at school."

Kendall waves me closer and I can't help but notice her perfectly shaved pubic area.

I quickly hand her the vial and turn to leave before she notices me staring.

"Great. Did I give you enough to cover it?" she asks.

"We're good, thanks. 'Bye!"

"Wait," Kendall says softly, pausing for a moment. "Why do you seem so nervous around me?" she asks.

"I'm not."

"I'd like to be friends," she says, smiling with ease.

"We are," I stutter, backing up.

My heart's racing.

"Do you want to work out? 'Cause I can do arms again if you want me to go with you."

"No. That's okay, thanks. Another time. I think I'm just going to go home and get started on my homework. I'll see you later."

I stumble into a plant on my way out.

Nine

Kendall's intensity overpowers me. The thing is, I'm not sure what I am feeling or why I am drawn to her. I decide to spend time away from the Mansion and reconnect with my friends at Beverly High.

It's the Beverly vs. Palisades football game and Liz, Amber, Sonya, Hunter, Michelle, and I crack open cans of beer in the alley and place them in extra large McDonald's cups. We make our grand entrance up the bleachers blaring Run-D.M.C.'s "It's Like That" from an oversize ghetto blaster.

"You guys should come out with me tonight. I know this slamming nightclub in Hollywood. A bunch of girls are going."

"Let me guess, Playmates?" Sonya rolls her eyes.

"I'm rushing right over," says Michelle sarcastically.

"Why would I want to be seen with a bunch of sleazy Playmates?

I mean, what's the dealio? You've been dissing us, big-time," Hunter says, studying me curiously.

"They're cool," I say protectively, watching them exchange glances among themselves. "They're not what you think."

"Embarrassing?" Amber smirks.

"You have to admit, those girls don't have the best image. I mean, they're whores," Liz states matter-of-factly.

"They're fun and totally down-to-earth," I say.

"Listen to you defending them," Hunter laughs and I turn red.

"You're in, right?" I nudge Michelle.

"I would, but I lost my fake ID." She shrugs.

"I keep telling you, we don't need ID," I say, exasperated.

Hunter holds an unlit joint between her lips and rolls her eyes at me.

"Seriously, Jennifer, why the sudden change?" Hunter eyeballs me over her Vuarnet sunglasses.

"It's either them or us," Amber says. I don't respond, once again torn between my teenage life and the adult life I have at the Mansion.

"Whenever you're ready to get back in touch with reality, you know where to find us." Sonya flips her long hair, smacking me in the face.

Ten

I hit all the hot spots in town: Nicky Blair's, Vertigo, Helena's, and Eva's. Dad's out every night and encourages me to meet him since my friends are unavailable.

He and I have it all worked out.

At Helena's, the valet takes my Mercedes and I push past the crowd of wannabes milling in front of the door. The doorman knows who I am and smiles when I slip him a twenty. It doesn't matter that I'm only fifteen. Normal rules no longer exist.

I enter Helena's drenched in makeup, strutting in three-inch heels and wearing a silver sequined top that catches the strobe lights. Disco balls hang from the ceiling as tweaked-out girls stride by in rayon jersey Issey Miyake jumpsuits that shine with wildly printed patterns. The DJ spins a remix of Exposé's "Point of No Return" as Stoli gimlets, coke, and Quaaludes flow down the

throats and up the noses of tan and thin-limbed actresses. I ask
Robert Downey Jr., Rob Lowe, and Emilio Estevez if they've seen
my father. They point me in the right direction.

An effortlessly hip, gorgeous soap opera actor laughs with a
group of friends. He's twentysomething, tall with sandy-blond hair
and a rare killer smile. He's pompous, but in an unoffensive way.

"Hey dipstick, where have you been? Rehab?" I overhear one of
the guys ask.

"No, son, I've been sticking your mom," the actor responds.

His friend wraps his arm around a cocktail waitress, whispering in her ear, "Sweetheart, you know, you actually look good when
you don't try so hard."

"Let it go, dorkbag," she smirks.

"Seriously, when are we gonna fuck again? You know you
want it."

The waitress rolls her eyes at him.

The actor pats his buddy on the shoulder.

"Easy, tiger," the actor says to his friend before continuing to
move through the crowd. I look at him and then away, peering
around casually until I spot my father at a booth. He greets me with
a warm welcome, proudly introducing me to friends left and right.
Dad escorts me down a hallway into the VIP room, where a muscular guy nods to my father, unclasps the velvet rope, and lets us in.

The women in the room are awash in Claude Montana's designs: skintight leather pants glued to their loins and futuristic-
looking shoulder pads under ruffled silk blouses. They teeter in
Tokio Kumagai shoes, hand-painted and reflecting the Expres-
sionist styles of Kandinsky, Pollock, and Mondrian.

We stop at a table filled with middle-aged men who crane their
necks when hot young girls glide by. Dad can't sit still for two seconds. The Whispers' "Rock Steady" plays in the background.

I order a cocktail. Dad pats my ass and I cringe.

"You look so delicious I could eat you up," he says.

"Don't," I answer.

He takes my arm, pointing to one of his underage hotties.

"I want to introduce you to Chase."

"Another bulimic teenager?"

"She's twenty-two," he admits with no qualms.

"She must've cost a pretty penny."

"Free, actually. Flew in from Arizona all by herself." Dad's foaming at the mouth.

"Yeah, well, she looks like she's about to die. Maybe you should take her to McDonald's for a Happy Meal."

Dad and I are then distracted by two stunning girls locked in a heated French kiss. Their boyfriends lurk beside them on standby.

"It's called intergroup dating," I inform him.

"Friends of yours?" Dad questions.

"Interested?" I ask as Dad reviews his choices.

By now, checking out girls with my father is too familiar to seem scandalous. I wave to Hef and the circle of young beauties by his side. I nudge my dad.

"What are you waiting around for, sloppy seconds?"

"Very funny." He grimaces, but we both know it's true.

I give Hef a kiss hello.

"Hello, darling," Hef says. "Your father actually made it out tonight."

"You know he's been shacking up with Chase again, he just won't admit it," I say, and we laugh quietly.

Kendall smiles at me and excuses herself from the table. I watch her walk away. She's slinking like a panther, her black dress barely covering her body. She owns the room, easily and without even trying.

My gaze is interrupted when the waitress hands me my Long Island iced tea. I drink it greedily, loving the sweet mix of vodka, tequila, rum, and gin.

The soap opera actor stands in front of me when I look up. My father makes the introductions.

"Jennifer, this is—"

"Hayden Winters," the actor finishes, extending his hand.

He is fatally handsome: all-American face, flawless cheekbones, and piercing blue eyes.

"He's an actor on some soap," says Dad, looking around uninterested.

"Cool," I say nonchalantly.

"What do you do?" he asks.

"I'm in school," I answer casually.

"Which one?"

"Beverly."

"You look much older," Hayden says. My father takes off with the bulimic as Hayden reaches into his pocket and pulls out an invitation.

"I'm having after-hours at the Beverly Hills Hotel if you want to cruise by."

"I have tennis in the morning, but we'll see," I say, accepting the invite.

"You don't want to hang out with me?" Hayden smiles and his white teeth sparkle.

"I didn't say that."

I flip my hair carelessly while staring at his arms, his chest, and his stomach, which is rippled underneath his tight Polo shirt. He's perfect, like a Calvin Klein model.

One of his friends yanks him away.

"I better see you later." Hayden winks, grabbing my arm affectionately.

He turns around one last time and our eyes meet.

I continue roaming, bumping into Tommy, one of the regulars from the Mansion.

Tommy leans into me and whispers, "Hey, hon. Have you seen the Minister?"

"I haven't seen a minister since I dropped out of Sunday school," I laugh.

"Your father knows him. Where is the Big Q?"

"What are you talking about?" I ask, completely confused.

"Your father," he declares, surprised I'm unaware of his nickname.

I look at the big smile on Tommy's face.

I finally nod, knowingly: the Big "Q" refers to Quaaludes.

"Have any?" I ask.

"I don't, but the Minister does."

Tommy pulls me over to a man wearing all black, with a barely visible white collar.

"I want you to meet Doc's daughter," Tommy introduces me.

"I've known your father for over twenty years," the Minister says jovially, taking out a business card and handing it to me.

"Nice to meet you, Minister."

"Call me if you need anything," he offers sincerely, inconspicuously slipping me a few Quaaludes.

"It's a gift—treasure them." He winks.

"Thank you." I smile as Tommy and I walk away.

"He's huge. He's the biggest dealer in town," Tommy whispers as he spots his wife from afar. "I gotta split. Catch you later."

Dodging my father, I head down a neon-lit hallway. I bump into Kendall and am instantly pulled into her luminous green eyes. We let others pass as we lean against the wall. For some reason we're both surprised to run into each other. This is the nature of the club scene, after all: being surprised by the familiar and pretending it's new.

"Hey, kiddo." She wipes her nose. "What are you up to?"

"Nothing," I say. "You know, just hanging."

"Hey, promise me you won't say anything to anyone about the other day?" she begs. "You know, about the special delivery."

"No worries. I won't say anything."

"It's our little secret." She places her hand over mine, nestling her fingers in between mine. My nerves take over for no reason. I pull my hand back.

"I just met the coolest guy. He's so nice and he's got the cutest ass ever!"

"Good for you," she says.

Kendall leans in and kisses me sensuously on the lips. A warm, tingling sensation runs through me. She pulls away before I have time to think or respond. She steps back, smiles, and disappears into the club.

Moments pass before I can move.

Paranoid, I look around to see if anyone might have noticed, but no one's looking. I glance down at my drink. How many cocktails have I had?

I pull Hayden's invite out of my pocket and decide it's time to leave.

I arrive at the after-hours in the Beverly Hills Hotel at 3:00 A.M. The valet takes my car and I ride up the elevator to suite 1011. Entering the room, I look around for familiar faces, but find none.

Suddenly an arm wraps around me. Hayden welcomes me with a big smile.

"So, you did want to come see me!"

We examine each other, our attraction apparent.

"Can I offer you something to drink?" Hayden asks.

"Sure," I answer as a Persian princess in gaudy gold necklaces and matching hoop earrings joins us. She stands, awkwardly teetering in a pair of Patrick Cox platforms, like she'll topple over at the slightest gust of wind.

"Hi, Hayden," she says, shooting me a dirty look.

I glare back.

"Hi, Davita," Hayden responds politely.

The girl takes another assessment of me and continues moving.

One of Hayden's costars pours drinks at the bar.

"Yo, Winters!" he yells. "There's a shot over here with your name on it."

"I'm busy," Hayden answers.

"You're busy?" his friend shouts.

"Dude, I'll catch you on the next one," Hayden yells, and his friend finally notices me.

"Oh, I'm sorry, man. I didn't mean to interrupt you and your new *girlfriend*."

"Okay, *easy*, Slick."

Hayden affectionately slides his arm off me and walks over to do the shot with his buddies. The testosterone flowing at the bar is palpable. Hayden stands in the center of it, all eyes on him, his perfection, his status.

Hayden smiles over at me and winks.

Two Quaaludes later, Hayden and I have it all figured out.

We're chilling in the back bedroom, lounging on soft overstuffed pillows. We feel as though we've known each other for years. I lie back, admiring his great looks, knowing that every woman he meets must fall for him.

"Thank you so much for coming. You're really cool." Hayden stares at me with a look of desire. "I'd love to be in a relationship if I found the right girl." He strokes my arms and I roll my eyes.

"Shut up, I know you're a big player."

"Not true, I'm a monogamous type of guy. What's most important is to please the woman," he says. I put my finger over his lips.

"Listen, honey, don't speak. It's better that way," I tell him, patting him affirmatively on the leg.

Hayden brushes a strand of hair from my face as I adjust my butterfly clip. He gently runs his fingers over the body glitter on my neck. His trademark smile sweeps across his face. I flip him over on his back and straddle him.

Hayden laughs, pulls me in close, and kisses me. Our bodies are pressed against each other and I can feel how excited he is. Rubbing my hands over his jeans, I tease him for a while until I get up, over it.

"I gotta go," I say. My Swatch watch reads 4:30 A.M.

"Are you sure you can drive, sweetie? I'd love for you to stay. We can have breakfast at the Polo Lounge in the morning."

Hayden wraps his arm around me and I immediately throw it off.

"Listen, sweetie, I'm not impressed by your B-list celebrity status. I've been going to the Polo Lounge since before you got off the airplane from Iowa. I'm sure you're a great lay, but let's not waste any time. Call me when you're ready to be my boy-toy," I say, applying Chanel No. 5 lipstick.

The next day, I'm in the med room having a late lunch with Austin, Tobey, and Charlie, who are wearing leotards and magenta headbands. Kendall is in the foyer talking to a girl I've never seen before. I eavesdrop on their conversation.

"I'm in town for a few days. We should definitely get together," says the girl, moving closer to Kendall.

"Whatever, Jet Set," Kendall says flirtatiously, playing with her wraparound skirt.

"You know I'll make time for you."

"You should," says Kendall. "I miss you."

Kendall runs her fingers over the girl's stomach.

"I don't think of girls in that way anymore," she says, smiling, batting her lashes.

"Me either. It's so gross," Kendall confirms as the girl slowly clasps her fingers around Kendall's gold mesh belt.

I look away, unsure of exactly what I'm feeling. By the time I glance back, they are gone. Curious, I excuse myself from the table and hurry into the foyer, taking a left toward the bathroom. The door is slightly ajar and through the crack, I can see their reflection in the mirror.

Kendall and the girl kiss, sexual energy swirling around them.

I am fascinated.

Kendall's kiss from the night before enters my mind. The flames of jealousy flicker through me for a second. Averting my eyes, I leave before they see me.

Days later, Hayden and I pull up to the wrought-iron gates and I introduce myself to the gigantic rock outside the Mansion. A camera in the trees turns in my direction.

"It's Jennifer Saginor."

"Hi, Jennifer," greets the familiar voice. "Who do you have with you?" the voice asks.

"My favorite new boy-toy, Hayden," I say, pulling him by his hair and playfully pecking his lips.

We drive up the scenic driveway and Hayden's eyes widen when the castle comes into view.

"See, honey, isn't this better than the Polo Lounge?"

A valet takes my car.

I lead Hayden through the foyer and out to the backyard, showing him off like a prized trophy. He holds my arm and looks around wildly at all the commotion, the flowers, the flamingos, and the Playmates. As we roam the grounds, feeding the monkeys and birds, I see Kendall watching us from a window upstairs.

When I look up, she places her hand on the stained glass as if to say hello.

Hayden and I make our way over to my father, who's talking to three topless girls by the pool. Dad introduces Hayden to a few Playmates when Kendall, now standing by the outdoor bar, waves me over.

I leave Hayden as Kendall takes my hand and drags me to a nearby pathway where no one can see. We end up ducking into the Playmate of the Month's house, where we drop onto the bed.

"So, is that your new boyfriend?" she asks, turning to face me.

"No, just my new fuck buddy. Why?" I ask, with a half smile.

"No reason." She shrugs, sounding aloof. "I'm just . . . concerned.

He looks dangerous. Like he has diseases or something." She licks her bottom lip.

"Dangerous?" I ask, thinking of Hayden's angelic pretty-boy face.

I look at Kendall strangely.

"Are you high?"

"Dump him."

"What's the matter with you?" I laugh.

"I don't want to see my girlfriends being played by some player," she says seriously.

"Don't worry, I'm not going to be played by anyone."

"All right, well, I was just checking," she says, offering me a cigarette, drawing out our time together. We smoke, giggling and leaning into each other.

"You know, you're really not so bad. You're actually kind of cool sometimes," I tell her flirtatiously.

"Sometimes? Gee, thanks," Kendall laughs.

"You know what I mean."

"So are you."

Kendall pushes her shoulder into mine. We smile at each other as she grabs my hand and leads me into the backyard.

Later that night, Hayden and I watch movies on my big-screen TV. Cuddling underneath the sheets, we feed each other popcorn. Hayden touches my arm, running his fingers down my thighs. He kisses my neck, draws my mouth close as my lips melt into his. He undoes my bra, slips off my shirt, and grazes his fingers over my breasts. I unzip his fly and touch him. My hands find his warm chest and slowly pull his shirt off as he leans his body against mine. I close my eyes and Kendall's face appears out of nowhere, looking at me with an all-knowing smile.

Startled, I jerk my head back. What the hell is going on?

"Is everything all right?" Hayden asks.

"Everything's great. It's wonderful."

I kiss him with no emotion as he runs his hand across my

stomach. He gently squeezes my nipples and Kendall's face reappears, shining radiantly. Eyes closed, I smile back at her.

"Kendall," I sigh.

"Kendall? Who's Kendall?" Hayden asks.

I snap out of my daydream, open my eyes, and see Hayden's brows raised.

"Light a candle," I say, trying to cover up.

I reach for a votive, my hands shaking as I light it.

I feel like I'm tripping.

Hayden grabs me and I kiss him playfully. He pulls off my underwear and our bodies are now naked, rubbing against each other.

"I think I'm falling for you," he says.

"Me too, honey. Just focus. Do you have a condom?" I ask.

"No," he answers.

"I'll be right back."

I throw on a robe and run down the hall to Dad's bathroom, where I grab a few condoms.

Hayden and I fuck softly then roughly. I straddle him from on top. I can tell I'm turning him on and the sense of power excites me, driving me higher and higher as he begs for more.

I can't help but compare Dad's view of women to mine of men. My conditioning sets in and I critique his impeccable features, his perfect abs, and tight ass. Then another part of me recognizes men as disloyal, selfish pigs who must be punished.

I pull him in close, ride him hard, hate him intensely, and fuck him senseless. He deserves it. He loves it. His desire and hunger throw me into orgasm. Ten minutes and a cigarette later, I tell him it's time for him to leave.

The next morning, I lie in bed thinking about why thoughts of Kendall kept popping into my mind while I was with Hayden. The phone rings and I leap up to answer it.

"Hello?" I say.

"Hey, baby," Kendall says.

"Kendall?" I ask, surprised.

"Who did you think it was?" she asks.

"Oh, I was expecting a call from someone else."

"Does that mean you're not happy to hear from me?" she toys with my head in a sweet little voice, covering up her hint of disappointment. "Why don't you come up here?" she asks. "Your father's by the pool with Hef and the guys, and I'm sitting here with no one interesting to talk to."

"Maybe next time," I tell her.

"Come on, we'll have fun. We can play a game."

"Yeah, I heard you're into playing games."

"Only with you, sweetie," she claims with conviction. "Seriously, I did just get the new highest score on Pac-Man."

"What?" I leap off the bed. "You did not beat my highest score on Pac-Man!"

"Hey, champ, it's hard to keep up if you're not around," she says, drawing me in, knowing precisely how to divert my attention away from myself—not that anything is keeping me at home anyway.

There's something new pulling me toward the Mansion and it is no longer my father. I have shifted alliances.

Fifteen minutes later, I race through the foyer in tight nylon parachute pants, a shiny turquoise jacket, and two blue-and-white striped wristbands. I find Kendall waiting for me at the bottom of the staircase, grinning from ear to ear. Grabbing her hand, I drag her out to the game room, tugging at each other playfully like best friends.

After a few games of Pac-Man, Kendall's name is now in fifth position and she is passed out on the couch.

"Let's order drinks," she suggests, while I'm still preoccupied, maneuvering the joystick, truly satisfied as it gobbles up the last of the little dots.

"For sure—I'm ready for my champion's cocktail," I swing around, all smiles as Kendall walks into the carpet room and plops down on the comfy pillows.

She grabs the phone and orders two pitchers of strawberry daiquiris from the kitchen. We turn on the television and channel surf. Within minutes, the butlers arrive with our pitchers. We clink glasses and stare at ourselves in the mirror above. I catch Kendall looking at me and I smile back. She reaches slowly for the remote and my arm tingles as she strokes her fingers over mine. A strange, warm sensation moves through me. She clicks on the Nature Channel.

"Will you rub my neck?" she asks innocently.

I look away, shy.

"Oh, come on—it's just my neck."

"I know," I answer nervously.

I'm aware that I should probably not be here, but instead of leaving I pour myself another strawberry daiquiri.

Kendall pushes her hair to the side as she leans against me, unclipping her lacy bra. I run my hands over her arms, shoulders, and neck. Her skin is soft and warm. My fingers tingle every time I touch her. She gets really into it, letting out sighs here and there, and I feel this unusual, intense energy between us.

"I'm going to lie down, 'k?" she asks and I don't answer.

I'm apprehensive, yet I don't stop.

She turns over onto her stomach and leans against the pillow.

"Don't you miss having a mother around?" she asks out of nowhere.

I nod, full of feelings I cannot express. Little does she know, the pain of not having my mother is far worse than anything I have ever experienced.

"I'll be your mother," she whispers, playing with my fingers, my hand. What's always fascinated me most about Kendall is how she talks to me. It's as if she can read my mind. When Kendall speaks to me, she answers questions I have not asked. When she looks at me, I feel safe and cared for. When she takes my hand, leads me down a path, I eagerly follow, wanting nothing more than her love and approval.

Her absolute beauty is compelling in its flawlessness, its perfection.

I quickly look away.

When I look back, she is still there, only closer. My breathing becomes erratic. I cannot speak. A rush goes through me. We look at each other with a deep, meaningful stare. My heart pounds. I can feel the heat from her tan, silky skin. She changes positions, brushing her leg against mine. She looks at me longingly, grabs my hand, and pulls me closer to her.

"Come here." She smiles sweetly, tugging gently at my shirt and drawing me near, inches from her lips.

I close my eyes and we kiss. A warmth courses through me. I am taken by surprise.

"You feel so soft," she says.

Kendall moves a few strands of hair out of my face, spreads her legs apart, and pulls me even closer. We search each other's eyes.

"Just relax. I'll take care of you," she whispers in my ear.

There is something supernaturally comforting about her. I cannot convey my fascination for her with words, so I allow my hands to become like language.

I breathe in as she holds me tighter, feeling safe in her arms. I try to respond, but Kendall pushes her fingers over my lips, her hands eager to explore my body. Every touch is sensual, magical.

Kendall takes her shirt off, exposing her bare breasts, which I can't help but touch like forbidden pleasures. She guides my head, my lips pressed against her skin. She places her hand in between my thighs and I can feel her energy go right through me.

Everything is happening so fast.

She pulls her jeans off along with her lavender satin G-string. Her sexuality is overwhelming. She continues to kiss me and I am so aroused that there is no stopping the inevitable. She spreads her legs wider, pushing my hand toward her wetness, and I giggle like a nervous schoolgirl.

"I'm so wet, if you don't go down on me I'm going to have to go upstairs and get my vibrator," she warns, chuckling.

I yearn to keep her near me. I would do anything to keep this warmth, this gentleness. She kisses me, her mouth moving from place to place, as she speaks slowly and touches me softly. She tells me what I feel like, what I do to her, who she wants me to be.

"I don't know what I'm doing," I say with a sheepish grin, and a huge smile creeps across Kendall's face.

"I'll show you." She slowly pushes my head lower and lower down her stomach. My body turns to liquid. Questions run through my mind so fast I can't decipher one from the other. Kendall positions me in between her legs and I am startled by her thrusting movements as she clutches a pillow. She pulls me on top and our bodies writhe against each other. Hers is like a weapon wrapped in silk, dangerous and teasing all at once. I feel a tingle in between my legs.

"That feels so good," she says, guiding my body over hers. "That's it. Don't stop. Good girl," she repeats over and over, her moans telling me she likes what I'm doing.

She moves uncontrollably. It's like having an out-of-body experience.

I can feel her move under my touch. Our intensity is magnified with each simple breath. "Ooh, Jennifer!" she screams, and then it is all over. There is a new dimension to our relationship now. A door has been open and anything is possible now.

"I knew you could do it." She exhales and cuddles up to me.

Our warm bodies feel so good next to each other. She strokes my hair, my arms. I swallow her affection like a starved child. She makes me feel loved in a way I have never been before. She offers a sense of fulfillment, better than any drug I've tried. With Kendall I feel whole.

Kendall gives me what she can: love, parenting, and friendship. She gives me these things in the only way she can, the only way she knows how. In the end, we are both children, both searching.

We lie on the thick carpet staring up at our nakedness in the mirror above. She gives me a look like this is our little secret. I have never known such closeness or felt so safe in chaos.

Sometimes we don't know why we make the choices we do.

I am fifteen when I have sex with a woman.

Eleven

At home I shower, letting the water run over me for almost an hour. I trace my hands across my stomach and my breasts, my body now new to me and unfamiliar.

I want to make sense of what happened. I want to push the memory into the realm of rational behavior. The phone rings, shaking me out of the need to justify myself. I get out of the shower as water drips all over the floor.

"What are you doing?" Hayden asks.

"I'm in the shower, silly."

"Should I come over now?" he says.

"You wish."

"Call me later, will ya?"

"Maybe . . ."

"Maybe?"

"All right, I'll call you," I say sweetly.

"Okay."

We hang up.

I catch a glimpse of my nakedness in the mirror and my night with Kendall replays in my head. I hope nobody finds out.

It's 1985.

On my sixteenth birthday, Dad throws me a party at Vertigo. I invite everyone I know and don't know: high school friends, Mom, Savannah, Hef, Kendall, Playmates, butlers, and even some of the security guards from the Mansion.

I'm decked out in sequins with a short Christian Dior mini-skirt and Gucci heels. Hayden styles leather pants and an untucked Hugo Boss shirt. We look incredible as we make our way through the sea of people. Hayden and I are pulled in different directions, but our eyes meet every few seconds.

The club smells of Obsession perfume and clove cigarettes. Girls dance in short satin cheerleader skirts, high, clumpy patent platforms, and sequined gloves. Guys with layered hair and ears studded with silver earrings tap their ostrich cowboy boots.

Kendall yanks me into an empty stall in the bathroom.

"What are you doing?" I pull away, nervous.

"Happy birthday, sweet girl. You look beautiful." She draws me close.

"So do you," I mutter.

Kendall looks like a rock star in her gold snakeskin jacket, pale knee-high suede boots, and cutoff Calvin Klein jeans.

I look around cautiously.

"Someone might come in."

"So what? Kiss me."

Kendall squeezes my hand.

"I can't," I whisper.

She clasps her fingers around my waist, pulling gently at my sequined butterfly top. I feel a spurt of excitement before nervousness sets in.

"Where's your token boyfriend?" she says as she touches me in places I shouldn't be touched.

"You torture me," I whisper.

I hurry out of the bathroom, find Hayden, grab his arm, and pull him onto the dance floor. I am moving between two worlds. There is tenderness in Kendall that I can't find in anyone else, not even Hayden.

While Hayden and I dance, people swirl around us. Girls dance by in rhinestone minis and sheer tank tops, teetering in Claude Montana heels. Guys smelling of Polo cologne and wearing unbuttoned black-and-white Armani shirts watch the girls dancing, their grins and stomach muscles clearly visible.

Kendall watches Hayden kiss my neck and then she smoothly cuts in for a quick dance, guiding Hayden's arms around her waist.

My eyes are glued to her every move.

Kendall looks over at me with a dangerous smile as they dance. Hayden follows Kendall's gaze and smiles when he sees me. He's clueless.

I hear my sister's voice in my ear.

"What is that lezzy Kendall doing dancing with Hayden? He might catch something," Savannah says.

I look at Savannah and her self-satisfied smirk. "Shouldn't you be entertaining Mom?"

We turn and wander separately back into the party.

I find Hayden, grab him by the arm, and pull him off the dance floor and out of the club. We end up in a graffiti-scarred infamous unmarked bar hidden behind the unlikely front of a Chinese restaurant.

The doorman unclasps the velvet rope and lets us in. A door mistress greets us, eyes us carefully, and leads us down a hallway to an eighties glam-punk after-hours party.

We're in a carnival of funky chandeliers, guys in drag, black-lit walls, four-inch shag carpets, and Nag Champa incense. Hipsters with tattoos, wearing ski caps and Stray Cats T-shirts, stand around posing. Skinny girls in retro slips, body glitter, and baby blue fur coats and black hats dance to Prince's "1999."

"This place is like Studio Fifty-four—anything goes," Hayden informs me as we wander around.

A colorful drag queen in a turquoise rubber jumpsuit swings a pink faux-fur scarf around his neck. I refrain from laughing until I hear him yell, "Kendall!"

"Jamal!" a voice yells back.

I look over and see Kendall running toward Jamal. She's with Natasha.

"Hey, girl!" screeches the drag queen.

Jamal hugs her, waving a cigarette filter around her back, careful not to disrupt the hair. I catch myself staring because I've never seen a drag queen before.

Natasha and Kendall turn around. A surge of energy rushes through me as Kendall undresses me with her eyes.

Jamal offers us a small brown bottle. "Whip it?"

"I'm cutting back." I smile.

"Well, then, that's definitely not the room for you, honey." Jamal points to a room separated by crushed velvet curtains. Guys with tinted big-frame sunglasses exit the VIP lounge.

"Beware when you enter the buffet of euphoria. Everything's for sale in there, honey."

Hayden and I peek our heads into the VIP lounge, where glamorous divas indulge in their drug of choice. I ponder how quickly after-hours can go from a simple night out to a whole new lifestyle.

Twenty minutes later, we're all in the VIP room sitting around a table with lines of cocaine cut up and ready to be snorted. Kendall rolls a hundred dollar bill and inhales the line deeply. Hayden's face lights up as the bill is passed in his direction. He leans down with ease and sniffs hard. He hands it to me without a second thought. I pass.

Kendall looks over at me.

"It's not going to kill you," she says.

"You do blow, right?" Natasha asks.

"Not really," I answer.

"You'll love it," Hayden tells me as he does another line and hands the bill to me.

"Trust," he says with fixed pupils.

The wrongness of it makes it even more attractive. I lower my head, cover my right nostril, and sniff with the left. My eyes water. My nostrils sting. I swallow hard. A drip slips down my throat.

Two eight balls later, we are edgy, chasing a lost high. The crowd has suddenly become annoying. Everyone is sitting way too close to me. I feel claustrophobic. I nudge Hayden and tell him it's time to leave, but he is too busy chatting with Jamal to notice. Kendall looks at me with void eyes as she and Natasha vogue each other. They look like movie stars. I pull out an emergency Xanax, trying to dull my sketchiness.

It kills me that I feel so empty inside.

Twelve

It's the middle of the night when Dad receives a phone call that Hef has had a stroke. Dad hustles to quickly gather his belongings. Hef doesn't feel comfortable in hospitals so he asks Dad to move into the Mansion and monitor him bedside until he feels better. Dad moves out and leaves me all alone. His affinity for bachelorhood and the freedom it allows causes a lingering loneliness that continues to grow over the next year.

Walking into an empty house day after day unnerves me and makes me feel even more disconnected from the rest of the world. At night, I walk around the neighborhood and get a peek into other people's homes. I get a glimpse of the kind of family I've always wanted: a mother baking cookies in the kitchen, children's drawings hanging on the refrigerator door, a father playing basketball with his kids in the driveway. I smile the kind of smile that doesn't last very long; the kind that, without one even knowing it, turns into a frown.

The annual Midsummer's Night Dream party rolls around, and Hayden and I enter the foyer of the Mansion in striped pajamas. The house is awash in decadence and high style. Glam rockers, celebrities, and models prance around in outrageous transparent costumes flaunting themselves for all to see. There's a sea of platinum, feathered hair, and glitter. Playmates stroll by in floor-length spaghetti-strap gowns that drip with tear-shape Tiffany beads clinging to their bodies like a second skin. Others glide by in Trashy lingerie bikinis and faux-fur scarves that drape to the ground. A striking statuesque woman wears a Vivienne Westwood creation composed of a synthetic white cape and black satin minidress with a tutu skirt.

The Mansion's great hall is lined with television screens. A buffet of appetizers and finger sandwiches are spread out. Tommy slips me a brownie full of reefer. Hayden and I take a few bites as we pass Emilio Estevez, Charlie Sheen, and Scott Baio on our way to the bathroom. I accidentally walk in on Tom Cruise urinating in the bathroom by the foyer. He has long brown braided hair and I only see the back of his Levis. I apologize, close the door slowly, look down at my pot brownie, and toss it. I shake my head when I see my father in the same Snow White and the Seven Dwarves Doc T-shirt and slippers he's worn to every pajama party for the past decade. The other backgammon boys are in robes, boxers, and briefs.

I continue roaming, passing other Brat Packers Rob Lowe and Judd Nelson. I bump into the gang of Playmates. Tobey wears a strapless top with sequins and bugle beads in fuchsia flower patterns with a pleated aqua skirt.

"Where have you been?" Tobey asks.

"We haven't seen you at the gym," Charlie adds.

"I've been laying low. Hayden and I have been doing our own thing, but I miss you guys."

Tobey rubs me warmly on the back.

"Where's Kendall?" I ask, scanning the room.

Austin points. Kendall looks totally wild in a silver wig, knee-high boots, and silver chains that dangle from her silver bikini bottom. She acts remarkably composed for someone in such a skimpy outfit, but I know Kendall loves to be in the nude. She looks in my direction and I smile at her outrageous outfit. As she walks past me, I grab her hand.

"Hey, you," I say, smiling.

She grinds her teeth and pulls my arm.

"Come with me," she urges.

I grab Hayden and the three of us rush to the game room in a whirlwind. When we reach the blue room, it's crowded with other people. I turn to leave, but Kendall moves us swiftly through the blue room and into the red room, which consists of a red seventies-style round bed with mirrors on all the walls. Jamal is in there doing lines of coke with another flamer.

Kendall locks the door behind us.

"What's up, girlfriend?" asks Jamal, who's dressed in yellow and royal blue Spandex.

"I'm in need," says Kendall.

Jamal uses his acrylic fingernail to scoop coke out of a little Baggie and shoves it up her nose.

"I owe you, big-time," Kendall smiles.

"You're golden, girl."

He pours the coke on a hand mirror and cuts it with a razor into six lines. Hayden's eyes light up. Jamal hands Kendall a crisp rolled-up bill and she bends down to do a line.

I light a cigarette.

Kendall comes up for air.

"You saved my life," she tells him.

"You rock," Hayden chimes in, waiting for the bill to come his way.

I exhale smoke.

"You guys are so glamorous," I say.

Jamal offers me the coke.

I lean down and sniff hard. My eyes water.

"I don't feel anything," I say, immediately wanting to do more.

I inhale another line and sit down beside Hayden, who's busy snorting from a small spoon. He turns to me, but his eyes look past me.

"Just wait; you'll feel it," Hayden informs me.

Ten minutes later, Kendall, Jamal, Hayden, and I are flying high.

"I'm on fire!" Hayden shouts.

"I have to get back to the house. Hef might be looking for me," Kendall says, worried. Jamal winks, and he slips me a vial on the way out of the game room.

The cool air hits my face and makes my whole body shiver. I grind my clenched teeth as we try to find our way back to the main house. The castle finally comes into view as Hayden and I are bantering back and forth at high speed. We kiss before entering, acutely aware that everything feels very intense.

Over the next few months, Hayden and I fuel ourselves with cocaine and the nights begin to run together. Suddenly it's December, which is more hectic than usual. The social season is in full swing.

Hef has a huge Christmas party and we are greeted by festive decor, all the sights and smells that fill the Mansion: a massive Christmas tree, poinsettias, strong eggnog, Christmas carols, and hundreds of candles.

The party looks like something out of a Ralph Lauren ad. Tan girls with blond hair glide by in Diane von Furstenberg wrap dresses and stiletto heels, their faces shiny with lip gloss and blush. Guys wearing Armani blazers, and Christian Dior or Pierre Cardin suits, in slate gray, navy, and black, strut by while sipping eggnog and Manhattans.

We move from the great hall into the med room peering in at all the familiar faces. The fireplace is blazing in the living room along with the dimly lit lamps on the wall. The buffet table has an incredible spread as Mansion regulars sit at the mahogany table and enjoy.

Kendall's watching me.

The lights throughout the Mansion catch her gold mesh bib necklace, which dazzles me. It looks like liquid gold is pouring down her chest. She sways slowly to the music, poured into her cream-colored silk charmeuse Halston dress, her toned brown-sugar shoulders sensuously exposed.

We make eye contact as Atlantic Starr's "Secret Lovers" plays on the stereo.

I greet Austin, Tobey, Morgan, and Charlie as they return from the buffet. The backgammon boys throw air kisses as Troy, a hip, twentysomething butler, and a DJ offers me a glass of eggnog. We clink glasses.

"Merry Christmas," we cheer.

I look around the med room at my new family.

Kendall and I play childish games, passing notes underneath the table. I open mine carefully, making sure Hayden does not notice.

"I miss you," Kendall writes, signaling me to meet her upstairs. I shake my head no, with a silly smile on my face.

Hayden catches the tail end of our silent dialogue and assumes we're talking about coke.

He nudges me, all excited.

"Let's go."

"Not now," I whisper, but he urges me to get up anyway and the three of us end up in the foyer.

Kendall points out mistletoe above our head, so I lean up to kiss Hayden. He turns and quickly inhales a bullet of coke before our lips can meet. Pissed, I shove him aside and Kendall giggles.

"Are you okay?" Hayden sniffs, wiping his nose. He looks concerned. I guess my paralytic smile is obviously unconvincing.

"Yes." I couldn't think of what to say.

"What's wrong?" he asks again.

"Nothing's wrong. I'm having a fabulous time. In fact, I'm so happy I can't eat a thing."

My father comes gallivanting over in his Gucci loafers and Italian suit, waving his manicured hands. His gold Rolex watch sparkles halfway across the room. He's been here all day. He glides by women floating in paper-thin chiffon Victor Costa gowns and elaborately patterned draped jersey Missoni dresses. He grabs Kendall and strangles her affectionately as we all laugh nervously.

"He can't deal when he's not the center of attention," I joke, trying to lighten the mood.

"Hi, dear; sweet as ever I see," Dad responds in a blasé tone.

"I'm your daughter; I'm entitled to act bitchy."

"That's what they all say." He shrugs.

"Stop confusing me with your teenage girlfriends," I snicker as everyone gathers around for a holiday picture.

We huddle into place. My lips curl upward as I fake smile for the group photo.

The holidays come to an end and thoughts of another year passing start to hit me. Even though I'm still a junior, I know somewhere inside I have to start thinking about what I am going to do after I graduate, if I graduate. I need to avoid going to the Mansion and start concentrating on homework. I need help and fast.

I decide to visit Grampy Joe, my seventy-five-year-old paternal grandfather, at his condo in the Valley. He is thin with tiny spectacles covering his personable, wise, yet worldly eyes. Dickens, Keats, and Yates line his bookshelves. Stacks of *The New Yorker, Time,* and the *Wall Street Journal* lie on the kitchen counter. CNN is perpetually on in the background.

He looks dapper in the wrinkled suit he puts on every time I come to visit. Since my grandmother passed away, Grampy keeps himself busy by reading, swimming, and burying himself in lots of paperwork. We usually watch the news and debate politics, but today I need help with my homework.

I'm sitting at the faded oak table in the living room as Grampy finishes a phone call in the den. His voice is harsh and stern, and for a second reminds me of my father's.

Perhaps at one time, my grandfather was a two-timing lady's man, a man like my father, who created my father; however, I barely see those sides of him. They are small glitches left over from a lifetime ago. Today, all I see is a kind, wise, loving soul who wants the very best for his granddaughter. I see a man who is my mentor, my confidant, and in many ways my truest friend.

He sits down and shakes his head.

"Now, where were we?" he asks.

I move my sunglasses higher onto my nose, hoping he does not see my glazed eyes. Grampy's thinking is so clear: he's so astute, both politically and socially, that it's almost painful to be around him.

"I don't know how you can go to school and never read," he says.

"I read; I just can't remember anything," I tell him, wondering if he smells the pot on my breath.

"Do you still want to be a writer?" he asks.

"Maybe," I mumble.

"How do you expect to be successful if you don't read? Who's going to listen to what you have to say?"

"I don't know . . . people," I say like some burnout. "I want to raise awareness."

I'm struggling to make sense.

"You develop opinions by reading," Grampy stresses.

"Maybe I prefer to be sheltered."

"Nonsense. That's a cop-out. You need to prepare for your future."

"I'm not even prepared for algebra tomorrow."

"If you'd stop monkeying around you would be. Go to class. Take journalism. Do something," Grampy repeats over and over. But I cannot hear him.

I look at my life and can see only what is missing.

The next day, I'm in my bedroom filling my stained-glass bong while Modern English's "I Melt with You" is on KROQ. The phone rings. It's Kendall.

"Hey, kiddo, it's me," Kendall whispers in a groggy voice.

"Hey, you. What's up?" I ask, casually.

"The girls were over last night. We had a little slumber party. I'm so beat," she tells me.

"What slumber party?" I ask, putting my lighter down.

"A post-holiday slumber party," she answers.

My stomach drops because she purposely didn't include me.

"Thanks for the invite," I snicker.

"Hey, I would have, but every time I see you, you're always with that boy-toy of yours."

"Oh, come on."

"It's true. No guys allowed."

"Whatever. I would've come solo. Who was there?" I ask, dying to know how left out I've become.

"Everyone. Charlie, Natasha, Morgan, Tobey, Austin, even Rebecca," she rattles off.

"You invited Rebecca and not me?"

"I can't deal with this shit right now, okay? My head is throbbing."

"No, it's not okay—fuck you for not including me in your little party!" I scream and slam down the phone.

At school, I kiss ass to my old crew, quickly handing them flyers for another rager at Dad's house with no less than five hundred people.

The Go-Go's' "This Town" blares through the outdoor speakers. I'm on my portable phone running through the house like a crazed teenager. Mirrored balls hang from the ceiling next to bright neon lights. Confetti is strewn everywhere. Caterers in uniforms dash by with trays. Bartenders set up outdoor stations. Troy, the DJ from the Mansion, spins records while a few security guards on loan scope out the backyard for trouble.

Three hours later, "White Lines" screams through the house and backyard. I'm in the bathroom getting ready when Hayden strolls in and lays out a huge line of coke for me. He hands me a cracked used straw. After I'm done, I run my finger along the mirror and lick the remainder off.

Friends start to arrive, lining up at my bathroom door. I dip into my pill drawer and grab handfuls of Xanax, Quaaludes, Valium, and Percocet. I'll bet Kendall's little party is no match for mine.

"What's up with your dad? We never see him," Hunter asks, swallowing a 'lude.

"I thought I'd spare myself the embarrassment of watching him come on to all my friends," I say as Amber comes running up to us.

"Your sister is here and some senior is totally hitting on her!"

Blood rushes to my face.

"Where is he?"

"In the backyard," Amber reports.

I run down the stairs with a parade of followers trailing behind.

Time stops when I see my sister. She's fourteen now. Her sandy-blond hair is long, past her shoulders. Her skin is flawless and her blue eyes huge and innocent. My heart sinks. Sisters aren't supposed to be separated like this. I never meant to leave her. I thought it was temporary, that I could change my mind. I never knew it would become legal. I am too numb to admit that moving out of my mother's house cemented a division in our relationship. Unconscious of my real feelings of anger toward my parents for allowing this disruption to occur, and clearly unprepared to take responsibility for my choice, my instincts tell me to attack others who may come between us.

I spot the senior predator making the moves on her. I race over and shove him aside.

"Get the fuck off my sister, asshole!" I scream in his face. "I don't want to see you touch her, look at her, or see you in the same fucking room as her! Do you understand me, asshole?"

The security guards stand behind me ready to make a move.

"Jennifer, it's okay. It's fine. He wasn't bugging me." Savannah touches my arm.

"Are you sure?"

"Yes," she answers, petrified by my temper, which I've now clearly adopted from my father.

"All right, well, let me know if he bothers you again," I say protectively.

I am unable to get anything else out. Savannah smiles at me. We hug for a long time and then I retreat back upstairs to my bathroom and continue doing lines.

The next morning, the house is a disaster and the backyard is even worse. Hallways are cluttered with leftover friends. Stragglers lie on rafts in the pool. I'm sprawled out on my bed in my clothes, while Hayden is passed out on the leather chair in front of the TV.

Out of nowhere, Kendall hops on my bed, surprising me while I'm still dead asleep.

"What are you doing here?" I ask, barely able to open my eyes.

"I came to see you," she whispers.

"How did you get here?" I ask, half asleep.

"Troy drove me." She runs her fingers up my back. "Don't be mad. You know I'm not even supposed to be here."

"Oh, well, I guess you better hurry home, princess."

"Listen, kiddo . . ." She rubs her hands over my arms and legs.

"Hey, Hayden's . . ."

"Sleeping," she finishes.

I allow our eyes to meet.

"I've missed you," she says.

"Me too," I admit softly.

"Come with me," she whispers. "The limo's downstairs waiting. We could go to Mexico and no one would ever find us."

I giggle like a child, struck again by her audacity.

"You want to take Hef's limo to Mexico?"

"Why not?" she smiles, tickling my side.

I forget about Hayden asleep on the chair. I am lost in Kendall's deep green eyes and insane plans. She's out of her mind, but it's so easy being with her. We communicate without even having to speak.

She kisses me lovingly and I move my hand underneath her Ton sur Ton sweatshirt. Kendall yanks her fringe leather boots off and lies back down, but before her head hits the pillow, she jerks suddenly. A chill rose through her as she felt an unexpected apprehension. Rebecca, my father's latest twenty-year-old girlfriend, stands in my bedroom doorway. I sit up, trying to play it off.

"Hi!" I stutter.

"What are you guys doing?" Rebecca asks, trying to peer in at Kendall, who's hiding underneath the sheets.

"Just fuckin' around. What are you doing here?" I say lightly.

"I just came by to pick up some clothes for your father," Rebecca says.

Hayden's eyes open. He sits up and scratches his head.

"Great, well, see ya in a bit. . . . Oh, and don't worry about the mess, I'm gonna clean it up before Dad gets home."

Rebecca half smiles and leaves.

I turn to Kendall and whisper, "We're dead."

I'm in the car driving with my father; he is explosive, his stare intoxicating. I roll the window down to let in some fresh air.

"Why did you bring that slut to our home?" he demands.

"She came on her own," I tell him.

"Let me make this crystal clear. Under no circumstances do I want you hanging out with Kendall!"

"Why?" I ask defensively.

"Because she's a manipulator and a user!"

"Says who?" I shout back, my hostility mounting.

"Says everyone! I trusted your judgment! Obviously I made a huge mistake!" he yells and I look away.

I did not purposely betray him. I simply need her, her affection. I need what she gives me, what no one else can provide. I won't let anyone take her away from me.

"Let me tell you something, young lady." Dad spits out. "Let me reinforce this for the last time. You are crossing a thin line here. If Hef finds out about your little escapades, you are over. Over! Do you hear me?"

What I really hear him say is that he's threatened by his loss of control over me. He feels powerless and knows the feelings between Kendall and me won't keep us apart for very long. His need to control me is now suffocating. He sounds more jealous than concerned.

His love has become my enemy.

My resentments begin to escalate into anger. Though I still don't know how to voice my feelings, I shut my mouth and concede to his demands, feeling more and more like a prisoner. My father drops me off at home and drives up to the Mansion.

Rattled, I walk into the house and out to the backyard, where I find Hayden by the pool. As I come through the French doors, he climbs out of the pool, runs up to me, and plants a big kiss on my lips.

"You're gonna be so happy!" Hayden shouts with vigor. "I just got off the phone with Universal and I got the lead for that film I auditioned for!" he shouts.

"Oh, yeah? That's awesome, Hayden; I'm so proud of you!" I say, vaguely recalling some meeting in the distant past.

"They're filming in Italy."

"Italy?" I stop in my tracks. "How long are you going to be in Italy?"

Hayden looks at me dumbfounded.

"Between two and four months, depending on how the shoot goes," he responds casually.

"Four months? You're leaving me for four months?" I shout like a child. "I thought I meant something to you."

"Here I get the lead in my first major motion picture and you're giving me shit because it's on location?" Hayden yells.

"Just go. Leave, now," I say. I should've known I couldn't count on him. I can't count on anybody. Hayden reaches into his bag, pulls out his vial of coke, and sniffs a few bumps.

"I don't get you anymore!" Hayden responds, wiping his nose.

"What are you waiting for? Get out!"

"I don't believe this!" Hayden grabs his duffel bag. "I thought you'd be happy for me."

"I am happy for you," I hear myself say as tears swell.

I thought you loved me and now you're leaving me.

Hayden walks to the side gate and lets himself out. When he is gone, I collapse to my knees in tears, deeply saddened by a vacancy that lives inside me, crippling me as the anxiety that comes with it washes over me.

Thirteen

I attempt to call Hayden, but he does not answer. Finally, I pick up the phone, only this time I call Kendall. She and I never discuss the fact that we are forbidden to see each other. Instead, we make clandestine arrangements to meet.

It's midnight and I'm in my bathroom tying sheets together. I turn up Madonna's "Papa Don't Preach" on KIIS-FM and stop to do a line of coke off the cobalt-blue tile counter. I tiptoe through my bedroom to the door, opening it slightly. I look down the hall and see a dim light coming from my father's room. I peer downstairs and see that the alarm system is set. The red light stops me from using the front door but the windows on the second floor are unsecured. I retreat back into my bathroom and continue tying knots in the sheets.

The phone rings. I answer it.

"It's me. We're outside," Kendall whispers excitedly.

"I'll be right there," I say.

I tie the end of my homemade sheet-rope to the doorknob and toss the rest of it out the window. I begin climbing down the wall of my second-story bathroom window. I jump the remainder of the way, scraping my tight stonewashed jeans along the side of the house. I bypass the creaky gate and hop over the backyard wall. A black stretch limo waits for me on the other side. The back door is ajar and I hop in. Kendall and Austin are glammed-out and drunk. Troy's in the driver's seat.

"Hey, Troy." I flash him a smile.

"Right . . . what's up, girl?" He winks.

Kendall immediately places her sweater over my legs as she discreetly moves her hand underneath it, running her fingers over my left leg. We sip champagne, crank up the Rolling Stones, and cruise down Sunset Boulevard.

"I need to stop at the market for a sec," Kendall says, motioning Troy to pull into the 7-Eleven.

Kendall grabs my hand.

"We'll be right back," she tells Austin as we jump out.

We run in and Kendall asks for the bathroom key. We get in and Kendall locks the door. She grabs my arms, pins me against the wall, and kisses me playfully, but for me her affection has become more of a physical ache: a gaping hole deep inside me is suddenly filled when she touches me. When she lets go, it's as if I am drowning again and cannot breathe.

On the way out, Kendall buys a pack of cigarettes.

"Let's get our asses over to Vertigo!" she roars with enthusiasm.

Moments later, we roll out of the limo, strut past a line of clubgoers, and head straight through the crowd to the purple velvet rope. As soon as the doorman sees Kendall, he lifts the rope. Kendall throws him a kiss. We enter the mass of decadence. After the first round of drinks, we drop 'ludes, turning the night into a fog of dancing, laughter, and general fabulousness.

It's almost morning. The haze begins to clear when we go to Ed Debevic's, a twenty-four-hour diner in Beverly Hills. Kendall, Austin, and I chill in a corner booth. The decor is pure camp with red booths and checkered floors.

"So, what are you going to tell Hef? I mean, where does he think you are?" I ask Kendall.

"Not with you, that's for sure. He thinks I'm with Austin and Jamal. He knows Jamal's gay, so he doesn't care. I'll just say I got drunk and crashed at his house," Kendall answers.

"Where's Hayden?" asks Austin.

"He left me to become famous in some European shithole," I tell them. "I hope he catches gonorrhea."

"Typical self-centered asshole," Kendall chimes in.

The waitress puts plates of omelets in front of us and I look down at mine and can't conceive of eating anything. The thought of food is so disconcerting. We decide to leave and on the drive home Kendall holds my hand, squeezing it every few seconds. I feel a tingling sensation run through me as she presses her fingers into my palms. Most of me wishes we could sleep next to each other just for the night so I could feel the warmth of her body next to mine, a comfort and closeness surpassing the realm of sexuality: it's a deeper connection I am searching for and have somehow found in Kendall. But I know the simple fact that we are out together is risky and my heart pounds as the limo drops me off at the side of the house. Kendall whispers, "Call me tomorrow."

" 'Bye, hon." Austin throws air kisses from the back.

I make my way toward the front door and decide to chance it with the alarm. I turn it off and quickly run in, holding my breath as the numbers make a beeping noise. I wait to hear Dad's footsteps coming from his bedroom door, never knowing when he will wake up. Nothing happens. All is silent. I tiptoe upstairs to my room.

At school, I'm chilling alone on the second-floor patio as friends in side ponytails, rolled-up sleeves, and ripped sweatshirts breeze by me but I barely notice; I am consumed by thoughts of Kendall.

I'm talking to Troy up at the Mansion.

"Are you sure my dad's not there?"

"Girl . . . he left. I saw him drive off the property myself."

"You're a cool cat, Troy. I owe you, big-time."

"Who takes care of you, babe?"

We hang up and I leave school, arriving at the Mansion to show off my new rooster-bang haircut, sleeveless Breakfast Club T-shirt, and Molly Ringwald earrings. Kendall skips down the staircase in tight cotton pants and a white tee without a bra.

"C'mon, we're going to the beach," she says, and pulls me out the door and into my Mercedes.

David Bowie is on the radio as we head down Sunset, holding hands in the car. I keep looking in my rearview mirror, paranoid that we're being followed.

"So, did Hef ask where you were going?" I ask hesitantly.

"He knows I need to get out for a while. I get claustrophobic in that house all the time," she answers.

"So, he's cool with us hanging out?"

"He's not thrilled about it. He knows I always get myself into trouble."

She lights a cigarette.

"Is that what I am to you—trouble?" I ask, slightly hurt.

"Oh, don't be so serious." She slaps me on the leg.

We pull into the Sand and Sea Club, where my mother is a member. We cruise through the women's locker room and stop at the sauna. Kendall leans against the door, holding her cigarette in her slender fingers. We look at each other with a deep, meaningful stare, one filled with loneliness and longing. She reaches over and pulls me close. I can feel the electricity between us. My enslavement to her touch makes me feel loved and complete. We're both naked underneath our white fluffy towels and the hot air leaves us no room to breathe. I crave her in a way I cannot explain. Our bodies are on automatic as we reach for each other and our lips softly meet. When we finally pull away, she lies down and gently uncovers the towel revealing her firm, round breasts. She reaches for my hand and traces it slowly up her tan flat stomach. My hunger to consume her is lost in a state of recklessness. I lean my head down to kiss her voluptuous full lips as a high-society woman in her fifties comes in wearing a pearl necklace and sits down. There's a wall of aloofness between us as the woman closes her eyes and leans back against the wooden sauna. I instantly sit upright as though caught in the act of a criminal mistake. Kendall moves her hand without abandon underneath my towel, not caring what anyone thinks. She finds delight in people's discomfort, something I admire but am still afraid of at the same time. I try to move away from her, but end up giggling nervously. Sweat pours down my face as I maintain a plastered smile. The woman opens one eye and glares at me peculiarly. Out of nowhere, Kendall lets out a thunderous groan. The woman shakes her head and leaves. We laugh hysterically.

Kendall combs my hair with her fingers as we kiss. She trails her fingers up and down my spine and rolls onto her back. I trace my hand over her breasts, barely touching them as she sighs in desperation. I touch her softly, allowing my fingers to make their way in between her legs. Kendall's moans become louder and longer until another woman opens the sauna door, and I jolt to my feet. It's one of my mother's friends!

I grin awkwardly and run out; Kendall follows behind. I turn back once and see the woman standing there, staring. Nosy bitch. Kendall and I spend the rest of the day frolicking in the water and running around on the beach as if we've been best friends all our lives.

A few days later, I ditch school, pick up Kendall, and sneak out to Gregory's on Sunset, a trendy New Age candlelit furniture store with a full bar and slamming music. Kendall's friends with the owner, so we stop by to sip champagne and be glamorous. I watch her smoke Marlboro Lights, fascinated by the way she holds the filtered cigarette in her hand.

"I've been trying to get a hold of you for weeks," the owner says, waving his crystal glass of Dom Pérignon.

"I've been . . . ," begins Kendall.

"Fucking your brains out?"

"If your friends won't fuck you, who will?"

Kendall spins around in a Coco Chanel hat, posing in front of the mirror.

"Oh look, she twirls," the owner laughs.

I watch quietly, infatuated with Kendall's seen-it-all eyes and how comfortable she is in her body.

For a moment, I feel my age, my youth, my awkwardness, but stifle it. Just being with her makes everything okay.

"We need to go on a real date, to Disneyland," Kendall says as she jumps up and wraps her arms around me lovingly. "We could ride in the teacups and wear Mickey Mouse ears. Or move to New York together and be really outrageous."

Kendall leans in and kisses me sensuously on the lips as Culture Club plays in the background.

"That, my friend, is the future," the owner says, popping open another bottle of Dom.

"What used to bring us shame now brings us status." Kendall pulls away, licking her lips naughtily.

After Gregory's, we stop by Mirabella's for a quick strawberry margarita, sitting at an outside table as we watch packs of Euro trash go by. We parade down Melrose wearing colored fur scarves and tinted winter sunglasses. Strolling hand in hand as best friends do, we stop and look at our reflection in a storefront window.

I know we're being careless. I turn around with a funny feeling that we're being followed, but tell myself I'm being paranoid.

Troy picks us up in Hef's limo and we cruise by Dad's house but keep going when we see Carmela's Pontiac parked on the side. He drops us off at the park across from the Beverly Hills Hotel, and Kendall and I tackle each other playfully as we race up the grassy hill.

Looking around, I notice a man who's wearing a long black coat. It strikes me briefly as odd, considering the warm weather.

Kendall and I pass the fishpond and slip into the public bathroom. We lean against the wall and kiss passionately as my fingers trace along the edge of her lavender lacy bra. She wraps her leg around my waist.

We're like junkies chasing the latest high.

My heart races in my chest as I catch a reflection of the two of us in the mirror grinding against each other, hungry for more. I quickly pull away, unable to withstand our intensity. Running outside, I inhale the night air and the scent of damp grass and mist.

Weeknights, I drive up to the Mansion with Dad to hang out while he plays cards with the guys. I am careful not to look over at Kendall while my father hovers nearby, rolling my eyes when he blows her kisses. Dad despises Kendall but will do anything not to disrupt his friendship with Hef. As soon as she's gone, his smiles turn to frowns. He tries to keep us from seeing each other, but his attempts are useless. The more he disapproves, the more I yearn for her. We meet in the carpet room and shut the door. I know I am treading dangerous water, but the excitement of something taboo turns me on.

"You're so bad," she whispers in my ear, and we kiss. "I have to go," she says, clawing her fingers through my hair.

"No, don't go," I beg, not wanting to be left alone. There is something so familiar about Kendall, but I can't quite place it. Perhaps it's the way she runs hot and cold, like my mother, enticing me as if she truly cares, but then shutting off without warning.

There's a knock on the door and we both freeze, looking at each other.

"Come out, come out, wherever you are," a man's voice says through the door.

"Who is that?" I whisper to Kendall, who shrugs, panicking.

"Who is it?" Kendall shouts back through the door.

"Whoever you want it to be," a man's voice answers.

"We're busy!" Kendall shouts.

"Kendall, is that you? It's Ron Jeremy."

"Ron!" Kendall opens the door. Hugs and kisses.

A troupe of people follow Ron inside.

"What are you doing?" Kendall asks.

"I'm looking for Bambi," he explains.

"It's just us." She shrugs as a bubblegum blonde appears from the bathroom.

Kendall and I raise our eyebrows in shock. We had no idea she was in there.

Ron and his entourage take over the room.

"How's your dad?" Ron asks, grazing my head affectionately.

"He's good."

Three blondes lean against the soft, cozy pillows. A man and woman, possibly boyfriend and girlfriend, sit across from them. I look around, hesitant to sit down.

God only knows what this visit will bring.

"I was looking all over for you, Bambi," Ron says as he turns up George Michael's "Freedom" on the radio.

The other blonde toys with her spaghetti straps in the mirror. Her blouse falls past her shoulders as her tan firm breasts burst out at us.

"Why don't you strip for us?" some guy asks.

"I'm a Playmate, not a stripper, but I love to dance." The blonde flails her arms wildly in the air as her perfectly round breasts bounce up and down.

"Dance for us, Playmate of the Room!" everyone hollers. She wiggles her body sensuously, lifting her skirt as she dances. Before you know it, most of the girls have their clothes off.

"Are you a lesbian? I've always wanted to be one of those," asks Playmate of the Room.

"I don't label myself," I tell her, looking around at all the free-spirited girls. Being heterosexual here is way overrated.

"The girls are a little horny. They haven't been laid in a while," Ron says casually.

"Well, then, why don't you fuck them?" Kendall blurts out.

"Sweetheart, women pay me to fuck them," Ron exclaims.

"They beg me," Kendall grabs the back of my head and pulls me in close.

We kiss, our lips curled into a smile as we relish the excitement.

A few minutes pass unnoticed until we start to hear moans. We stop kissing and notice that Ron has his fingers deep inside one of the girls as Playmate of the Room dances obliviously with her hands stretched out in the air.

Kendall and I crawl out of the carpet room, careful not to disturb anyone.

Laughing, we head back to the main house. We stop along the pathway and kiss hungrily one last time, but pull away and separate before reaching the front door.

There's a lonely pit in the middle of my stomach as Kendall runs over and plops down next to Hef on the couch. It seems nothing can fill me up for very long.

Later that night, my father confronts me in the upstairs hallway at home.

"Do you mind telling me what you've been doing?"

"What do you mean?" I'm instantly frightened someone told him that Kendall and I were in the carpet room.

"Where have you been the past few days?" he asks accusingly, distrust seething from his eyes.

"At school?" I answer cautiously.

"Why don't you tell me where you've really been?"

"Nowhere," I say, suddenly unable to breathe. The walls are closing in.

This was never part of the freedom plan.

"Do you think I don't know what you're doing?" His eyes narrow.

I look at him for an instant, not sure what to say.

"You're not fooling anyone but yourself, do you hear me?" He glares at me with irritation and contempt.

"I'm not trying to fool anyone," I tell him, trying to think of a way to explain how much Kendall means to me.

"She is a whore, do you hear me?" he screams. "I do not want you hanging out with her! How many times do I need to tell you?"

He dismisses Kendall with total disregard and speaks as if she, like my mother, were the enemy. His lack of sensitivity infuriates me. The more he belittles her, the angrier I become.

"Why would you intentionally do something that you know is going to piss me off? Unless what you really want is for me not to trust you anymore?" he demands in an icy tone. "Is that what you want?"

"No." I shake my head.

No one purposely sets out to cross him, certainly not me. But, somehow, he always interprets it that way.

"Why do you lie?"

"I don't!" I shout at him in total frustration, which fuels him even more.

"Yes, you do! You're a liar just like your mother!" he yells. "Let me ask you this since obviously you have the brain of a ten-year-old. Why would you do something that I specifically told you not to?"

I shrug, hoping to end this tirade. I blink my secret thoughts away, knowing it's easier to stand there in silence than to argue for hours.

"Let me make this clear, in case it isn't already. I do not want you spending alone time with Kendall! Do you understand? I'm warning you, if you as much as look at her, there will be serious ramifications! If Hef or anyone else finds out, you're finished! Do you hear me?" He threatens me with a look of loathing.

"You put me in this position," I say.

"And it can all be taken away just like that." He snaps his fingers.

"Then you'd never see me!" I scream. "Since you don't even live here!"

Dad storms down the hallway and slams his door shut.

Kendall and I continue to speak on the phone every day, but we are more cautious about meeting in person. We know there is always a risk that someone will see us.

It's overcast outside. My mother and I meet for lunch at Bagel Nosh. She looks impeccable in her deep red Thierry Mugler suit.

In between bites of our tuna sandwiches she asks, "How's school?"

"Fine," I tell her.

"Are you still spending all your free time with those positive female role models at the Mansion?" she asks, with a tone.

"You don't even know them and you put them down," I snap back defensively.

"I've been to that house; I know all I need to know. Do you think a girl taking off her clothes for money is normal?"

"You're so close-minded."

"Calm down," she whispers in a hushed tone, looking around

the restaurant to see if anyone overheard us. "I don't want to go in circles with you." Mom shuffles around for her wallet as she peers down at the check. There is an uncomfortable silence as we glance around at other people eating in the restaurant.

"Are you ready to go?" she asks, but it sounds more like a statement. We get up without another word. She heads straight to the register and I wait outside.

The next day, Savannah and I meet at Pastels in the Rodeo Collection. We sip daiquiris. She leans in close.

"What's going on with you?" she asks, always more straightforward than anyone else.

"Nothing."

"All of a sudden you're all dressed up and coming to places like this?" She stares at the Venetian-tile fountain a few feet from us.

Savannah checks out my new Gucci sunglasses.

"And what are those? Another gift from Dad?"

"Why not?"

I plop down Dad's American Express card.

"Must be nice," Savannah smirks.

"Are you going to scrutinize every little thing every time you see me?" I ask.

"Mom said you're still going to the Mansion all the time."

"What are you, the gestapo?"

"I never see you at school anymore. In fact, no one sees you at school anymore."

"Thanks, Mom."

"Someone's gotta be."

It's a valid point.

"Why don't you try being nicer to Mom? She picks up on your anger, you know."

"She resents me for leaving and you know it." I weigh my words carefully.

"However you want to look at things, Jennifer."

"How should I look at it? Close my eyes and pretend everything's fine when deep down she wants nothing to do with me?"

Years later, we'll learn favoritism caused this never-ending sibling rivalry, this competitive greed and need to be favored.

"What have you been doing?" My sister softens. I take a deep breath and exhale.

"Nothing. I've been hanging with Kendall a little bit," I tell her.

"Kendall? Hef's girlfriend, Kendall?" she fires back. "Ew! Isn't she into girls?"

"I don't know," I say defensively.

"You don't know? How could you not know?"

"I don't know, maybe she's bi. Who cares?"

"Since when are you into hanging out with bisexual girls? And more importantly, what is she doing hanging out with you?"

Savannah slams down her drink as if she's the older one.

"Whatever," I say, wishing this conversation were over.

I can see in my sister's eyes that Kendall sickens her. Her disgust pushes me further into secrecy. I am convinced she and Mother will never understand my strong connection toward Kendall, so I push them even further away.

"You are definitely Dad's daughter and I am definitely Mom's," Savannah snickers in a disapproving tone.

"He's my father until he sends you a check, then, all of a sudden, he's your father too, right?" I rebut, bleeding sarcasm.

"Actually, I want nothing to do with him." She shakes her head like she wants nothing to do with me either.

"In front of him you're like, 'Oh, Daddy, I love you so much,' but then you run back to Mom and tell her how much you hate him. How classic," I mumble.

"At least I don't check out girls with my own father!" she says.

"Of course not, because deep down you wish you were one of those Playmates just waiting to be discovered."

"Okay, attitude, I'm leaving." Savannah gathers her things.

"Maybe you should get your boobs done. Maybe then Dad will notice you more," I say, lighting a cigarette as Savannah takes off in a huff, her silky blond hair blowing in the breeze.

Fourteen

As summer rolls on, Kendall's phone calls grow less frequent. Mine are no longer put through or go unreturned as panic sets in that she is letting me go the same way my mother did. Hayden hasn't called since he departed for Naples. I feel utterly alone. I've alienated myself from my mother and sister. My friends at school don't understand. I turn to the one person who I know will be there for me: My father.

By this time, Dad's gone through a whole slew of women: Michelle Johnson, who was seventeen at the time (not that age matters), Victoria Principal, Kimberly Hilton, Shelley Fabares, Kelly LeBrock, Deidre Hall, and Debra Adair (to name a few). When he's in-between girlfriends, it is easy for me to slide back into my role as his running-mate. Dad may not know how to be there emotionally in the traditional sense, but he is always there for me by inviting me along with him wherever he goes. I follow him to pool parties, nightclubs, strip clubs, even out on dates. The distractions help keep my mind far from thoughts of Hayden and Kendall.

Soon Mansion parties aren't enough. Nightclubs, pool parties, and high-class party girls are common occurrences. The need for new thrills and more adventure becomes essential. I crave daily doses of chaos. My desire for stimulation intensifies and spending time with people whose lives revolve around drama becomes the quickest fix. It's an addictive lifestyle. When we cannot find the drama, we create it out of anything and nothing. It's a vicious circle, as I inevitably begin to believe the reality I've created.

One afternoon Dad greets me with a surprise.

"Go pack an overnight bag and meet me downstairs in ten minutes," he says joyfully, and I can tell he's sober by the clarity in his voice and the sharpness in his eyes. I relax momentarily because he's in a good mood.

"Where are we going?"

"I'm not telling."

"What's it for?"

"It's a treat just for us. A little daytime excursion like we used to do," he giggles, and I too become giddy. But mostly I am happy that he and I will be alone.

"Now go pack your bag." He smiles as I race into my room and quickly fill my Le Coq Sportif duffel bag.

Minutes later, I run downstairs to find a black stretch limousine waiting for us in the driveway. Dad helps me into the limo and we head off on our adventure.

"You look the best I've ever seen," he says sweetly, and I can't help but wonder if the bad times are behind us.

The driver pulls onto the tarmac at the airport, where a private jet awaits our arrival. A pilot greets us and takes our bags.

"Welcome, Sir, Jennifer," the pilot says.

"Where are we going?" I ask again, as we walk up the stairs into the private plane.

"It's a surprise," Dad gloats. The plush plane has cream leather chairs, a stocked bar, stereo, large television and VCR. Dad and I chill in the comfy seats as we fasten our seat belts.

"Sit back, relax, and enjoy your trip to New York City," the pilot announces over the PA system.

I turn to Dad, thrilled.

"No way!"

"Way," he responds calmly.

"What's the occasion?"

"No occasion. It's father and daughter day."

After a few minutes I ask, "So, why are we really going?"

"A high-profile prima-donna couple needs to lose twenty pounds in a week," he says, giving a shrug. "Junkies on a binge waiting to be squeezed in to see the bicoastal celebrity weight-loss doctor."

"Anything for those miracle diets," I say.

"I go to all lengths to please," he sighs.

The rest of the flight is relaxing as we reminisce about old times and enjoy the comforts of traveling in a private plane.

That evening, we skip the theater and instead hop from one club to the next finding nonstop distractions. We do a few loops at a party in SoHo, check out the scene at the Vault, find the sexiest woman in the room, add her to our entourage, and jump to the next hot spot. We're on a party binge, a mission with the attention span of twenty minutes at each stop. Our search for the next best female is always on our minds.

It's 4:00 A.M. by the time we return to our suite with a few girls straggling behind. We sit in the living room as Dad entertains us with tales of the Hollywood heroes he's friends with, and you can tell the girls are impressed by the mesmerized look in their eyes. I yawn because I've heard it all before.

I kiss him good night, head to our bedroom, and crash. Before

I doze off, I question whether anyone finds it odd that we're sharing a bed.

We return home the next day and Dad and I hit an array of pool parties in the Hollywood Hills. Dad's new friends he met out clubbing, Don Michaels and Eric Jacobs, middle-aged talent agents with dark complexions, dark shades, and huge cocaine habits, host elaborate daytime events sponsored by modeling agencies I've never heard of. Hundreds of underage disco-style girls fill Don Michaels' backyard. Human League wails through the speakers. Buffet tables display spreads of various meat, pasta, fish, salads, fruit salads, and gourmet desserts. The outdoor bars are stocked with Tab, Cactus Coolers, and every kind of liquor imaginable. Caterers serve rounds of champagne and caviar. Guests mingle in the Jacuzzi. Underage hotties in summer dresses stand around posing as guys in suits hunt their prey.

Dad and I check out the rooms inside. There are different colored cushions against every wall. The lighting varies from red to blue to light shades of orange. Stunning models in tiny Esprit tight skirts with glazed eyes lie around on cushions. Mounds of coke are piled high on tables while glass jars are filled to the limit with white tabs.

"Where did these girls come from?" I ask Dad as we wander.

"They live here," he explains.

"Why do they live here?"

"Why wouldn't they?" He gestures to the luxurious surroundings.

Dad introduces himself to a young model who strolls by while I veer off, venturing down a long hallway with mirrors on both sides. I hear the Motels' "Only the Lonely" coming from an obscurely lit room down the hall. I poke my head through the door and find five young girls sitting on the floor, shooting heroin underneath their toenails. I stare at them for half a second, not sure if they see me or even care.

I make eye contact with one. She looks as lost as I feel. I quickly turn and walk outside seriously in need of fresh air and a cigarette.

The sunlight blinds me. I can barely keep my eyes open as I help myself to a wine cooler. An older actor in his fifties introduces himself to me.

"Nick Randall. How ya doing?"

"Fine," I answer aloofly, because I no longer have the energy to be completely superficial.

"How do you know Don?" the guy asks.

"My father's friends with him."

"Oh, yeah, who's your father?"

"You probably know him as Doc."

"Sure, everyone knows Doc." The guy smiles while drooling over the underage hotties. "These girls must be cashing in on some serious allowances. Their payroll alone must cost a fortune. I don't know where Eric and Don find them."

"I heard they advertise in *Teen Beat*," I say, my words drenched in sarcasm.

"No shit?" The guy lights up, excited, and walks away.

I spot Dad surrounded by a group of girls my age. He smiles and waves me over. I pass, sitting down on a swing. I close my eyes for a second and see Kendall's face. She is telling me she loves me. The thought of her hits me like a quick knife in the heart. When my eyes open, the image is gone.

As if life wasn't full of enough complications, some of the girls from Don Michaels' move into Dad's house. Our halls are suddenly filled with porn stars and strippers. I never know which one I will bump into in the morning. Dad explains that they have nowhere else to go. These girls are notorious for spending every summer in Beverly Hills. They never once pay for food, rent, or entertainment. Each summer, they choose a new man to bankroll their lavish spending. Most of them met my father, their latest mark, at a Hollywood party in the Hills.

Carmela and I roll our eyes and make fun of the dolled-up hookers that seem to move in every week. One night, hearing them stumble in drunk, I open my bedroom door as one of the girls passes by me.

"Hey, cutie," she purrs, running her fingers over my belly button.

I instantly begin to feel nauseated and shut my door.

The next morning, I'm sitting at the breakfast table eating cereal before school. I recognize the girl who passed by my room the night before as she breezes nonchalantly into the kitchen. She is dressed in my father's infamous Snow White and the Seven Dwarves Doc T-shirt. She opens the refrigerator door and grabs the mocha mix as if she owns the place. Her hands shake as she pours herself a cup of the coffee that Carmela brewed hours earlier. Her skinny legs and big perky tits are shoved into my face as she reaches over me to grab the sugar. Disregarding my presence, she takes her coffee and dashes back upstairs.

Dad's kitchen countertops now feature blue and white handmade candy jars labeled Uppers, Downers, and Quaaludes. Carmela grabs handfuls from each container and concocts her famous party mix by tossing in M&M's and Jelly Bellies for color.

It's a hot summer day, so outside, girls in string bikinis with hopes of becoming Playmate of the Year lounge around Dad's pool showing off their new boob jobs and nipple sizes.

"Welcome to Los Angeles. We're going to baptize you—you have to lose twenty pounds," my father tells a new girl approaching him.

"I'm on a monthly plan with my plastic surgeon," she says.

"So why don't you get your fat ass over here?" he asks frankly as she swiftly moves her chair beside him. "Wait, let me see your ID first," he says.

She grabs a fake ID out of her wallet and shows it to my father, whose eyes pop out. "You have a fake ID that says you're eighteen?" He looks at her closer. "Do I know you?"

"My name is Phyllis."

"Oh my God, you're blond. I remember you now. You finally listened. You went blond. Now you'll finally get a date in L.A., and if you're lucky, you'll get a job."

Knowing my father is watching, one of the other girls casually takes off her clothes and walks naked into the swimming pool.

"Nice stroke," Dad comments as the tan eighteen-year-old steps out of the pool and shakes her kinky blond hair. Dad passes around the party mix as he walks over to a group of girls asking if they want to go upstairs and have some candy. One of the girls grabs the party mix out of his hands.

"I'll take this. It's worth thousands." She smirks as she steps into the house.

I go with the party brigade as they move into Dad's bedroom. His bedroom has always been a subculture of sex and excess.

Ten girls are now locked in "Doc's" bedroom. Dumb and blond, just the way he likes them. They vie for his attention, bitch-fighting over who has the tenacity and persistence to please the almighty doctor.

"This is the man who can get you into the Mansion," one of the girls explains to the other.

"Do you think I have Playmate potential?" one of them asks him.

"Why don't you come over here and show me how wild you can be, and maybe I'll introduce you to Hef," he brags. "I can make you a centerfold."

All the girls jump into his king-size bed.

"What's your name?" Dad asks one of the girls—he's never met any of them before.

"Lizzi, courtesy of an ex–porn star."

"I would love to wake up to your face every morning for three days," he laughs as the phone rings.

"I'll have to get back to you. I'm undercover," he says, handing the phone to me.

He loves to include me.

"What's your name again?" He turns to one of the girls in his bed. "Look at your big mouth. I bet you can shove a few cocks in there."

"I was very popular in high school," the girl says. Her best attribute is that she likes to swallow.

"Maybe if everything goes well, we'll spend the week together."

The next night, Eric Jacobs walks into Dad's house wearing an Italian suit, loafers, and dark shades. He looks overbaked from the tanning salon. He's with some smooth-talking PR guy named David, who's in his mid-thirties, handsome, and has two pagers attached to his belt. They show up sniffing nonstop. Big cokeheads. Where did these guys come from anyway? I've never seen them at the Mansion.

David extends his arm when I answer the door.

"Hi, how ya doing? David Meyers."

"Jennifer."

I shake his hand and he wipes his nose.

Eric gives me a kiss on the cheek.

"Hi, hon. Pops ready?" Eric sounds rushed.

"He should be right down," I tell them. "Do you guys want something to drink?"

"We're cool, we're cool," Eric repeats, and I watch as they pace around in our foyer, edgy, unable to stand still.

"I'll be right back," I tell them since I can't bear watching them any longer. I slip down the hallway to the kitchen.

"How's the new model from Sweden doing?" I hear the PR guy ask Eric.

"Oh, the hooker that just moved in?"

"I tap that ass ten times a day. Before she moved in, I installed cameras in her bedroom and now I watch her and her sexy little friends strip down to nothing. The other day, I walked into the room and took on five at once."

"When can I come over?" David jokes.

Dad comes downstairs wiping his nose.

"Jennifer, did you meet David? He does PR for all the hot spots," Dad explains and I nod like I'm interested. "Girls . . . let's go," Dad yells and an entourage of blondes descends the staircase one by one.

We pile into my father's Cadillac while David jumps into the back of a black stretch waiting in our driveway. Crammed uncomfortably in between two annoying blondes with enormous silicone boobs, I tell Dad I'd rather ride with David in the limo.

"Do what you want," he says, so I hop out of the Cadillac and into the limo.

"Your father's a great guy," David says.

"Uh-huh," I nod.

"Must see a lot of action coming in and out all the time?" he asks.

"It's incredible: between the eyes, cheeks, lips, and boobs, I barely recognize the girls when they leave," I spew sarcastically as the limo pulls into Don Michaels' mansion in the Hills.

David jumps out, quickly runs into the house, and comes out with six tall, thin models he ushers into the back of the limo, and then pops open a bottle of Cristal.

"The girls are visiting from Europe and as soon as they move here, we're going to make sure their careers take off. Isn't that right?" David nudges one of the girls, who giggles in a silly way.

"We want to be stars!" one of them yells as David whips out the coke and a small mirror.

The girls squirm in their seats, itching to inhale until they bend down and sniff the white lines of powder one by one.

He then takes out a joint and passes it to me. I take a strong drag off the joint and hand it to the model sitting to my left. David leans back, placing his arms around two of the girls.

The model to my left takes a hit and offers it to the others, who are more interested in blowing rails of coke. She passes the joint back to me, so I take another deep hit and begin to cough, passing it back to David. I'm fine until everything starts to become dreamy. Soon the inside of the limo starts to stretch and recede. Pedestrians in the streets blend together. Images of people appear out of nowhere. I start to hear hundreds of muffled voices in my head. Everyone's talking to me at once—or are they? My heart's pounding. I can't breathe. What the hell was in that joint? The girls beside me have deranged faces, swollen lips, and their breasts rip out of their tight tees. I blink a few times, hoping to shake off this horrible buzz. My eyes water.

David pats me on the back. "You okay, kid?"

"Was that pot?" I ask, my hands trembling.

"A special blend of pot and angel dust. Isn't it great?" he says as his face peels off and turns into a devil with horns. "I knew the girls would get a kick out of it," he finishes.

We arrive at the Bistro Garden and I'm so high I can barely speak. When I step out of the car, the ground seems a hundred miles down. My feet are heavy as I follow behind everyone else. Dad, Eric, and the other girls wait for us in front and we're taken to a round table where a Middle Eastern high roller from out of town sits alone. He stands up as we make our way over.

"Welcome," the man says.

"Ladies, this is my dear old friend, Sufian," David introduces us.

"Of course, of course, please come join me," Sufian offers generously as he motions for the waiter to deliver bottles of Dom.

Within minutes of our arrival, Dad gets paged and excuses himself. Sufian sips his Johnnie Walker Blue Label and turns to the blonde beside him. I zone in and out of their conversation, trying to maintain the plastered smile on my face.

"So, how long have you girls been in town?" Sufian asks.

"Less than a week," a blonde answers.

"How long do you expect to stay?"

"I'm only going to be here for a week unless I get a good job," the girl confesses.

"What type of job?" Sufian asks softly.

"I'm a model."

"Maybe I can help you out. What agency are you with?"

"My agency is in Europe. I don't have an agency here," the girl explains.

"I know the top agents in the city. I can get you work tomorrow. I'll call them later," Sufian mentions calmly as the bottles of Dom arrive. "You're so lovely, I bet you can get any kind of job. What do you do—print, runway? I bet you're a print model," Sufian says, leaning over to the girl.

"I enjoy print, but it's tough because there aren't enough jobs. No jobs, no money," the girl says with a Swedish accent.

"It's true. I bet you'd look really sexy in front of the camera. Have you ever done any nude photography?" Sufian asks.

"No, I haven't."

"Well, are you comfortable doing nude?"

"I love being nude," she smiles, and Sufian turns to the brunette with the fake boobs and injected lips.

"What about you? I bet you love to be photographed in the nude," Sufian whispers softly to the brunette.

"I always feel better naked," the brunette confesses.

"Seeing the two of you nude would make me so horny. Do you ladies party?"

"Of course," they giggle.

Sufian whispers in one of the girl's ears. "Let's step outside to my limo and start this party. Why don't you ask your friend to come along?"

Sufian takes the blonde and brunette outside and I get up unexpectedly, telling everyone I need fresh air. The whole room is spinning. I need to get out of here. Sufian notices me tagging along behind them outside.

"We haven't been formally introduced," he says as a series of hands extend from his body. I need to lie down. "It's a pleasure to meet you," he says and the four of us step inside his limo.

"Do you have any blow?" the blonde asks almost immediately.

Sufian takes out a little mirror from a side compartment and cuts several lines of coke and the girls begin to snort.

"Why don't you come over and sit close to me," he signals, giving the blonde to his right a kiss on the lips. I lean against the window and curl up as I hear Sufian say, "You're going to be so happy. I'm going to get you the best modeling job here in L.A."

He's said the magic words. The blonde automatically gets down on her knees. I blink a few times as she unzips his pants and starts sucking his cock. I must be dreaming: she is not doing that right in front of me. He doesn't seem to mind either.

"Both of you will be on the cover of *Vogue* next month. My cousin is the owner. You're going to be so happy," he says and the brunette gets on her knees and starts sucking his dick too.

Something weird is happening, but my head is too heavy to lift. I feel like I'm in Arabian porno.

Sufian lifts the blonde off her knees, pulls up her little plaid skirt, and starts fucking her from behind while the other coke whore does more blow. I lean forward and reach for the door handle as Sufian pushes the blonde off him and grabs the brunette. I jump out of the limo. The cool breeze hits me in the face and wakes me up a little. I stumble back into the restaurant.

My father is nowhere to be found. Sufian and the girls walk in a few minutes later. Before they sit down, Sufian leans over to two new girls at the table and softly whispers, "Why don't you switch seats. I want to get to know all you girls better."

They exchange seats obediently as Sufian flirts with two new girls, blowing off the ones he's just fucked in the limo. I excuse myself and go to the bathroom. As I enter, I recognize a young, skinny model with perfect skin and a bright, sunny smile. She leans against the counter snorting a line of coke. She can't be older than seventeen. She looks at me and smiles.

"Wanna bump?" she asks.

"Sure," I say, accepting free coke even though I have my own.

She hands me a little Baggie filled with white powder and her key. I take a few quick bumps and hand it back to her.

"Are you one of the girls staying at Don's house?" I ask.

"If that's the really old guy I fucked last night, then yeah, I am," she answers and I smile, not knowing how to respond. "I was so not into it, but he got me so drugged up that I ended up fucking him. I hope I don't have to do it again tonight," she says.

"I don't see why you would," I say, not knowing how to answer.

"My agent in Sweden set me up to stay with him and told me this guy was going to book me a lot of modeling jobs. I had no idea I had to sleep with him."

"That sucks."

"I told him today I didn't want to do it, and he said, 'I'm gonna charge you twelve hundred in rent.' I told him I didn't have twelve hundred, so he said, 'I need you to work for me.' He wants me to work twelve-hour shifts four days in a row. He said I have to strip and dance around with other women, and somebody's going to tape us."

"For what?"

"His own collection, I guess. Some people collect stamps; he collects girls doing stupid things on tape. I hear he's got thousands of videos in his collection. He's a power junkie. We don't have a choice."

"So, why do you stay with him?" I ask.

"Because I want to be an actress, a superstar." The girl lifts her hands in the air.

I can't help but feel sorry for her, knowing she will probably never get anywhere.

"Well, good luck."

As I leave the restroom, I see my father standing by the table. I take deep breaths and tell myself I'm going to be fine, the coke has leveled me out a little. Dad seems restless and he tells me we're leaving. We say our good-byes. Most of the women stay with Sufian while the rejects leave with Eric and David.

On the way out, I see Sufian slip David some cash with a wink.

"Good work," Sufian says to him. "Let's do it again tomorrow. Next time more blondes. I'm tired of brunettes."

Dad and I hop into the Cadillac and we cruise down Sunset Boulevard checking out strip joints. Thank God my buzz is starting to wear off. We discuss Cheetahs and the Tropicana, and then end up at Crazy Girls. The doorman lets us right in.

The host escorts Dad and me to a VIP booth where a few girls are waiting for us. Dad ignores them as he scans the joint looking for fresh pieces of meat.

He motions for me to check out a brunette at another booth.

"Go get her name. Tell her I can make her a Playmate," he boasts.

"You already have more distractions than you know what to do with."

"Yes, but the unavailable ones are always the most intriguing," he says and we both nod.

I slip out of the booth and make my way over to the brunette, waiting until her date gets up to make my move.

"Sorry to bother you, but my father wants to buy you a drink," I say, wondering if she's bi.

She blushes, but only slightly. She's obviously heard this before.

"What are you, his pimp?" she asks with her eyebrows poised.

"Something like that," I tell her, now wanting to flirt with her myself.

"Actually, I'm here with someone," she says.

In the corner of my eye, I see my father, who's signaling for me to get her digits. She is clearly uninterested, so I decide to change my strategy.

"I totally understand. I hate it when guys hassle me. The truth is my dad is really shy ever since he and my mother divorced. I had to drag him out. You looked so nice, I just thought that since he's a producer, you'd be perfect for his next film . . . but I don't want to bother you." I back up and she softens.

I hand her the small Playboy Mansion West notepad I carry in my back pocket.

"It's no bother." She jumps toward me as her eyes light up.

I return to Dad's table and slip him the notepad with her number.

"She's with someone," I say.

"I'm in love already," he says, grinning.

"She's too old for you. She's at least twenty-three."

"I'll make an exception," Dad cackles.

I order another drink and then slip into the bathroom, dipping into my supply of coke. I hold my left nostril, snort out of my right; my eyes water, I wipe my nose; I switch nostrils, grab my backup bullet, refill, and again sniff hard. Fuck Hayden. Fuck Kendall. I don't need anyone.

Later that night, I'm in my bedroom when I stumble for the phone and dial the Mansion, asking for Kendall. They tell me she's unavailable. I decide to call Hayden. I don't know why I call him, but hearing the sound of his voice makes me angrier with each spoken word. The simple fact that he hasn't called me back makes me more furious than actually speaking to him.

"Hi, it's Hayden . . . leave me a message."

By the time I hear the beep I'm in full attack mode. When it picks up I start screaming, "What is it you've been doing that you can't pick up the phone and call me, you fucking asshole! You're a real asshole, you know that? If you didn't know, I'm here to tell you! You're an asshole!" I scream, realizing I sound like a real psycho, which makes me even angrier.

"Fuck you!" I fume, slamming the phone down, missing the cradle.

I call and hang up at least a hundred more times in the next hour.

I'm riding in Dad's Rolls when Eva's, a new Hollywood bar on the bottom level of the Beverly Center, comes into view. A bouncer with a headset stands behind a velvet-roped-off entrance with a line around the parking lot. Pure attitude. Everyone's in black. My father ushers me out of the car.

"Tell the doorman you're with me," he says. I get out, closing the car door, forgetting to let his date out of the backseat. I push past the paparazzi and make my way to the front.

"No one gets in unless I know you. There is no list," the bouncer calls out. "I'll need for you to step back," he repeats sternly.

"But, I'm . . ."

"The back of the line starts over there." He points as bar divas in black vinyl breeze past me. I approach the bouncer.

"My father . . ."

"I'll need for you to step back!" His voice crushes mine as Dad walks up with his young blonde in a tight dress and heels trailing behind. The bouncer is suddenly all smiles.

"Right this way, sir." The bouncer unclasps the velvet rope and lets us in. I glare at him.

"What is wrong with you people?" I bark, passing the bouncer as we enter the new club.

Plastic surgery junkies are everywhere. It's a fashion flashback of feathers, beads, and fringe. They're models, celebrities, and Playmates, all sporting the size-two lollipop look. I recognize many of them from my father's office. The place is flooded with Mansion regulars.

Hef and Kendall and his other girls of the moment make a grand entrance and everyone rushes over. Kendall and I make eye contact, and she immediately looks away. Fuck her. Why am I attracted to people who are bad for me? There is a huge pit in my throat as I hold back the tears that well up inside. I hold them back as I watch her and Hef walk gracefully past me in the spotlight. She and the new Playmates who follow behind her act as if I do not exist.

Three hours later, I'm drunk and miserable. I hate everyone. I sit at the bar alone, shooting evil, deadly glares at everyone until Judd Nelson sits down next to me. He notices me staring at my father's date.

"How old do you think she is?" I ask.

"Twelve, thirteen tops," he answers, smiling.

"One more boob job on that one and she'll need a face-lift just to swallow."

We clink glasses. My father waves.

"I better hide before he and Romper Room make their way over," I tell Judd, ducking.

After a while, I say my good-byes and catch a ride home with Playmates Charlie and Morgan. I sit in the backseat of Morgan's Beemer and stare out the window the entire drive home. I find my-self wondering what the girls from school are doing tonight. What happened to watching Luke and Laura and *Friday Night Videos*? I feel so old. Mental note: remind myself tomorrow that I'm only a junior.

A Beverly Hills High School vs. Westlake tennis tournament is un-der way. As the home team we're stoned and blasting Blondie from our ghetto blaster. I slam my tennis racket against the net because some former child movie star with fake tits and pumped-up lips slams the ball down the line and I miss it. Speed demon.

My mother shows up outside the courts and demands to speak to me. I try to sort through my thoughts, but everything seems so surreal that I cannot speak properly. Plus, I'm stoned and on the verge of a cocaine-induced heart attack.

We discuss everything but what is really going on. We never talk about my appearance, my weight, my hooded eyes, the sluggish, grunge style I've suddenly adopted. The changes in me over the past few months have been so profound that neither one of us has the courage to acknowledge them out loud.

"You seem a little restless. Is your father still giving you Xanax to help you study?" Mom asks, obviously annoyed. My mother's frustration is so extreme it transcends into hostile insult.

"Yes. And it's not helping."

"Maybe if you cut down on the medication you'd have more energy," she says with a tone that insinuates that she's pissed he's prescribing pills—but she'd never confront him to his face.

By now she knows he won't listen and half of her has given up on me too.

"Some of the parents say you're still doing drugs," Mom presumes with conviction, a look of disappointment in her eyes. "I've heard you stay out late, drink, and God knows what hour you get home."

"I'm sure your sources really know what I'm doing." I sip my Jolt cola and watch happy, normal kids with knapsacks walk by.

"If you're not going to tell me anything, then I'm forced to find out through other means. I am your mother. I do have your welfare in mind even when we're not living under the same roof."

I shift in my white Fila tennis skirt, uncomfortable in my own skin. I want to tell her how much I miss her, how much I need her, how much I hate her, how cruel she is, and how screwed up I am without her. She's telling me she cares, but it's difficult for me to trust her. Too much has happened. Fear and paranoia have taken root and twisted themselves around any hope I might have had about being open and honest with my mother.

"I had a conversation with your math teacher, who says you haven't been to class in weeks. You may not want to abide by my rules, and there's not a lot I can do about that, but there is something I can do about your not going to school."

I can see in my mother's eyes that she thinks I'm a drug addict. I can almost hear her and my sister cracking jokes about the lavish lifestyle I supposedly chose over them. I wish I could tell them, explain to them, that luxury comes at a dreadful cost, and that the edges of a gold card can be very sharp.

"You know, Jennifer, you make it very difficult to have a relationship with you," she says. There is nothing but ice and pain between us.

After a few seconds I find my voice.

"Stop making me feel like I'm the one who's crazy. If a client came to you, you would be empathetic. But for some reason, you can't be that with me."

"You act like I owe you something. You chose to move out, remember?"

"No. I don't remember. I don't remember anything," I say, unaware of the depths of my feelings. "It wasn't a choice. I didn't feel comfortable there. I don't feel comfortable anywhere." I lower my head, returning to that place in my mind where fantasy takes over and real life fades away.

The thought of vomiting four pounds off races through my head, though I am interrupted by a fever of self-loathing. Suddenly I don't feel good enough, smart enough, or pretty enough. I try to remember a time when I felt my mother loved me, but the memories won't come.

I turn around and head back toward the tennis courts. When I reach the center of the court I slam my tennis racket into the net as hard as I can.

Fifteen

The night of my seventeenth birthday I don't have plans with friends, so Dad invites me to a party at a ritzy condo in West Hollywood. We ring the bell and a brunette in a turquoise miniskirt, heels, and red lipstick answers, welcoming us in. The condo is sparsely furnished, mostly in black, white, and gray. Prints of Cindy Sherman's photography line the walls. There are a lot of model-type girls, many of whom my father knows and greets warmly. I notice there are very few men, and the ones I see are old and don't look very happy. The smooth-operator hostess offers us a cocktail. Dad and I roam through the girls waiting for more guests to arrive.

"So, how did it go with your date the other night?" I ask.

"Which one?" Dad answers, scratching his head.

"The one from Eva's," I specify, wondering if he's on something.

"Oh, right. Poor thing's in dire need. It'll take her weeks to get out of the position I left her in. She calls me all the time to tell me how much she loves doing me," he boasts.

"That's because she's too young to know any better."

"You sound jealous."

"Concerned," I say with conviction.

I notice a gross older man staring at me hungrily and I shoot him a dirty look. Dad excuses himself and wanders down a hallway, where he disappears behind closed doors. I saunter outside to a candlelit balcony, where I look down at the city lights until someone with a familiar face grabs my hand. It's Paulina, one of the coke whores from the Bistro Garden.

"How do you know Heidi?" she asks.

"Who?"

"Heidi." She looks around the condo. "You know . . . it's her party . . ."

"Oh, right. I don't know her. My father does." I sip my drink, scanning the room for my father.

"Which school do you go to?" She wipes a piece of hair off her face and for a second Paulina looks like Kendall.

"Beverly," I peer into my cocktail. "But soon I'm going to college," I say semiconfidently.

"You must be really smart." She looks me up and down, and I blush, flattered because she's striking and therefore it matters to me what she thinks.

"Do you have a boyfriend?" she asks as she moves closer, tracing her hand over her miniskirt.

My father is still nowhere to be found. No other guests have arrived. The women are sitting on red stools playing with their hair. Christian Lacroix accessories are left on tabletops. A pair of embroidered gloves, a leopard-skin hat, and a patchwork cape are slung over the backs of chairs. I've never seen a party like this before. And then it hits me: exclusive guest list, attractive women, a few older men, condo in West Hollywood, and the hostess, Heidi. My father has brought me to an upscale whorehouse for my seventeenth birthday.

I turn to face Paulina and let out a half smile.

"I gotta go," I say, stepping back inside.

I find my father sipping on a martini.

"Dad, why are we here?"

"One of my friends asked me to watch his date for the night. I told him that's like leaving a plump hen with a fox," he laughs. "Who should I take home with me?" Dad contemplates taking home three first-class broads standing across the room. They're not the usual whore types.

"Who's on your pimp roll?" I ask.

"The redhead."

"I heard strawberries are in season."

Dad approaches the sexy redhead, the kind of girl who only pays attention to wealthy men. The three of us take off moments later.

That weekend, Dad invites me to an annual party in Malibu reserved for Hollywood's A-list stars. He tells me that list can be tougher to get on than the ones for the Mansion parties.

I go with Dad and Eric, who take off roaming as soon as we arrive. Dad is in a hurry to hook up with some girl who is in a relationship and can never talk because her boyfriend is always lurking nearby.

I wander around the party checking out the scene. Label whores pose by the pool as caterers in black-and-white suits pass by with trays of hors d'oeuvres. They spared no expense. Women in short off-the-shoulder sweater dresses and Jean Paul Gaultier heels nibble shrimp as they take turns running to the bathroom every two seconds. Others stand anorexic and tan, seemingly unaware that their neon skimpy string bikinis could fly off at a moment's notice.

The six outdoor bars are sponsored by some vodka company. Girls in black stilettos and miniskirts the size of headbands sip clear drinks with pineapple in them while they survey their options. I see a table filled with magnums of Cristal and Dom. Three sushi chefs cut up fresh fish and there is more caviar than the party can consume. I make a beeline for the bathroom and bump into Paulina, who's running around in a G-string and body paint. She's so high she can barely speak.

"I'm going crazy," she yells past me as she runs up to two guys and starts giving them head by the pool. Nobody even pays attention.

In the house there's a huge dance floor with a big-screen television against the wall. A DJ spins the latest records as an old black-and-white porno movie plays in the background. Two girls in bikinis dance on cubes beside the screen. Turning around, I see two police officers standing behind me. I jump, paranoid I've done something wrong. And within seconds, the owner of the house comes running over.

"Hello, officers; how are you doing today? How can I help you? I'm the owner of the house. My name is Mr. Malcolm."

"We had a complaint about the noise," the officers explain.

"I'll try to keep it down. Thanks for letting me know. Sorry if it was an inconvenience for you. By the way, what department are you from?"

"Malibu Police Department."

"How is Captain Walker? He's a dear personal friend of mine; in fact, he should be stopping by this evening."

The officers appear somewhat surprised, almost embarrassed.

"I'm a fellow LAPD reserve myself. I always enjoy seeing a man in blue. After your shift, please feel free to stop by and have a drink on me. In the meantime, I have a little surprise for you guys." He snaps his fingers and his Asian assistant runs toward him with four center-court tickets to the next Lakers game.

The officers' faces light up. "Thank you, Mr. Malcolm, we sure do appreciate it. We'll be out of your way now. Have a nice evening. If there's anything we can do, don't hesitate to call."

The officers accept the generous gift and leave as quickly as they came.

I continue roaming through the house, passing wasted guests left and right. I reach a door that is slightly ajar and go in. It's filled with entertainers in costume. A woman in a black vinyl cat suit holds a whip as she walks on a naked man's back in high heels.

She screams, "Tell me what a little bitch wimp you are!"

"I'm a little bitch, I'm a little bitch," the man whimpers.

"No, you little bitch; cry and tell me that you are a little bitch!"

He begins to cry as she steps on his balls, which are tied together with a tight little string.

"Who do these balls belong to, bitch?" the woman screams.

"They belong to you, Mistress," the naked man yelps.

"Spread your legs, you pathetic little bitch!"

The Goddess kicks him hard in the balls using the tip of her stiletto heels.

"Another one, Goddess, please," the man cries and she kicks him again.

"This is my ass, you fucking bitch. You hear me?!" she yells and whips him on the back. "Now bark like a dog!"

The man tries to bark.

"Bark like a dog, not a pussy!" she whips him again.

As I step out of the door, a guy grabs my hand and I gasp slightly.

"It's not about sex, it's about entertainment," he whispers.

I push past him and bust out of there, moving quickly down the hall. I pass another room and stop when I see a young woman dressed in a schoolgirl uniform kiss another girl dressed as Raggedy

Ann. I turn around and accidentally bump into Paulina again, relieved to see a friendly face.

She grabs onto my arm.

"I'm so fucked up. I don't know what to do. I've been throwing up. I need a bump, one bump, please, you've gotta give me a bump," she begs.

"I don't have one, hon, and honestly, I don't know if you should do anymore," I say, as gently as I can.

"I'm fine." She zooms off and approaches a strange-looking guy. "I'll give you a blow job for a bump," I hear her beg.

The sniffling guy looks both ways before he takes her by the arm and leads her into the nearest bathroom. Curiosity gets the best of me and I can't help but stand outside the door listening.

"What's your name, little girl?" he asks in a perverted voice.

"Paulina," she mumbles, barely able to speak.

I can hear them sniffing inside until I don't hear anything for a while.

"What the fuck? Your nose is all fucked up! You got blood on my fucking dick, you stupid cunt! What the fuck are you doing?" the guy yells as the door flies open and he runs out. I stare at Paulina on the floor with a pool of blood surrounding her face. Her body is wiggling up and down. She's having convulsions.

Instinctively, I scream, "Help! Someone call 911!"

"Chill out!" someone calls after me.

I can't find my father. It feels like hours pass before I find a phone. I pick it up and dial, but there's no dial tone. Shit! I'm running around frantically. I go back to check on Paulina and see that the door is still wide open and no one has stopped to help her. I shout again for help and finally Mr. Malcolm comes running over. I'm in tears as I show him Paulina. I know she needs to get to the hospital and quick. The owner peeks into the bathroom, looks at the girl, grabs a security guard, and walks over to a phone. I follow him.

"I have a situation," he says into the receiver.

Within minutes, a man dressed in business attire arrives. Mr. Malcolm announces that the girl's going to be okay as two security guards wrap the lifeless Paulina in a blanket and carry her upstairs. They put her in a bedroom and close the door. I try to go in but they stop me.

"Thanks, kid. You've done all you can do. We'll take it from here," Mr. Malcolm assures me.

"But I know where she lives and everything," I plead, eager to help.

"We've got it under control."

He slams the bedroom door in my face. I stand outside, eavesdropping.

"It's too late. She's dead," one of the guys whispers.

No one calls the police.

No one calls an ambulance.

I am terrified that nobody cares or wants to interrupt their fantasy and be slapped back into reality. I am frightened and race out of there without saying good-bye to my father.

I run frantically down Pacific Coast Highway until I reach a pay phone and call Carmela to ask if she can pick me up. Sitting on a block of cement, I see a family laughing, having a picnic on the beach. The mother puts sunblock on her little boy as the husband gives the mother a kiss and a cold drink from the cooler. For a moment, I forget that I just saw a young girl die right in front of me.

I'm relieved when I see Carmela's green Pontiac.

I can barely force myself to go to school anymore. I show up late, skip my first two classes, and walk out on my teacher when she is talking in third period. I chill on the second-floor patio smoking a cigarette with Liz, Hunter, Sonya, Michelle, and Amber.

"We are so worried about you, girl." Sonya flips her black hair and plays with the Velcro fasteners on her Keds.

"You've been totally MIA," Michelle exhales.

"For real. We haven't seen you in ages." Amber passes the stogie to Hunter.

"Sorry, it's been crazy." I tilt my shades so I can see clear blue sky. A group of guys flick paper footballs in our direction.

"By the way, I finally took your father up on his offer and called him for connections," Hunter says. I instantly feel my body heat rise ten degrees.

"You called my father?"

"Don't you remember?" she says as a paper football breezes past my head. "He said he knew some people in the biz, so I sent him my head shots."

"Did he say he wanted to meet to talk about it?" I ask suspiciously, my blood boiling.

"Yeah, he said to come by his office after school tomorrow. I think he wants to introduce me to somebody," Hunter says innocently.

I can feel my muscles twitch.

"Why don't you just fuck him and get it over with!" I yell as a paper football smacks me in the forehead. "I'm gonna kill somebody!" I shriek and run toward the guys who flicked the paper footballs in my direction.

I can tell which one did it by the look of pure terror on his face as I approach him. The next thing I know, my knee is in his chest and I'm choking him as hard as I can. Blood runs from his nose, staining his blue Quicksilver T-shirt. People gather around but I don't see them. I refuse to let go of his neck. I knee him in the groin several times until faraway voices seep through my head. I feel someone yanking me off him. It's a teacher.

"Jennifer, stop!" he shouts.

More teachers hurry over. They're hovering over me. I don't know what's going on. Where are they taking me? What happened? Next thing I know, I'm in the principal's office.

"Your behavior is unacceptable! You have a real attitude problem, young lady," the principal exclaims, but I don't care.

Later, my sister finds me down an isolated hallway sitting against the wall crying with my hands curled into fists. How much time has passed? We're alone.

"What is wrong with you lately?" Savannah places her hand on mine. "You're in trouble all the time," she says apprehensively.

"What a surprise, considering the hell I'm living in!" I declare harshly, my hostility ever present. "And no one gives a shit."

She stares at me, clearly shaken by my tone.

"That's not true. Mom's been calling you for weeks. You don't return any of her calls. She doesn't know what to think anymore."

"No one gets it. No one's there for me." I place my head in my hands.

"Has Dad been there for me, Jennifer? No. He's been off chasing girls since I can remember and you were never far behind," she says.

"Yeah, and look where it's gotten me." I feel vacant, like my insides have been scooped out and all that is left is an empty hole.

"So, what are you gonna do, blame your whole life on them?"

"Whose side are you on?"

"I'm your sister. I'm not on anyone's side. I just don't think it's healthy for you to be so bitter."

"All of a sudden I'm the fucked-up one?"

"Maybe you should try rehab."

"Now you want to lock me up? Just leave me alone!" I cry and bail out of there, hopping into the light blue Cadillac convertible I borrowed from Dad. I fire up a Marlboro Light, crank up Run-D.M.C., and speed down Moreno Drive, running the stop sign in front of the high school. A horn blares at me.

"Fuck you!" I yell. "Fuck everybody!"

My drama rush is fading fast, so I pull out an emergency Vicodin, call Austin, and we decide to go dancing. That night, we walk along Santa Monica Boulevard in West Hollywood.

"Everyone's blowing me off in the worst way," I say.

"I know what you mean."

"You won't believe the shit I've seen over the past few months," I tell her.

"Like what?"

"First, I meet these transient models who live at Don Michaels' house, and then I find out the girls have to fuck him in order to stay there."

"I stayed at a house like that once when I first moved here," Austin says casually. "The guys would wine and dine us, take us to clubs, get us super fucked-up, and introduce us to rich old men, who would pay them off. We were being prostituted and we didn't even know it!" she explains.

"Really?"

"Swear. My agent in Canada set it up for me to stay with a guy who had a house in the Hills. When I first got there, I thought he was just a rich man who liked to have pretty girls around. But then one night I overheard him talking to this other model that had been around for years. She was a little bit older. They were saying how they both wanted to fuck this new eighteen-year-old who wanted to get into porn. They kept saying how much they loved the power of taking an innocent girl and corrupting her. It turned them on. 'Let's get her drunk and fuck the shit out of her,' they kept saying. I think they slipped something into her drink because the next morning the young girl came into my room in tears because she had slept with them. She says they got her really drunk, video-taped her, and took pictures. It was horrible. I felt so bad."

"How did you get out?"

"They tossed me. I refused to sleep with the old fuck so he kicked me out. Guys like him are everywhere in this town—lifelong losers who buy self-esteem by fucking young girls they could never get when they were younger. The trick is learning how to get ahead without having to fuck them," Austin says.

Neon lights flash as Rage, a predominantly gay male nightclub, comes into view. Attention whores pose outside wearing tight Levi's or Calvin Klein jeans, their Moschino shirts either unbuttoned or completely missing. We pay a few bucks and enter the sea of sexy men. Janet Jackson's pumping, the energy is bouncing, and soon Austin drools after a muscular boy-toy at the bar.

Meanwhile, a girl in a miniskirt, white tank top, spiked heels, and blond bobbed wig smiles at me from the dance floor. Our eyes discuss whether or not we're really flirting as she slowly makes her way over to me, introducing herself as Skyler. We dance for hours, and I can't help but notice how Skyler keeps putting her hands around my waist as she grinds behind me. But I don't mind. I like the attention. She asks me where I live and I tell her with my father in Beverly Hills, but I try to stay away from details.

After a while, Austin tugs at my arm, ready to go home. Skyler and I exchange phone numbers, mention hooking up for after-hours, but we both end up flaking.

The next day, my father is in the middle of telling me about a chick he's going on a date with when the phone rings. He talks for a minute, smiles, and hands me the cordless phone.

The voice on the other end says, "Does your father know you dance at gay bars with girls in blond bobbed wigs?"

I stare blankly at my father.

"Who is this?" I respond aloofly.

"This is Skyler from last night."

I lose my ability to breathe.

"Remember me? I finally put it together when your father kept talking about his daughter Jennifer, who lives with him," she says in a soft tone of voice.

"Small world," I barely get out, turning bright red.

"I have a date with your father tonight. You should come and say hi," she giggles. I half smile as I hand the phone back to my father.

"I'll be there with bells on," Dad says into the receiver.

I shake my head as he hangs up.

"How do you know her?" Dad asks, smiling.

"I met her through a friend of a friend," I say, diverting my eyes away from him.

"That's unbelievable. She's really incredible. I mean she's nuts, but she's great. You should join us for dinner," he offers, generously.

"I don't know . . ."

"Come by. What else are you doing?"

Hours later, I'm sitting across the table from my father and Skyler at Trader Vic's, an upscale Polynesian restaurant in Beverly Hills. Tonight, Skyler has long brown hair and wears a conservative Donna Karan skirt suit and a white silk blouse. After a few Scorpion bowls, Skyler and I retreat into the bathroom to touch up our makeup. We crack up laughing. Though it is an unspoken connection, it is clear we like each other.

I apply more powder. "How bizarre is this?"

Skyler coats her lips with liner. "Your father wants me to go with him to Hef 's New Year's party."

"Shine that, come to the Arena—it's an awesome nightclub. You'll love it," I tell her.

"Your father will kill me. By the way, what's with the Uzi in the backseat of his car?"

"He's a little paranoid. Besides, everyone in L.A. has a gun; my dad just keeps his close," I say indifferently.

We return to the table to find my father outraged. He taps his watch repeatedly. Who knew twenty minutes had passed? He waits until we sit down to command our full attention. Then he points his finger at Skyler.

"I'm only going to ask you this once, lady. Do you want me or my daughter?" Dad questions.

My stomach drops. Skyler is speechless. I immediately excuse myself from the table, not wanting to deal with my father's temper. Fear and anxiety take over, fueling me to my feet. I ignore my "ew" feelings as I make a mad exit through the restaurant.

On my way out, I bump into a guy at the bar.

"Excuse me," I say and regain my balance.

I see the familiar image of a sexy smile out of the corner of my eye. It's Hayden.

"Hey, hon," he says sweetly.

"Hayden?" I manage to get out of my mouth, still flabbergasted that I'm looking at my "boyfriend" who hasn't called to tell me he's finished his movie and is back in town after four months of silence.

"You look good, honey," he says, knowing he looks radiant in his Italian suit and European tan.

"So do you," I hear myself say. "I guess the movie's finished."

"Yeah, actually, we wrapped ahead of schedule so I came back to town hoping to see you," he says smoothly, sliding his arm around my waist. "It's a real shame you didn't come to visit me on location. You would've loved it."

"How the fuck do I visit someone in a foreign country who doesn't call to tell me where he is?"

"I guess I was kind of mad at you," Hayden confesses, breaking out that trademark smile. "The bottom line is we're together now. Let's just move on from here. I've missed you," he says and my negative thoughts subside.

His arm slips into the small of my back as he pulls me close.

Then I remember my father and Skyler at a booth a few feet away.

"Let's get out of here," I whisper to Hayden.

"Sure." He grabs my arm and it's as if no time has passed.

He walks me around to the passenger side of his turbo Porsche, opens the car door, and makes sure I'm comfortable before he shuts it. We speed down Wilshire Boulevard and cut up to Sunset Plaza, straight to Hayden's condo.

Come New Year's Eve, I'm at the Arena nightclub, and Hayden and I are in the middle of the dance floor. Mirrored balls hang from the ceiling. White confetti and balloons with glow sticks litter the floor. Banners scream WELCOME TO 1986!

Girls dance suggestively in silver heels and twirl around in short Vivienne Westwood skirts. Baby-pink and silver sequins flood the Arena. The men lurk around the room in Ralph Lauren slacks and tight black T-shirts under Lagerfeld blazers.

I spot Skyler on the other side of the room wearing a miniskirt, white tank top, heels, and the blond bobbed wig. I laugh, but she reminds me of Kendall—I wonder what she's doing tonight. I think about Kendall all the time. She haunts me.

The following week, Dad and "his girls" fly off to Hawaii so he can judge the Hawaiian Tropics Beauty Contest. Alone in the house, I call Kendall, whom I haven't spoken to for a few months.

"Playboy Mansion."

"Is Kendall there?" I ask.

"Who's calling?" the butler says.

"Jennifer Saginor."

"Hey, Jennifer, just a minute, please."

I fidget nervously with the buttons on my brown cable box.

I assume she'll avoid my calls but am pleasantly surprised when they put my call through.

Kendall answers in a sexy voice, "Hello."

"Hey, what's up," I say nonchalantly, trying to hide my burning desire to be with her, to have her hold me. She sounds so distant and the distance cuts into me as I seek but find no connection. I yearn for closeness.

"Nothing much, kiddo. What are you up to?"

I want to tell her how much I've missed her. I want to ask if she's missed me too.

"My father and his entourage left for Hawaii. I'm in this big house all alone."

"Is he still hanging with all those bimbos?" she asks.

"I can't tell you how thrilling it is to wake up to a different hooker every morning."

My call waiting beeps and I click over. It's Hayden.

"Hey, sweet cakes, what's shaking tonight?"

"Hi, honey. Um, actually, I'm on the other line. Let me call you right back."

"When am I going to see you?" Hayden asks, sort of annoyed, as if he can walk back into my life and do whatever he wants. I click back over to Kendall.

"So, I thought maybe we could hang out sometime," I say to Kendall impulsively.

"Oh, Jennifer, do you really know what you want or do you just think you know?"

"I know," I answer.

"You sound so young," Kendall whines.

"So do you."

Part of her knows better than to continue this affair while another part of her can't resist. There's silence as she thinks.

"Well, I would come over, but I don't want to take the limo," she says after a while, as if a ride has anything to do with why she hasn't called in months.

"Everyone is going to Helena's tonight but I don't want to go with a little girl who may flake on me," Kendall says.

"Flake? Since when have I ever flaked on you?" I ask.

"All right, fine, but don't come here. Pick me up outside of Nicki Blair's in forty-five minutes" she says.

"Okay, you better be there" I tell her.

"Okay, child. 'Bye," Kendall laughs.

" 'Bye."

I toss down the phone and want to scream because I'm so excited to see her.

An hour later, Kendall and I strut into Helena's wearing sequined halters, colored Day-Glo miniskirts, and black fishnets. "Jam on It" by Newcleus blares through the joint as we walk around, drunk and uninhibited. We touch each other innocently, our hands finding reconnection. Our longing, our need for attention, so apparent. We lean against a flourescent light.

"I've missed you," I tell her, searching deeply into her eyes for something, though I'm not quite sure what.

"I've missed you too." She clasps her hand tightly around mine until I pull away suddenly because I am standing directly in front of my friends from Beverly High.

"Hey, guys. What's up?" I ask, hoping they didn't see us all over each other.

"Whatever, dyke," Sonya says, flipping her hair as she walks away.

Michelle won't even make eye contact as she mutters "disgusting" under her breath. I try to reach for Hunter's hand but she pulls away repulsed. The others trail behind laughing, pointing, and looking us up and down as my eyes fill with tears. How quickly my It girl status and popularity has plunged to my being a total freak show and outcast.

Kendall grabs my hand.

"Fuck them. Let's go do a bump," she says, and as we head toward the bathroom we run into my sister with the club bouncer, who's twice her age. I'm taken aback by how stylish Savannah looks. She's wearing a tight white minidress, Chanel heels, and tons of makeup. A Nolan Miller Roman coin pendant hangs around her neck.

"What are you doing here?" I ask, my eyes glaring up at the muscular bouncer towering over her.

"Same thing you are," Savannah answers.

"Does Mom know you're out this late?"

"Does Dad?"

"You're fourteen!"

I shoot poisonous glares at the tough-guy bouncer, who continues chomping on his bubble gum.

I pull Savannah to the side.

"This is insane! He's twice your age! What are you doing?"

"What are you doing with that lezzy Kendall?"

"She is not a lez!" I declare with conviction.

"Whatever," she rolls her eyes, totally grossed out. "Everyone knows you're having an affair with her," she informs me.

"Not even! Why would you say that?" I gasp as if the thought horrifies me.

"Probably because you spend so much time with her and everyone knows she's into girls, duh."

"You're starting to sound like Mom."

"You're starting to act like Dad."

We search each other's eyes for a few seconds. We used to be so close. I miss who we once were. I want to say something but don't know how and instead blink the tears out of my eyes.

The bouncer pulls her away.

She is gone. My heart aches as I watch my sister blend into the crowd.

On our way home, Kendall talks to me but I don't hear her; my mind is racing.

It's clear to me now that my sister is searching for a father in her choice of older men while I am searching for a mother in my relationship with Kendall.

They say our lives are shaped not by those who love us but by those who refuse to love us.

Perhaps it is true that we find our parents in other people, re-creating the same dysfunctional family we are used to.

Sixteen

I wake up to someone knocking incessantly on the front door downstairs. I lie in bed pretending that no one is home. A faint voice begs, "Please, is anyone there? I'm looking for my daughter." I tiptoe downstairs, place my eye into the peephole, and see a tan European man in his fifties.

"Hello?" he repeats.

"Can I help you?" I finally ask through the door.

I've never seen him before.

"Is your father here?" he asks.

"No, he's not."

"I understand he has a daughter named Jennifer. Would that be you?"

"Can I ask what you want?"

"I'm very sorry to trouble you, but I'm trying to locate my daughter," he explains, still speaking through the door.

"I'm the only one home right now, so I can tell you that she's not here."

The man shifts his weight. He looks very tired and weak and truly seems harmless.

"My daughter's name is Paulina Svenson. Do you by chance know her?" he asks, pulling out a small photograph of his daughter.

I can't take my eyes off the peephole. This kind-looking man is the father of the girl who overdosed at that party.

"She is a model from Sweden. She was visiting the States and I was told she knew your father. I have been to a Mr. Don Michaels' estate."

"I knew a Paulina once, but I think she was from Connecticut," I answer almost too quickly, afraid he may see right through me. The father leans in closer to the door.

"Are you sure you never met my daughter Paulina from Sweden?" he asks in a really nice voice. My palms are sweaty. I try to stop my hands from shaking as I recall the image of Paulina's lifeless body on the bathroom floor.

"No, really, I'm sorry. I don't know your daughter. Wish I could help."

The words are pressed against the tip of my lips and so much of me wants to say something, but the fear of someone finding out I've exposed them keeps me silent. The man lowers his head, thanks me, and walks back over to the blue Dodge rental car parked along the side of the house.

Paulina's path, one that once seemed so foreign, seems more real to me than ever. I can't help but wonder if I am a few days, a few months, a few introductions away from becoming her: a lost young girl searching for escape in a world of scavengers. The way she was so ruthlessly disposed of will remain with me forever.

Through the window, I watch Paulina's father get into his car and drive slowly down the street.

Dad returns home from Hawaii and everything starts to change. The summer ends. Everyone has disappointed me. There are not enough pills to medicate me anymore. The skinny models are thrown out and Vicki, a nineteen-year-old coke fiend, moves in. Vicki walks around with a huge attitude, bragging about her ex-boyfriend, Marco Santiago, an infamous Colombian drug lord, an invisible Godfather who watches over her.

She left home as a teenager and has been running ever since. Vicki is a natural brunette with dyed blond hair, bony, shaking limbs, and a sunken face with a perfect complexion.

She makes my skin crawl. I don't know what Dad sees in her. They are suddenly sleeping at the house every night and I never see him at the Mansion anymore.

On one occasion, not long after Vicki moved in, I go into Dad's bathroom to restock my pill supply. In the back drawer, I come across a vial of coke. I pull it out and stare at it until Carmela sneaks up on me and yanks it out of my hand.

"Jennifer!" she screeches. "Give me that!"

We each fight for the vial in a tug-of-war.

"What are you doing?"

"This is your father's!" she hollers in her high-pitched accent.

"So, why are you taking it?" I yell back, grabbing it.

"Your father says he doesn't want anything moved from here!"

Carmela grabs the vial forcefully from my hand and I fall backward. My arms flail wildly, accidentally knocking a towel holder that pops open. An enormous pound-size Baggie filled with white powder falls to the floor from a secret compartment in the wall. Carmela and I stare at each other utterly stunned.

"What the hell? What is going on?" I ask.

"I know nothing. Your father no tell me nothing! I just work here! He says no touch, I no touch. He tell me no look, I no look," she chants like a crazy person.

"You no look! You no look!" I too now chant, sounding equally insane.

Carmela's facial muscles are twitching. Our eyes meet and uncontrollable smiles creep over our faces. Next thing you know, we're rolling around on the floor laughing hysterically. My stomach muscles ache. We regain our breath and agree not to tell anyone about the bag.

That night, I lie in bed awake. Things have turned so shady around here. Three Xanaxes later, I hear voices coming from downstairs. There's a lot of commotion and people are walking in and out. Things seem to be more hectic than usual. I recognize Eric Jacobs' and Don Michaels' voices, and a few others as well. The clock reads 3:45 A.M. as I pop a Halcyon, pull my pillow over my head, and try to fall asleep. After what seems like hours of tossing and turning, I hear loud noises coming from my father's bedroom. Lots of furniture is moved around. Banging and screaming echoes down the hallway. Then all is silent. I lie in bed frozen, like a scared little girl.

I've learned not to knock on Dad's bedroom door until at least two or three in the afternoon. Up all night, in bed all day, Dad and Vicki don't eat and barely leave his room. I've stopped asking why he's never at work anymore.

One night his door is slightly ajar, so I burst in to load up on more Xanax but stop because the shades are drawn and I realize they are home. Everything is dark and there's the grotesque odor of syringes dripping with heroin residue. There are two figures passed out on Dad's king-size bed. I try to back up quietly, but they sit up, groggy, eyes completely bloodshot.

"Sorry," I stutter, unsure of what I see.

"It's okay," Dad says, scratching his head, and I immediately forget why I came in. Dad gets out of bed and slips on his underwear. I turn my head, trying not to look at his penis.

"I need to give her another shot," he utters in a muffled tone, walking to his dresser.

Vicki is clearly drugged up on something and I can't imagine what else she needs. He rummages through his drawers as Vicki props her head up, reaching for a compact mirror and vial on the dresser. Her hair is messy and she has black circles underneath her heavy eyes.

Dad unwraps a needle in a plastic package and grabs a small bottle out of the refrigerator in his bathroom as Vicki snorts a quick line of coke off her compact. I doubt she sees me. Dad opens the bottle and inserts the needle and the syringe slowly fills with liquid. I want to somehow disappear, slide underneath the crack of the door, but fear keeps me still. There is something sinister and corrupt about watching him prepare her injection.

"She's been like this all day. It's some kind of bad flu," he insists, heading back over to the bed. I can tell he is lying to me.

I freak out because I've never seen needles around the house.

His shadow towers over her. Vicki makes groggy noises as he flips her over with one swoop and pumps the needle into her ass. Within seconds, Vicki is more looped than ever. She gazes over in my direction, mumbles something, and lays her head back down. My father laughs, a weakening sound that penetrates my bones.

His eyes, which were once warm and friendly, now emit a look of distrust. He is haggard and withdrawn. I barely recognize him.

It's around ten on a school night as Grampy and I sit at his dining room table working on my term paper. My eyelids are heavy from lack of sleep.

Though I am not interested in school, classes, or homework, I gravitate toward my grandfather more these days because I love him and he is the closest thing I have to a parent. He reminds me that I am only a teenager by frequently asking questions about schoolwork and my friends. I can tell he is concerned about my state of high anxiety, but his deep devotion to his son keeps him silent. Instead, he tells me to focus on reality and my future. He forces me to use my mind. Though I may not be ready to hear him or change, I know he is the only person who can lead me in the right direction.

I never want to disappoint him and therefore never admit to not attending classes. I turn my ear the other way when he talks about how to make a living or survive on my own because my father always tells me that I will never have to worry about money or anything as long as he is in my life. Therefore, I couldn't give two shits about my studies, college, or anything outside of my own secluded world.

"I don't understand why we need to know about all these World Wars," I complain while flipping through my American history book.

"If we don't learn from our past, ignorance repeats itself in the future," he informs me.

"Is that why people get so out of control? They don't resolve problems from their past and their past shapes their future?" I ask.

"It is how we interpret experiences from the past that tells us how to act in the future," he explains.

"Maybe we're all just running from times we don't want to remember?"

"Yes, but make no mistake. The past is the past. You are responsible for today," he clarifies, lowering his glasses so I can see his eyes.

At home, my father's house has turned ugly. I never know when I'll find my father and Vicki passed out on his bed. His mind is filled with scrambled, irrational thoughts, leaving him overly suspicious of everyone.

"They're after me, but I can outsmart them!" Dad repeats wildly over the next few months.

His paranoia scares me. He and Vicki become more out of control and I become more perplexed and terrified. I detach from my sister and everyone else who is close to me. I isolate more at school as things at home become strange and unpredictable. Things are unraveling.

It's late in the evening when I open my bedroom door and quietly peer down the hallway to see if anyone is coming. I approach the staircase and head downstairs to the kitchen. I open the refrigerator door, pull out a wine cooler, and jump, startled to find my father standing behind me in his underwear clutching an Uzi. I have developed such a high tolerance for his inappropriate behavior that I actually stand there and don't even think twice about it.

"What are you doing?" I ask, opening the wine cooler.

"Get down!" he screams, pointing the gun out the window.

I duck, losing my breath as anxiety takes hold. I hide underneath the counter as he aims the Uzi toward the backyard.

"Games!" he screams out loud as beads of sweat form on his forehead. "I'll give them games!"

"Who?" I ask, trembling.

"The men out there."

"What men?"

"The men who are after me!" Dad screams, lost in his delusions.

He must be mixing. Life has become one big emergency as I stand witness to my father's paranoid hallucinations.

"Follow me! Stay low!" he orders.

We walk low to the ground as I follow him past the window above the kitchen counter. I am scared to death.

"Who's after you?" I ask again.

"The Mafia!"

"Why would the . . ."

"Shush! The house is bugged!"

His stare alone is an implied threat, an inner hardness that didn't used to be there.

"What do they want?" I say, shaking.

"I'm a doctor. What do you think they want? Drugs!"

I find myself on my knees following my father in utter dismay. I wonder whether or not there really are men with guns outside.

Dad checks out the back door and slowly opens it, instructing me to follow him along the side of the house.

"Stay low and behind me!" he commands, whispering as we walk with arched backs down a side pathway through the backyard. "People think they're smarter than me, but they're not! They say one thing, but I like to figure out what they really mean. I am one step ahead of them! People always want something from you. You can't trust anyone!" Dad instructs.

He thinks he's teaching me invaluable lessons on how to survive in the world, but what he's really doing is scaring the shit out of me. Fear pulses through my veins as this unsettling experience numbs my entire body. Life with him is becoming a constant merry-go-round of fear and terror—he's a far cry from the fun-loving Hollywood scenester I used to know.

Later, we end up in Dad's bedroom, where I watch him sort through various types of guns, petrified as he hands me a loaded revolver and shows me how to use it.

"Keep this by your bed at all times," he urges. "It's for your own protection."

I nod before walking slowly down the hallway to my room.

I close my bedroom door and head straight into my bathroom, popping numerous Xanax and Halcyon pills to relax. I pull a large bong from underneath a cabinet, fill it with pot, and open the window. When I'm done, I cautiously reenter my bedroom, taking one step at a time, concerned he may come in. I place the gun carefully underneath my bed, near the headboard. My entire body and fingers tremble uncontrollably.

I see shadows beneath my bedroom door. My eyes zoom up

close to the door, where no lock exists. Inexplicable, terrifying images of someone bursting through my bedroom door to kill me
race through my head. The house used to be so quiet and now
every noise makes me jump. My bedtime tremors for unpredictable behavior make the nights nearly impossible to sleep.

Living my father's suspicious and distrustful delusions will
haunt me forever. The paranoia will creep up on me when I least
expect it.

Nothing will remove the voices from my head. The slightest
turn of events can turn a peaceful afternoon into a thundercloud
of anger and confusion as the entire world crumbles to despair.

There are no answers. There are no solutions. By this time, I
have learned to run and hide, to isolate, to numb myself, and lash
out at those who get in the way.

Anything to avoid feeling my feelings.

Seventeen

On my way to school one day, not long after the night when Dad gave me the revolver, I close the front door to Dad's house when across the street, I notice three suspicious, shady-looking men smoking cigarettes against a shiny four-door Mercedes with dark tinted windows. The men don't look American; in fact, I'm not sure what they are, but they have dark complexions with mustaches and appear to be looking around every few seconds as if they are waiting for someone. I attempt to brush it off like it's no big deal and tell myself I'm being paranoid. I am not ready to deal with everything that is happening, because I don't know what is happening. All I know is that my father continues to reinforce that I not mention any of this absurdity to anyone.

At seventeen, I am sworn to secrecy and told to keep a gun by my side at all times.

The freedom package has officially crumbled.

For Dad's fiftieth birthday, Eric Jacobs throws him a birthday dinner at his exquisite estate in Beverly Hills. It's the kind of home you see in magazines: lavish furniture, gallery-style paintings, impeccable decor that seems so perfectly placed. There are hundreds of sexy young models running around in silky dresses.

"Where's Pops?" Eric hugs me hello.

"Late as usual."

"He can't be on time even to his own birthday," Eric chuckles.

"What do you think of your father's new girl?" he asks sincerely.

"I'd rather not say," I smirk and he laughs.

"Listen, kid, if you ever need anyone to talk to, you come see me, okay?" Eric offers in a creepy tone; I can tell he's the type to take advantage.

There's commotion by the front door as Dad and Vicki arrive. They're perspiring, rushed, and scattered as guests dash over to greet them. I venture around the house, making my way into the living room before everyone is seated. The place settings are exquisite with extravagant floral arrangements and a bottle of Dom in the center of each round table. Name cards are perfectly displayed, though my father's seat has no name tag. Instead, an oversize plastic hypodermic needle is set in front of his place setting. My eyes rush up close to the needle. I stare at it for a while, unable to move. I don't know why I am so surprised to see it out in the open.

I thought it was a family secret, the dirty kind people don't talk about in public or even to those closest to them.

If others knew what evil lurked behind our doors, how come no one did anything to help?

Dad comes up from behind me, draping his arms around my shoulders.

"Need a tranquilizer?" Dad jokes. I jump, noticing glossy sweat running across his face.

He picks up the large plastic needle and begins poking everyone near him in the ass.

"Come here, little one; Dr. Feel Good has a little something for you!" he teases a friend's wife, who shrieks and runs away.

Everyone laughs as Dad chases her for a moment and then stops to catch his breath. I suppose in a world of partiers, a plastic needle as your name tag is commonplace, even funny. But somehow I am far from laughing. Eric wraps his arm around Dad's shoulder.

"We knew it was your birthday and we know you don't sleep with hookers, but we ran into a couple old friends who wanted to come say hello. You might recognize them." Eric coughs to himself as four skinny girls with size-D silicone boobs step forward.

"Oh my God," Dad chuckles cheerfully.

"Doc, I haven't seen you in so long!" One of the girls plants a big kiss on him as Vicki enters coked out of her mind.

"What are you doing? You're cheating on me! I knew it! You motherfucker!"

Vicki picks up a china plate, throws it at the skinny girl, and runs after her. A catfight ensues. Vicki throws a punch at the hooker but misses, hitting Dad in the eye. He flinches and reacts by throwing an arm in the air and accidentally knocks Vicki in the nose. Blood pours out. The girls stop fighting. Someone grabs a napkin and hands it to Vicki. She pinches her nose with it, but the bleeding is so intense that the napkin is quickly drenched. Another girl brings her a towel.

"Don't worry, honey, you needed your nose reset anyway," Dad assures her and the guys laugh, a deafening tone that resonates through the room.

My mind wanders, preoccupied with thoughts of Kendall, my mother, safety. I need an escape. A phone will work. The den has a warm feel to it with mahogany wood and lots of reds, greens, and browns. Books line the shelves. I pick up the receiver on the desk and dial while staring out at the spectacular landscape hoping Kendall answers.

"Hello?" Kendall says softly. My body heat rises.

"Hey."

"Hey . . ." She lingers and I can feel my stomach turn, craving her affection more than ever. The urge to see her day or night regardless of the consequences beats inside to such an extreme that I would risk anything to be with her, to hold her in my arms. My desire for her has turned into something much deeper, much more uncivilized.

"I miss you. I need to see you." My heart pounds, wishing she could reach through the phone and comfort me.

"I can't," she whispers.

"Why?"

"Oh, Jennifer, what am I going to do with you?"

"Anything you want," I try to flirt, but it comes out sounding more like a plea for help.

"I'll figure something out, okay?" she says quietly.

"When?"

"Soon," she assures me. "I gotta go." She hangs up.

The phone goes dead.

I rejoin the party, where a group of coke whores are playing Twister.

Blood drips from their noses onto the mat.

The scene is horrifying. My tolerance for this deranged behavior has peaked. I leave abruptly and drive to the Mansion, searching for some kind of normalcy. Thank God Tobey is there. We end up ordering milk shakes and watching reruns of Dallas in one of the upstairs bedrooms. My entire childhood was a perfect cliché. Tobey falls asleep and I stare out the window lost in the hours that go by.

Eighteen

*M*ost days after school Kendall and I meet at the park across from the Beverly Hills Hotel. Our passion is rekindled whenever we haven't seen each other for a while. Usually we meet at the last minute. We are in the bathroom kissing, hungry to be touched. Our desire for each other is so intense it startles us both. The feelings I have for Kendall are different from anything I've ever felt before. There is no reasonable explanation; it is simply a connection we both seem incapable of stopping.

We lean against the wall, our bodies pressed close as she plays with my hair softly and then pulls on it harder. I sigh, wanting her to hurt me. She moves her hand slowly in between my legs, making me beg for more. Once I'm aroused and totally helpless in her arms, she smiles alluringly, knowing she has me. When we are done, we separate. Kendall slips into the limo while I cross the street and walk two blocks to my father's house on the corner.

At home, I look in my desk drawer for my journals and notice that they are missing. I bump into Vicki, who looks thin and haggard, which makes her appear twice her age. Our relationship has turned openly hostile. She wipes blood from her nose as her nosebleeds are common these days. She avoids eye contact.

"Are you okay?" I ask, feeling momentarily sorry for her.

"Mind your own business. I'm warning you, stay out of my shit," she threatens with gangster attitude.

"What shit would that be, Vicki?" My voice overflows with sarcasm.

I move in closer as she uses her sleeve to put pressure on her nose, and we both pretend there's not blood oozing out of her nostrils. "You took my journals, didn't you?"

"Listen, you little punk. You shouldn't talk to me like that. I'm watching you and if you're not nice to me, I can put you and your father in serious danger."

Her words are meant to be threatening, but she looks so pitiful that I try hard not to laugh. Vicki moves in close and points her bloody finger in my face.

"I can have you and your father killed—do you hear me?"

My stomach tightens, all urge for laughter is gone as adrenaline rushes inside me like a volcano ready to explode. Rage rips through my skin and starts to pulsate. However, I stand there in silence because a part of me knows that she is linked to the Mob and really could have us killed.

I leave abruptly and drive around aimlessly until I find myself parked in front of Hayden's condo. I rush in without warning and find him alone, doing blow on his living room table. He barely looks up when I enter.

"Hayden?"

"Yeah?" he answers, distracted, inhaling.

"I need to talk to you."

"Oh, now you want to talk to me?" He finishes an enormous line, stands, and pulls up his Levi's, showing off his tan muscular stomach and white Calvin Klein boxers.

"I'm sorry, but a lot of shit has been going on at my father's house since he met Vicki. Her ex-boyfriend is a huge Colombian drug lord, and Carmela and I found kilos of coke in his bathroom, and Dad's walking around the house with an Uzi."

"Sounds like a bad TV movie."

"Minus the commercials."

"What else have you not kept me in the loop about?" he asks, a look of distrust emanates and I become immediately fearful that he knows about my affair with Kendall.

"Well, since we're being honest, a relationship has sort of developed."

"What, are you seeing another guy?"

"No . . ."

"Then what?"

"Kendall," I say blankly.

"Kendall? What are you a fucking lesbo now?"

Clearly, it wasn't the reaction I was expecting.

"Let me get this right—you can fuck whomever but I'm expected to stay monogamous?" I retaliate.

"I was trying to reach you for weeks!" he screams.

"Next time try picking up a phone, it might work better!" I shout.

"Get the fuck out of my house! By the way, since we're being honest, I've been fucking Austin," Hayden yells, his eyes full of hate as he grabs my arm and shoves me out the door. He slams it inches from my face and I twitch as though I've been slapped. Tears slide down my face and there is nothing I can do to stop them.

The house is a disaster area by the time I get home. Phones have been taken apart and opened. Men are installing surveillance

cameras and from the windows in the living room you can see police cars driving by. Dad passes right by me with a bodyguard trailing behind.

"What are you doing?" I ask.

"This is my new bodyguard," he says, introducing me to a man
in a suit.

"We are checking the house for bugs. I think the phones are
tapped."

"Why?" I ask, staring at the various workmen.

"I'm being watched," Dad insists.

"By who?"

I have a sudden sick feeling in my stomach.

"We're not sure. That's why I'm upgrading our security system.
It's for our protection." Dad and the bodyguard wave something
that resembles a metal detector along the walls.

"Is that why there are people trying to break in late at night?"

Neither one of them answers me. There seems to be a lot Dad isn't
telling me these days. They continue checking corners of each room.

"How was your day?" Dad asks in the midst of chaos.

"Terrible. Hayden's an asshole. I hate him." I wipe my sore, red
eyes. Dad strokes the back of my head affectionately.

"Did he hit you? If he did, he made a big mistake," Dad intones,
truly concerned.

"No, but he's completely irrational. He threatened me and
threw me out."

"I'm sorry you're upset. I promise you, honey, I will take care of
him later," Dad says as he rubs my back, peering into a mysterious
hole in the wall.

"No. It's fine. I can deal with Hayden on my own," I tell him,
hoping he heard me.

Filled with despair, I walk upstairs and close my bedroom
door. I don't know whether to laugh or cry. I no longer have any
secrets, privacy, or personal space. I pick up the phone and call
Kendall at the Mansion.

"Is Kendall there, please? It's Jennifer Saginor."

A few seconds later Kendall picks up.

"Hello?" her voice is soft and sexy.

"Hey" is all I can get out.

"Hey, kiddo. What's wrong?"

Tears form in my eyes. "Things are so fucked up around here," I cry.

"Are you okay?"

"No."

"What happened? Wait, I hear Hef, I gotta go," she whispers, cutting me off midsentence as the phone goes dead.

I then decide to drive over to my mother's house. I'm in a hysterical frenzy, cigarettes falling between my fingers.

She answers the door and doesn't seem overly thrilled to see me. My defenses immediately go up out of habit. I find myself standing in the doorway wishing she would embrace me in her arms and never let go in order to shield me from a man and the demons that follow him. At this point, I'd rather live in a Dumpster than have to bear another sleepless night in his house. I want so much to move back in with Mom so I can hide, but I'm afraid she isn't strong enough to tackle him. And when Dad does find us, he will hurt us. My grandfather's alliances are with my father.

I have nowhere to turn.

"I need to talk to you," I plead. She lets me in and we move into the living room and take seats across from each other. There's a glass table between us.

"I need to get out of there," I tell her.

"Why do you say that?" my mother asks.

"Because Dad and Vicki are partying and fighting, and all this weird shit is going on," I say.

"Partying meaning drugs?" she asks blankly as we are speaking a foreign language.

"Of course drugs!" I scream, pissed off that she's so naive. I'm still in shock over the past twenty-four hours and furious at my mother for not being able to read my mind and comfort me. Sadness fills me up because I know she is not tough enough to fight this battle. I want to cry with the intention of self-pity, yet the longer I cry it turns to anger and then vengeance. It is clear her animosity toward my father has now been transferred to me. I begin to teach myself to define what I really feel toward my mother—an uncontrollable anger over her letting me go.

"Like what?" she asks, in a level voice, still unable to comprehend the severity of it all. She peers at me skeptically like she doesn't believe me, which really annoys me. She seems to have total disregard for my feelings or what I am going through.

"All this stuff is happening and I can't tell anyone, and I want to leave but I can't because he'll never let me go," I say, sounding just as paranoid as my father. I shiver. My legs are light and I can't move my toes. I begin to have that nervous feeling again, the butterflies in my stomach. I'm in danger. My days are numbered, but where will I go? Who can I turn to?

"Do you think I can move back home?" I ask, even though the thought of defying my father terrifies me to death. I think of how fun-loving he used to be and now I'm never quite sure what state of mind he'll be in, or who I am when I'm alone in his house, or how I'd be if I left him.

"Your father has legal custody of you and did a damn good job of making a mockery of this family. If you want to move back in, then you'll have to get his permission. He is too stubborn and I'm tired of fighting," she states matter-of-factly.

"He's not going to let me move out." My hands tremble. She rearranges her plastic expression of vague concern into one of smugness. She looks at me as if I am now a stranger, but maybe I always was and never knew it.

"I guess you should've thought of that before you decided to move in with him," she says, clear and in control, like a good psychologist. Her eyes are hollow; I do not see myself in them.

It's as if I'm not really her daughter after all.

My eyes lock on to hers and I can almost see hers fill with bitterness and resentment. It's not always the person who harms you that you're angry at, but the person who let it happen.

"I can't believe I tried to talk to you," I say, feeling the blackness of betrayal swirl around me. I walk out, convinced I am the daughter she hopes will disappear.

Years later, she decides to hear that my cry for help was real.

My father's house has become a war zone. Things have gone from bad to worse.

Vicki and Dad stay up late screaming, knocking and banging. Dad stalks around his room enraged. My insomnia is no longer from anxiety or depression: it is because I am too petrified to shut my eyes. Each night I think of ways to avoid sleeping. I am petrified someone will come in and do something. What, I'm not sure, but just seeing Dad and Vicki both on drugs, their unpredictable behavior and words, is enough to terrorize me into hysterics.

I peek through my bedroom door, which is slightly ajar. Dad is dragging Vicki on her knees, while she's clinging on to him, as he storms down the hallway with hypodermic needles protruding from the pockets of his open terry-cloth robe. The expression on her face is childlike, and so vulnerable, that for a second I actually feel sorry for her.

She glances up at him with a look of pain. He dismisses her with complete disdain as she begs him to stop. Her pleading makes it worse. His voice never registers any emotion; it is harsh and contemptuous. He grabs her hard, wrestles her shoulders to the ground, and turns her over. She is completely helpless, trapped beneath him, unable to move. When Dad sees me standing in the doorway, he winks while dragging Vicki across the carpet. It's as if he is giving me lessons on how to treat dumb whores.

Dad was always on the verge of splitting up or getting back together with some young girl, especially Vicki. They each looked different, but in the end, the story was always the same. According to him, they all had "agendas" and "serious psychological problems." They played mind games. His thrill in life was finding out information people didn't want him to know. I was always amazed at the effect he had on these women. He convinced them that they deserved to be treated like shit.

He never got close to anyone—except me of course.

"I respect *you*, that's all that matters," he would say.

Sometimes he'd throw Vicki's clothes off the balcony and kick her out of the house, making her stumble around outside naked, begging to be let back in. His dead eyes would come alive for an instant.

They were the eyes of a man without a conscience.

On a few different occasions, I hear the sound of people in the backyard. I move to the bathroom, where I turn off the lights and look out. I'm petrified because I'm home alone and there are moving shadows underneath the lights on the tennis court. I run back into my room, grab the gun, and hide underneath the bed. The phone rings. I reach for the spiral cord and pull, yanking it off the nightstand.

"Hello," I answer in a whisper, worried it's someone from outside.

"Hey, it's Hunter. We need to talk."

"I can't. The Mafia's after me," I whisper before hanging up.

My hands tremble as I grip my gun, ready to shoot anyone who enters through my bedroom door.

The next morning, I'm still half asleep with my gun in hand.

I lift my head, hitting it on the box spring. I'm wearing the same robe from the night before. My neck is stiff. My shoulders are sore. Slowly, I realize that I am still under the bed.

At school, friends pass me in the halls and whisper behind my back. I've withdrawn from everyone, and everything around me feels like it's moving in slow motion.

I overhear my friends say, "I heard she's having an affair with Hef's girlfriend."

"Gross."

"That is so nasty," another says.

"Ew, do you think she looks at us when we're naked in the girl's locker room?"

"Not even," Hunter says. "She's so into that actor, and besides, I've never even seen her in the locker room."

Nobody knows what to think of me anymore. I'm in a spaced-out daze that doesn't wear off. My friends distance themselves from me even more. I don't let myself wonder what is affecting my entire life or why everyone keeps asking me what's going on. For some reason I keep turning to the one person who pushes people away yet continues to tell me he is the only one who understands what I am going through.

That afternoon I pass Dad in the upstairs hallway and ask if we can spend some time alone. I am anxious to talk to him about Vicki. He looks at his watch and tells me about some pornographic-art gallery opening in a few hours. "It's a must," he insists, so I agree to join him.

"Oh goodie, I have you all to myself," he giggles.

On our way, we stop by the Mansion so he can check on Hef. While he's upstairs I ask one of the butlers if he can let Kendall know I am here. He tells me she is unavailable.

At the gallery showing, Dad and I sip champagne. My father

stops at a black-and-white sketch titled "The Butler Did It." The picture depicts a man dressed in a butler's uniform having doggy-style sex with a woman on all fours.

"I really love this one. Something about it," Dad chuckles. He motions to a salesgirl.

"Hmm, could it be the leash or the fact that she's on all fours?"

"If they want to be treated like dogs, I am more than happy to accommodate them," he scratches his head. His eyes look a little bloodshot, but I try my best to ignore them.

"So I assume we're replacing the tennis court with the your own Kennel for Dogs?" I laugh with him.

"I was thinking more along the lines of an Obedience School for Girls," he giggles like a boy.

"I'll screen them to make sure they don't have a mind of their own," I say matter-of-factly as Dad puts his arm around me.

"I'm glad to see you're finally getting with the program," he says.

We approach a life-size portrait of an olive-skinned brunette with big boobs. "Now this one I like," I tell him, knowing the portrait reminds me of Kendall.

"It's a little hard for my taste, but if you want it, get it," Dad offers generously, our subliminal battle coming to an end. He signals for the salesgirl to wrap it up. I thank him and we continue roaming. He glances at his watch and I can't help but notice how tired and stressed he seems.

"I have to go. I'm rushing to meet a private investigator and then I'm off to play gin with Hef."

"What's the private investigator for?" I ask.

"I can't get into that right now," he says.

"Why?" I plead.

Dad signs his bill and walks briskly outside. He hands the valet our parking ticket. "It's a long story. But the truth is, I think Vicki may still be involved with her ex-boyfriend in some capacity," he says.

"How do you know?"

"I have my sources," he confirms.

"You should dump her. She's bad news."

"Her ex-boyfriend runs the largest West Coast operation from here to Colombia. Why would I want to get into a big thing with him? I'd rather not do anything until I have all the facts."

"I don't see what her ex-boyfriend has to do with you dumping her?" I ask, confused.

"Let me handle it, okay? I'm the one getting life-threatening messages on my answering machine every day, not you!"

"Fine," I say, at a loss.

He never gives me a real answer. I am confused yet sworn to secrecy. We get into the car and drive. Dad picks up his car phone and calls his bodyguard, telling him to check the house before we return. We pull up in front of the house and get out. Dad looks around and paranoia sets in. It's difficult to tell whether he is acting delusional and suspicious or if there really is something to fear. Either way, it frightens me.

It's a Saturday night and I'm still in bed when I hear someone ring the doorbell. After a few moments, the doorbell rings again. I throw on a Puma jersey and boxers, walk downstairs, and look through the peephole. I am surprised to find my mother standing there, looking worried. I open the door.

"I'm so glad you're here," she says. "I called you all morning but your father said you weren't home. When I saw your car in the driveway I realized he was lying." She is shaking nervously and I suddenly suspect my father is lurking nearby. His reaction to my mother being here makes my anxiety level skyrocket.

"Why would anybody want to kill your father except me?" she laughs half jokingly. I shrug. Small tears fill my eyes as my mother pulls me in close, and for an instant, nothing else matters.

"Everything's going to be okay." She rubs my back soothingly, trying to console me. But a little rubbing is not enough to make everything okay. I haven't been okay in years.

"What can I do?" she asks as I hold on to her for dear life, never wanting to let go.

"Nothing." I shake my head, petrified Dad will find me speaking to his enemy. There is no way she can pull me away from such a powerful man. She is too weak. He will destroy her. She cannot save me. No one can.

"Honey, why don't you come with me now?" But her voice quivers as she says it, and hearing her trepidation sends chills down my spine. I am a prisoner, yet somehow that is less frightening than the thought of actually defying my father.

"Everything will be fine. I just need to get back to the house before he gets home," reassuring myself that he really loves me.

"Are you sure?"

I nod.

"As long as you'll be all right, sweetie." Mom seems relieved to return to our usual state of denial. We hug and for a moment, for one moment, I am safe. She will never know how much I need her approval and love like the child I was when I left her.

The moment quickly evaporates as we say good-bye and I hurry inside, using the side gate. I enter the French doors by the pool, run upstairs to my room, swallow two Xanax, and slip into bed.

The next morning, the phone rings, startling me out of a heavy haze. It's my mother. The next thing I know, I look up to see my father looming in my bedroom doorway. He's rocking back and forth in his blue terry-cloth robe. My hands shake because I am talking to the one person my father despises most.

A thick rubber band is now aimed inches from my face.

"Who are you talking to?" my father demands, hovering over me with crazed bloodshot eyes.

"A friend." I flinch, hoping my mother does not say a word. He pulls the rubber band back even farther as if to spring it at me. The rubber band is now pointed directly at my face.

"Who are you talking to?" he asks again. Anger clouds his eyes. My heartbeat is so irregular that it almost stops. I can't speak and part of me is too scared to face him or what he'll say if I open my mouth.

At this point, I would welcome death.

"I gotta go," I mumble into the phone.

"Well, let's try to meet more often," Mom says, unaware of what's happening.

"Okay."

"Call me when you have time, honey," she says.

We hang up and Dad lowers the rubber band, but continues to sway back and forth. There is an awkward silence.

"How are you?" he asks, momentarily calm. His bloodshot eyes peer right through me. I feel naked and uneasy. I hate that he's just barged in.

"Good. You?" I say in a trembling voice, still shaken by his psychotic behavior.

"Fine," he says, and walks out like a zombie.

I lower my head, ashamed of how easily I was bought. How readily I walked toward a life that promised me freedom but turned into a prison.

By Monday, I can't wait to go to school. I stop by my tutor's house to pick up my term papers that are due and waiting for me in a manilla envelope on the bench outside her front door. She has been kind enough to write them because she knows I couldn't graduate without her help.

I'm a senior now and therefore afforded the luxury of flicking cigarettes at freshmen who walk by in the courtyard. Out of nowhere, I hear some annoying loud-pitched screech: "Hunter, you slut, you fucking slept with my boyfriend, didn't you?" I get up and race over to where others have gathered around in a large circle. A catfight ensues. A high-fashion Euro snob, a label whore from Bel Air wearing Gucci everything, slaps Hunter across the face. Hunter turns bright red, shrieks, and holds her hand on her face. My old group, along with everyone else, backs up and leaves Hunter all alone in the middle surrounded by the Gucci label whore clique.

I slowly take off my sunglasses, light a stogie, and walk casually up to "Gucci."

"Listen, you little knockoff queen. Why would Hunter fuck your nuevo Euro trash boyfriend who reeks of Drakkar?" I say, pressing my finger into her fake gold-plate oversize "G" necklace.

"If you so much as look or lay a hand on her again, I can make you disappear and no one will ever notice," I add, exhaling smoke from my Marlboro Light into her face.

Students clear the way as I pass, clapping, high-fiving me, and rooting me on. My old group smiles warmly as I quietly and honorably regain my status as a very cool chick and someone not to fuck with.

I skip PE and stop by the Polo Lounge to call Kendall while having an afternoon martini. I'm hoping she can meet for a quick rendezvous at the park across from the Beverly Hills Hotel. I know we won't be followed there. When I call she is not there, as usual, so the butler takes a message. We have been discreet since the phones have been tapped and I miss talking to her.

That evening, I'm alone, curled up on the couch in my Nike sweats, and I order in kung pao chicken from my favorite Mandarin restaurant. I'm watching *The Breakfast Club* when the phone rings. Someone listens and says nothing. For a moment, I am frightened until I hear Hayden's voice.

"I don't know why I'm calling. It's probably the thirty Percodans I've swallowed, but I just thought you should know some asshole got their hands on my car," he mumbles as if there's something in his mouth.

"Your car? What happened?" I ask, knowing that only a crisis would lead him to call me.

"Someone loosened all the bolts on my tires and two of them fell off coming down Laurel Canyon!"

"Two bolts?"

"No, two tires! The police told me the bolts were sawed off, so at high speed they'd break instantly! It's a miracle I wasn't on the freeway or else I'd be dead!"

"Oh my God. Are you okay?" I say, instantly forgiving him, as feelings of guilt and fear wash over me.

"If you call a broken leg, a broken arm, and back brace okay, then yeah."

"Who would've done this?" I ask, immediately remembering my mother's car being bumped by some strange man on her way home.

"How should I know?" he barks.

"Where are you?" my hands tremble.

"Cedar Hospital."

"I'm on my way."

"Don't bother," he says with little emotion and hangs up.

I stand by the window finishing my cigarette until I walk downstairs to raid the fridge for food, anything to ease my anguish. The house is pitch-black so I feel my way around the hallway, reaching for the light switch that I know is inside the kitchen. My body halts when I see my father standing inches in front of me in his underwear.

I try to take a casual step back but am frozen by fear. He's not alone. Vicki is standing beside him with a spooky grin across her face. Her eyes are so dilated that you cannot see any color, only a black-and-white socket. My father rocks back and forth, scratching his arms. Their eyes have an evil shimmer and it doesn't take long to realize they are both high. What the hell is going on? Why are they standing in the pitch-black kitchen?

I can feel Vicki's stare on the back of my head as I turn around and move briskly back up the staircase. I close my bedroom door and head right for my bathroom, pack a big bowl of chronic, and suck the whole thing through. There are footsteps outside my door and I know it's Vicki. I grab the phone and dive underneath the bed. The only person I think to call is my sister on her private line.

"Hello?" I hear Savannah answer in a groggy voice.

"Savannah, it's me."

"Who's that? I can't hear you."

"It's me, Jennifer," I whisper again. "I just wanted to tell you I love you."

"What's wrong and why are you whispering?" she asks.

"Shush. Vicki can hear me. I can hear her breathing outside my door."

"Why would she be breathing on your door at this hour? Do you know what time it is?"

"Listen, she just tried to kill Hayden and I think she's going to kill me next."

"Are you stoned?"

"No. You have to save me!"

"Where are you?"

"I'm underneath my bed. Help me!"

"You really shouldn't do drugs so late at night and call me with these paranoid delusions," she says.

"I'm not the one who's paranoid."

"Go to bed."

"I can't. She'll get me."

"Fine, sleep under the bed. Maybe they won't find you there. Good night." Savannah hangs up and I realize my only link to the outside world has just been cut.

I look around with wild eyes, reach my hand above the bed, feel around for my pillow, and snatch it quickly.

Savannah's right—they will never find me down here.

In the morning, after sleeping for four hours, I am stiff from being curled up underneath the bed all night. I slip on sweats and a tank, and rush over to Cedar Hospital. The weatherman on the radio tells me, "It's going to be another sunny California day," but I'm not so sure.

I buy armfuls of balloons and flowers, and locate Hayden's room. He's covered in bandages. One leg is elevated in the air while his arm is wrapped in a white cast. The bed is raised a few feet from behind so his back brace has plenty of room to adjust. The balloons and flowers fit perfectly into a vase on the end table.

"Hayden, I'm so sorry." I place my hand on his, but he moves away, barely acknowledging me. "I know you already hate me so what I have to say will probably seal the deal," I say, full of guilt. He slowly turns and looks in my direction. "I think I know who did this to you."

"Who?" he asks without another word.

"I know this sounds crazy, but I think it was my father's crazy girlfriend."

"What?" Hayden shouts, with cold menace. "The shit just piles up faster and faster with you."

His voice is powerful and there is still something very seductive about him. His muscles bulge through his hospital gown. His baby-soft cheeks are rosy, though the whites of his eyes are bloodshot, and in many ways he resembles my father.

"Get the fuck out of here!" he yells, shifting himself in painful ways. "And stay away or I'll file a restraining order against you and your psycho father! You hear me? I never want to see you again!" he screams, slamming the vase to the floor.

The crashing noise scares me as I turn and hurry out into the sterile white hospital hallway. I'm heading toward the exit doors, which seem so far away. I burst through them and into the parking lot. Leaning over on the hood of my car, I inhale deep breaths, desperate to pump the life back into myself.

At home, I head straight for the kitchen but stop cold when I hear Vicki's voice coming from upstairs. I can't help but listen to her conversation. I have a strange feeling in my gut.

"Boy Wonder doesn't know if it's day or night. He thinks somebody wants to kill him. The only problem is that little bitch Jennifer. I've been trying to get her out of here, but she has nowhere to go," she hisses.

My body temperature drops as I process this information. I pick up the back office line and try to call my father. It rings and rings but there is no answer. I look up to see Vicki barreling into the room, rushing at me, yanking the cord out of the wall.

"What the fuck do you think you're doing here?"

"I live here."

The sunken, black circles underneath her eyes pale in comparison to the purplish bruises on her arms. What alarms me even more is that she seems to have no comprehension as to the absurdity of it all. She has a psychotic expression on her face as she uses both arms to pin my head against the wall. The possibility of danger begins to sink in.

We stare at each other. I stay quiet as she grabs my chin firmly. Inside I was hysterical—there were Uzis and a coke whores in the house—but outwardly I knew I needed to remain absolutely composed. I couldn't believe what was happening. My instinct is to scream, but no one can hear me. I can't move or speak. My heart is beating so fast I can feel my pulse throbbing in the palm of my hands.

I duck swiftly, catching her off guard, and run down the hallway as she follows closely behind. I spin around the corner, searching for something, anything to defend myself. I grab an iron statue of a female nude and hurry into the den, hiding behind the swinging door and clutching the statue for dear life. I can hear her breathing as she turns the corner.

"You little bitch!" Vicki points her finger at me, but the gesture is so powerful it might as well be a gun.

Her features are distorted and a look of disgust floods her face. She blocks my path. Both of us are yelling when someone shouts,

"Get away from her, you stupid whore!" I look up to see my father looming over us.

I'm not sure which one of us he's talking to. He steps forward and pushes Vicki aside.

"Are you okay?" he asks me. His voice is muffled, like he's at the end of a long tunnel.

He lifts me up. My legs are shaking and can hardly hold me as he puts his arm around me for support. He hugs me assuredly, comforting me, telling me not to worry, that he is going to take care of everything.

I am still a little girl in his arms.

He orders Vicki to get the fuck out and never come back.

In light of all the hateful things we've said to each other, I am grateful for the reassurance that my father would never put one of his girlfriends before me. Vicki's physically out of our lives for good, but she leaves a permanent scar. She began a surge of destruction that will outlast her memory.

I will sleep fitfully, waking at the slightest noise, terrified Vicki or one of her friends has returned. In my dreams, I see her thin drug-racked body, my father hobbling down the hall, needles falling from the pockets of his robe. Remnants of the smell of unwashed sheets and rubbing alcohol make me sick to my stomach. I will fight demons and dragons late at night when everyone else is sleeping, never seeing my father's face behind them.

One morning, my father wakes me; he's shaking.

"Wake up, wake up. We have an early appointment!" Dad coughs. It's clear that he hasn't slept in days. He has a scary grin across his face.

"An appointment?" I sit up, my heart coming to a crashing stop. "With who?"

"I don't want to discuss it now. Get dressed," he urges, and I can see his skinny legs beneath his blue terry-cloth robe as he leaves my room.

Ten minutes later, we're driving in his car. He's shivering. He's put on the same blue jeans and striped Izod shirt he's worn for days. "What's going on?" I ask.

"I need to make arrangements," he answers.

"For what?"

"My will."

"Why would you need to do that now?"

"Because I may not be here," he confesses.

"Where would you be?"

"It's all going to be over soon," he says with impending doom.

"What is?" I ask as he speeds up. Things are happening so quickly.

"I'm in danger. At risk."

"From who?"

"If I knew, I wouldn't be in this situation, would I?" he says condescendingly. "I want you to have the house, the cars, CDs, bonds, everything."

"Why are you saying this?" I am choked up.

"There's too much to explain. It's just better this way," he assures me as we pull into the parking lot of Century City Towers. I am relieved to get out of the car, but my mind is floundering. We wait for the elevator, rush up to the twentieth floor, and are buzzed into a plush office to meet with Gregory James, attorney-at-law. Dad and I sit across from his mahogany desk as he hands my father a few papers. Dad quickly shuffles through them, reviews them, and hands them back to the attorney, with a new draft he pulls out of his briefcase.

"Jennifer, I am appointing you as the executor of my will. You are now my beneficiary. I am leaving my entire estate to you."

I listen without blinking.

I can tell he wants to cry but he controls himself. The pain in his eyes is almost too much for me to bear. I stare at him in disbelief.

"I took care of everything related to my burial, and the hospital knows you have power of attorney to arrange everything related to my death." I am frightened by the figments of his imagination that tell him he is dying or could be killed. I manage to listen to him continue.

"I want a quiet burial without too much fuss. Twenty or thirty of my closest friends, you know the drill. It's time for me to go and I am determined to go peacefully," he rambles as I am consumed with guilt for not knowing how to help him.

I peer over at the attorney, whose eyes are as icy as Dad's can be at times. Today Dad's eyes are full of gloom and sorrow as if he has seen the evils of the world. I want to reach out and touch him but it's as if he is already gone.

"I want to thank you for everything. Forgive me if I've been too harsh on you at times, but I did it out of my deepest love and devotion for you. I've only ever wanted you to lead a happy, fulfilled life," he says, and all I can do is nod and accept this peculiar act of contrition.

I sign the papers, and Dad and I leave the office. We ride down the elevator in silence. Neither of us mentions the attorney visit again.

That evening, I sit on Grampy's balcony smoking a pipe. I can no longer move or speak. My insides are shriveled into a tight ball. My eyes are red from crying.

"I need to get out of that house," I tell him.

"Running away never solves anything," he replies.

"Spoken like a true escapist."

"I keep telling you to broaden your horizons. Get involved with something outside of yourself. Why don't you go to college on the East Coast," he suggests.

"I'm afraid Dad won't let me go."

"If you had any discipline you wouldn't be concerned with what others demand. You would do what you need to do."

"No one seems to understand, school is not the issue. I can't live in that house anymore."

"I am telling you to focus on your future."

I am frustrated with his response.

"My future? At this point, if I don't get out of there, I may not have a future."

"What you need is a real education," Grampy demands.

I take my dark shades off so he can see my face. "Do I look like I'm ready for finals?"

"You look like you're ready for a change," he says. "Most of the time we make up stories in our head that aren't even true. They're illusions to keep us from doing something."

"The only illusions I see are Dad's hallucinations on the tennis court late at night," I tell him, a cloud of smoke between us.

His loyalty to my father runs deep. He seems to overlook my father's lack of boundaries, his antagonistic, condescending ways of making even the smartest person in the room feel stupid. He knows I am right about the drugs, his neglect as a parent, as a human being, his inability to differentiate between fantasy and reality; yet Grampy continues to enable him out of guilt, out of pure love for a son he can no longer reach.

"Darling, there are many ways of looking at your life. There is what happened, the story of what happened, and the story of what can happen. And depending on how you interpret it, you can make it mean something negative or you can create new possibilities for yourself. That's for you to decide." He lowers his head so he can see me over his thin spectacles.

"You make it sound so easy."

"You can't control what other people do. But you can control how you respond to it, whether you allow it to eat you up and occupy all your thoughts, and how much you let it affect you."

I try to digest what he is saying.

"You have everything you need," he tells me.

But I can't understand what he's talking about. I'm so used to the little voice in my head that believes the world owes me something and that civilized behavior is a waste of time.

Nineteen

*I*t's 1987. I graduate Beverly Hills High School with the rest of my class and when the ceremony ends, we shoot confetti and champagne corks high into the air. Though we have grown apart, we will always be there for each other.

We are reunited again as we were as kids.

We may not see each other every day, but our old bonds will stay in our hearts forever.

Liz, Amber, Hunter, Michelle, Sonya, and I snap photos of ourselves outside on the front lawn. We gather around making funny faces as we capture the last of our days together. A knot swells in my throat as I say my good-byes.

I turn around every few steps and watch as my old friends blend into the distance.

I drag through the next few days and think seriously about leaving town. I need a hiatus from my life. Somehow, it is less painful to run away than to face the insanity of my everyday existence.

One of Dad's friends owns a suite at the Plaza Hotel in New York City, so I arrange to stay there for a couple weeks. Three thousand miles away, I lock myself in my suite doing lines of coke all night until the next day. I keep the curtains closed at all times to keep the sunlight out. Cat Stevens' "Wild World" drowns out the street noise below. I spend my days on the phone with Kendall and order room service for every occasion. At night, I drop a Halcyon, sip vodka tonics in crystal glasses, and take cabs to clubs like Limelight and the Tunnel.

Around 1 P.M. I'm in a deep fog.

Hidden beneath two fluffy down pillows, I hear faint noises that begin to sound like ringing. Flailing my arm, I bang something off the end table and lift the receiver to my ear.

"Hello?" I answer, wiping sleep from my eyes.

"Hey, kiddo, it's me. I'm coming to New York," Kendall says. It's as if she read my mind.

"I'll be there tonight," she whispers and hangs up.

Hours later, there's a knock on the door. I slowly open it and see Kendall standing in the doorway wearing a sheer white linen dress. She is tan and toned and looks happy to be alive.

She jumps on me and we fall backward onto the bed laughing and rolling around like kids. She seems a lot calmer than the last time we saw each other. I tell her about my falling-out with Hayden.

"It's about time," she says, ordering up a bottle of Cristal. Within minutes room service arrives and we lie on the bed feeding each other pâté on French bread.

"Everyone thinks we're having an affair," I tell her.

"Aren't we?" she laughs.

"Are you going to tell me why you're here?"

"To see you, silly." She takes a small bite of pâté and licks her lips flirtatiously. It's difficult to ignore how sexy she is. Her beauty drives me to distraction as she gently caresses her fingers through my hair and we look at each other.

"Have you been a good girl?" she whispers and I blush.

"Tell me how much you missed me." She rolls on top and pins me down playfully, our bodies now pressed together. Her hand slides naturally down my stomach as she slowly unbuttons my pants. She slides her fingers gently between my legs.

"Tell me how much you need me," she says, and I swallow hard, breathing heavily, tortured, yearning to be loved, touched. I'm not sure if she's a game in my head or if she's for real. She draws me near, kissing me, teasing me, keeping me in her complete control, and the impulse to give her full power turns me on even more. She squeezes my hand and hesitates.

"I love you," she says softly.

"I love you too." I pause, absorbing the intensity of my feelings. She strokes my face and I put my arms around her, unsure of whether I'm her lover or her child. She leans her head against mine. We are far enough away from L.A. that we can say whatever we want, yet somehow I can't help but always feel like somebody is watching us.

It's past eleven at night by the time we motivate to go out. After painting our nails and taking a relaxing bubble bath, we rummage through our wardrobe trying on at least three outfits each. She ends up wearing a low-cut dress showing off her cleavage. I throw on ripped jeans and a rhinestone tank. We stumble out of the hotel room, kissing and holding hands in the elevator.

We go to Limelight, a converted church, where all the guests are on display in a sea of glitter and camouflage. Flooding the dance floor are partygoers in painfully bright short jackets and miniskirts.

Long-legged girls wear carefully ripped aqua jeans, neon-blue and candy-apple-red pantyhose with glow-in-the-dark stilettos.

Boys squeezed into tight leather pants and Spandex biker shorts circle the scene, shirtless beneath lambskin jackets. Girls sweat to Madonna's "Holiday," their blown-out bangs sturdily held in place with red glitter hairspray.

The energy in the church is perverted as fluorescent lights and wild sexual videos flash against the walls. Men wearing Calvin Klein underwear and combat boots and topless females in thongs and high heels dance in cages above the stage of clubgoers. Too many kamikazes later, we dance, surrounded by gays, straights, and strays. Kendall puts her arm alluringly around me and we make our way through the hedonistic crowd. We recognize the same openness toward sexuality and drugs as life at the Mansion. There is something very enticing and exhilarating about breaking free from restrictions that bind us to who we are rather than to who we are supposed to be.

In the morning, I can barely open my eyes as I hear faint, muffled sounds of someone talking.

"I have to go." Kendall whispers through my sinking haze. She kisses me gently on the lips and she's gone. My eyes droop and I go back to sleep for hours.

It's late in the day when the phone rings, startling me.

"Hello?" I answer, groggy.

"You're not going to believe what happened to me today." It's Savannah.

"Dad and I went to Nate 'n' Al's and he fell asleep in his soup! He told me the turkey made him tired."

"You're kidding."

"No, and then he made me drive him home!"

"You barely have a permit."

"It was a nightmare."

"Apparently."

"I wanted to call Mom to come get me but Dad was in such a hurry. You know how he's always in a frenzied rush, and I . . . it was really weird."

"Some things will never change," I tell her.

"Though we did meet outside the Mansion."

"Must've been an off night."

"That's the last time I'll be seeing him for a while," she says.

"Can't wait to come home," I hear myself say. We hang up and I fall back to sleep.

The next day, I finally motivate to check out colleges. I open my planner for the first time since arriving in New York and see I have a meeting scheduled at Mount Vernon College (now owned by George Washington University). It was one of the most exclusive high-end female colleges, full of young royals and southern belles. I take the train to D.C. and find myself sitting across from a warm-hearted, plump guidance counselor. Through the window, I can see the trees, the colorful spring leaves swaying back and forth. Students in casual wear and knapsacks stroll by in between classes. I squirm in my seat. "Normal" feels so thoroughly uncomfortable to me.

"Why do you want to move out of Los Angeles, dear?" she asks and I want to tell her everything: the fear I face daily, the guilt, the fact that I too have become a person without a conscience. I get unexpectedly choked up. The counselor looks into my damaged eyes and places her hand on mine. "Everything is going to be okay," she says sincerely, and I believe her.

I catch a flight back to L.A. and wait for my father to pick me up outside the airport. I look around but see no sign of him as a black stretch Mercedes limousine with the license plate 1HEF pulls up. Kendall waves out the window and jumps out. I hug and kiss her hello, both surprised and excited to see her. Then I hear a familiar voice over my shoulder. I turn to see my father stepping out of the limo. A huge rock falls to the pit of my stomach.

"We thought we'd surprise you," Dad chuckles jovially.

"You definitely did."

Inside the limo, the tension is unbearable. At first, I regard the surprise as an act of kindness. I take it as a genuine effort on my father's part to show that he finally understands my relationship with Kendall, although I'm puzzled by his sudden shift in behavior. He sits next to her and I sit across from them. We engage in small talk until Dad places his arm on Kendall's leg. I twitch because he's flirting with someone he's forbidden me to spend time with.

"Don't you think Kendall is phenomenal?" Dad rubs his hand over Kendall's thigh. "All right, so she can be a bitch sometimes, but everyone has their moments."

"Look who's talking," Kendall laughs, caressing his hand affectionately before she lets go. "Your father is nuts."

"I've been told that once or twice." He bats his eyes, but I cannot hear either of them. I feel like I'm the butt of some kind of sick joke.

When we arrive at Dad's house, I can barely wait to kick open the door and get out of the limo. I don't even bother saying goodbye to Kendall, who yells after me as I hurry inside.

The next day, I show up at the Mansion unannounced. I see Kendall sitting in the med room. My eyes say it all. We march out to the Playmate of the Month house so we can talk in private.

"What the fuck is going on?" I yell.

"Stop it."

"You fly to New York, feed me bullshit about how much you love me, how we're in love and best friends, and then you're flirting with my father? I thought you hated him?"

"Jennifer, there's so much you don't understand."

"Like what?" My eyes are fuming.

"Like stuff I have to do. I'm expected to act a certain way."

"Like how?"

"You're so young, you don't get it." She shakes her head.

"What don't I get?"

"You're going to hate me." She lowers her head, hands me a cigarette, lights mine, then hers.

"No, I'm not."

"Yes, you will," she states clearly. Kendall turns away from me, ashamed. She covers her face with her hands. She lets out a long sigh, as if making a decision within a matter of seconds, and then proceeds to speak.

"Your father was here one night and we all sort of . . . slept together."

"What?" I scream, afraid I might puke. "You fucked my father?"

Disgust rushes through my veins. My knees are weak. I lean against the wall and slide down to the floor. I feel like I've been punched in the stomach. My whole body hurts.

How do you explain a father's carnal desire to share female lovers with his oldest daughter?

"That's why I don't want you around all this crazy shit," Kendall says softly.

I pretend to listen to what she's saying as I raid the kitchen for alcohol. I ponder for a moment if this is my punishment for falling in love with someone so unavailable. All her words and the way she seemingly cared for me made me believe her intentions were real.

"I told you you'd be pissed," she insists. I find the Absolut and swallow continuously from the bottle. Kendall tries to reach for my hand, but I push her away.

"I trusted you. Traitor! You betrayed me. I thought you loved me."

"I'm sorry." She covers her face with her hands and I ignore her tears. "I was drunk and next thing I know a bunch of us . . . we're upstairs and . . . oh, I don't know . . ." She tries to reach out, but I am dead inside. "Talk to me . . . ," she cries, and I stare at her blankly.

Nothing seems familiar anymore.

I drive out the back gate going fifty, sixty, seventy miles per hour down a winding street toward Wilshire Boulevard. I speed up even more, hoping to hit something. I envision death. My head spins furiously as I plot revenge on my parents and everyone else—my long escape.

I snap out of my delusion because some asshole cuts me off in traffic and flips me off. "Fuck you, faggot!" I scream.

I've become the poster child for a vengeful generation.

Rounding a corner at high speed, I'm unable to make the complete turn. Headlights flash right at me! I spin 180 degrees and smash into a parked car. My head knocks against the steering wheel. Things are fuzzy and waves of pain move through me. I try to mumble for help but no one can hear me, no one is around. The sky becomes gray. There's a heavy weight shutting out all sounds until everything goes black.

Distant voices call out my name as if I'm in a tunnel and can only hear muffled echoes. There's a sense of dullness and heavy weight on my head as the voices continue and I slowly regain consciousness.

"Jennifer, wake up. Say something." Bright lights bombard me and I'm forced to shut my eyes again. Something tugs at my arm. There seems to be a lot of commotion: IVs, monitors, vital signs, X rays, EKG, CT, MRI results, tubes of fluids. It's daylight. I'm not sure how many hours have passed. Doctors and nurses hover around, mumbling. INTENSIVE CARE UNIT UCLA, the blurry sign above the door reads.

I think I'm coherent but no one is talking to me. My head is pounding. A doctor lifts my eyelids and shines a light in my pupils. My father is there.

"Are you sure there's no internal bleeding? I want you to check everything out. We need to do an MRI," my father tells the doctor when he lowers his shining light away from my eyes. The doctor finally notices I'm awake.

"You had quite an accident, young lady. You're lucky to be alive." The doctor clears his throat.

"Honey, are you all right?" Dad says, holding my hand as a nurse with blond hair stands beside him. "I've been so worried about you." I blink a few times, unsure of where I am.

"She'll be fine," the doctor informs him.

"What happened?" I ask in a groggy voice.

"You have suffered a slight concussion," the doctor explains. "All of the test results show only minor head injury. A few bruises here and there. I've seen situations much worse than this. Fortunately, you wore your seat belt."

Then I remember. All the oxygen is sucked out of me; the room spins as distant visuals of the car accident return. Headlights. Swerving. Crashing. And then I remember why I was so upset. Images of Dad and Kendall having sex flash.

"How do you feel, Jennifer? Can I ask you to move your arms and legs for me?" the doctor asks. "We may need to keep her here for a couple of days, to monitor her," he explains.

Faces lean over me as my mind races through possible excuses to justify how the collision occurred. My stomach sinks when the doctor leaves me alone with my father. I feed him a half-ass story about a hit-and-run accident as I'm squinting my eyes, cringing, and preparing myself for his wrath.

To my surprise, he waves the story off and mutters something about insurance and being late to the Mansion. He tells me he was able to speak to the chief of police about my alcohol level and somehow the DUI offense has been lifted. I thank him and apologize profusely.

"These flowers are for you," he says.

The bouquet is beautiful. Long-stemmed red roses in a tall vase.

I suppose these are my makeup flowers for fucking my best friend.

"Forgive me, but I have to leave." Dad kisses my forehead. "I'll be back in a few hours. Don't do anything I wouldn't do."

That leaves everything wide open. I stifle the impulse to laugh.

My father has a smile on his face as he waves good-bye and I grin back with a happy face that peels off. I obsess over the kind of mood he will be in later, but the throbbing headache makes it difficult for me to think. All alone, I pick up the phone and call my mother.

"Mom, are you sitting down?"

"Why? What's wrong?"

"I've been in a car accident. I'm at UCLA."

"Oh my God! Are you all right?"

"I'm okay."

"I'm on my way." She hangs up and I fall asleep.

When I wake up the room is dimly lit. There's a curtain around the bed and a tray of soft food and yogurt in front of me. Perhaps I have changed rooms. The doctor went somewhere and the nurses are gone. I don't know where everyone went. I'm dizzy in here and panic sets in.

"Mom?"

She's sitting on the edge of the bed. "I'm here. The doctor said the medications would make you a little out of it. Honey, what happened?" she asks, extremely worried. The thought of drinking and driving is more than she can handle.

"Don't ask," I say.

"You know better than to drink and drive." Mom frowns. She looks stressed and tired. "I'm really happy you're reaching out to me," she says as tears form in her eyes.

"I'm sorry. About everything," I confess, gently reaching out to her with an IV stuck in my arm.

"I'm sorry too." She squeezes my hand and we hug. She is here now. But we both know there is a bigger issue that neither one of us is strong enough to tackle. My father will never let me go and I don't have the courage to leave him. Mom offers to let me move in with her but we both know she doesn't really mean it. Somehow, it is easier to deny what is going on than to contend with going up against a monster, especially when everything is a game to him.

Savannah strolls in licking an ice cream cone.

"What the hell happened to you?" she blurts out. "Are you trying to kill yourself?"

"Actually, I think they've given me some awesome painkillers 'cause I haven't felt better in months." I reach for the bottle, but Mom yanks it away and hides it in her purse.

"Hunter called and said she saw your car in front of Dad's house," Savannah says.

"And?"

"She said it was totaled. The hood's up and smoke's coming out of it. The whole side is banged up, but that's nothing compared to the front of the car. The headlight is hanging down, like an eye popped out of its socket. Oh, and the front tire is flat."

"Thanks for the full report."

"You're welcome. Just don't expect to drive my car—that is, if I ever get one," she says, eyeballing Mom.

"You'll get one," I assure her.

"Yes, but I'll be too old to drive by then," she answers.

"I miss you. Maybe we can hang out when I go home," I say, sounding eight instead of eighteen.

"Okay, get some sleep," Savannah says.

My eyelids begin to droop as Mom kisses me softly and tells me to rest for a while.

When I am discharged from the hospital, Mom and Savannah gather my belongings. Dad is busy playing Monopoly at Hef's so Mom drives me back to his empty house. In the car, she and Savannah talk about clothes and new restaurants. Mom keeps asking me about my plans for college, but I'm not listening to a word. I have sobered up a little and realize how distraught and out of touch I have become. It seems hard to imagine feeling safe or sane, laughing or being lighthearted again. I wonder if I can ever go to the beach again, toss a Frisbee, have barbeques, go to street festivals, and talk about boys like most teenagers across the country are doing.

At home, days, maybe hours, later, someone pounds loudly on my bedroom door.

"What?" I yell from my bed. I sit up, lifting the covers off me.

"I need to talk to you," my father says, stumbling in. He is disheveled as he sways back and forth in the doorway. His hair is unkempt, his eyes half open. Two cowlicks stick up, scarily looking like two horns. He hasn't shaved in days. He appears more depressed than anything else.

"I'm going to stay at Don's guest house for a while. I think Vicki may have set me up," he says sadly. "It's only going to be for a few months until things settle down."

"Until what settles down?" I ask, trying to focus on what he's telling me.

"It's better for me to be gone for a while, but don't worry, I have my people watching the house," he says.

"What people? Who's watching the house?" My head is spinning. "Who's after you?" I find myself constantly asking. "The people who come by the house late at night?" The thought of being all alone turns my stomach. I think I'm going to throw up.

"I have a plan," he mumbles.

"What plan?" I ask.

"I can't get into details now."

"What if people try to break in?"

"Just don't answer the door," he says nonchalantly.

My look is one of sheer terror.

"How can you leave me here?" I could not formulate the words beyond panic.

"You handle your business and I'll handle mine!" he yells. "Stay out of it, you hear me? Just keep quiet!" But what I really hear him say is, "Shut up! Don't be a stupid little bitch like all women!" I stiffen, feeling once again like a child. I don't want to be a scared little girl so intimidated by her father's temper that I never confront him in a clear, adult way.

"I am not staying out of it!" I yell, trying to become a worthy opponent for the verbal battle ahead.

"What is wrong with you?" he reacts in a harsh tone.

"What is wrong with *you*?" I repeat like we're in fourth grade. I notice how quickly our anger escalates.

"You have serious problems!" he says.

"And that's coming from someone who can barely keep his eyes open!" I scream at the top of my lungs.

"If you don't like the way I do things, then leave!" he shouts, sticking his finger in my face. Something inside me snaps and I gather years of silent strength.

"I wish I could!" I scream.

"Well, let me make it real easy for you, lady. From now on, you're on your own!"

"I'd rather be on my own than living in your hell!" I'm enraged, feeling my own demons surfacing: my anger, my distrust, my venomous reactions.

I have been called to battle. Blood rushes to my head. Perhaps it is this ferocity that inspires natural-born killers. Violent images of his death take over but I allow them to subside, though every ounce of me wants to claim true retribution for the hell he has put me through.

"You're finished! We're through! You hear me? We're over!" he shouts as if I'm his lover and we're breaking up. The angrier he gets the further I retreat into silence. My face burns with shame; I'm sick of continuously swallowing his verbal attacks. My father takes pleasure in the fact that I now view the world as my enemy and no longer trust anyone.

"I do not want anyone knowing about this! Is that clear?

Under no circumstances are you to tell anyone about this!" He glares at me.

It becomes clear to me that I am the sad little girl hanging on Dad's office wall. The life-size portrait of the innocent girl holding a gardenia explodes in my mind. I am just as kept, just as lifeless, and just as out of place as that picture is. I wonder if I ever existed outside the frame, if I was ever born, ever breathed or thought on my own.

There is so much to say, but the words won't come out. When he is done screaming, he turns and stomps down the hallway to his room. I am relieved when he shuts his door behind him.

I look around at all the expensive toys my father has bought me. My life, which was once so privileged, now seems dark with nowhere to go. It's at this moment I feel myself begin to burn. They say the devil is a skillful liar in that evil is governed by appearances. It may present itself as something good when really it is not. It tempts us, draws us in with a glittering disguise, hooks us, and ultimately pulls us away from our true selves.

Twenty

Alone in Dad's house, I beg Carmela not to leave. But by 2:00 A.M. she tells me she has to go home to her family. I shiver myself to sleep, afraid that at any given moment someone will break into my bedroom and kill me. I keep the gun under my pillow and do not sleep.

One morning, I stop on Beverly Drive to pick up a coffee. I'm about to get out of the car when I see my father stopped at a red light in the lane right beside me. He's on his car phone. I stare at him for a while and try to open my mouth to say hello, but the words won't come out. I don't know why I don't say anything. I just don't. He never looks in my direction and I watch as the light changes color and he slowly pulls away.

It's my last Midsummer's party at the Mansion before I leave for Mount Vernon College in Washington, D.C.

I need to say good-bye to Kendall. I can't leave without her knowing how much I still love her.

I drive through the iron gates, a line of valet guys greet me at the top of the driveway. The doors open to the Mansion.

Strobe lights spin. Sexual ambiguity is now the rage. Rock star glam meets porn star chic. Lights and cameras flash all around. My feet melt into colored pillows as I waltz into the tented backyard.

I hug and kiss all the Playmates and begin making loops around the backyard.

Hours later, I'm running around with Natasha, Morgan, and Charlie. We've sworn off coke, so we're high on prescription pills. I shoot Austin the Death Look when I see her and debate confronting her about fucking Hayden, but figure he's not worth it. I pass Brigitte Nielson and Sylvester Stallone, and casually glance at Rob Lowe, but I look away instantly because he's such a babe and I don't want him to catch me staring. I catch up to Natasha, who makes a beeline toward Hef, Kendall, and the rest of the harem.

I hug and kiss Hef as the cameras flash, blinding us.

"Meet me in the bathroom," Kendall whispers and I tell myself not to go.

Ten minutes later I'm standing outside the bathroom door looking for her. Everyone around me is on supersonic time. It's as if were moving in slow motion. Everything takes so long, there's no air, and no one completes full sentences. The bathroom door opens and an arm appears, yanking me inside. Kendall and I don't say a word until we close the bathroom window. She hops on the sink and I lean against her knees.

"I'm still mad at you, you know," I mutter, half pretending I don't care.

"I never meant to hurt you."

"Yeah, well, I never meant to do a lot of things."

"You know what I mean."

"I'm leaving. I'm getting out of here," I say, trying to articulate what I'm really feeling. I mention the name of the college I'm attending, and she says she thinks she's heard of it.

"You'll be back. Real life is going to bore you to death," Kendall assures me. "Just remember, normal people are the enemy," she laughs, straddling me. She leans back on the sink, holding her breath, loving the naughtiness of it all. "I'm going to miss you," she says.

My anger turns into longing.

"Come with me," I beg like a child.

"I can't," she says sadly.

"You're going to forget about me," I say with tears swelling.

"How could I ever forget you?" she says softly. We filled voids that neither of us knew we had. I hold on tight until she breaks away. She leaves the bathroom first, then me. I watch as Kendall blends into the crowd. She turns around one last time and we both smile, a sad but sincere smile, one only meant for us.

I call my old friend Hunter, whom I haven't spoken to since graduation. She comes to pick me up. I tell her to meet me in the circular driveway. When Hunter arrives, I get into her car, but stop when I look up to see Kendall peering out of the castle from her bathroom window. A few seconds pass and Kendall waves. An odd sense of déjà vu overcomes me. I wave good-bye.

I never see Kendall again, though a day doesn't go by when my mind doesn't find her. There are some people you never forget. She is one of them.

I wake up early one morning and hear someone playing the piano downstairs. I ease quietly down the stairs, not knowing who I'll find. My father is sitting there with his back to me wearing his blue terry-cloth robe. I knew he'd move back into the house eventually, but I expected his arrival to be more dramatic. I expected cursing and thrown luggage and a parade of blondes following behind him.

What I see now is the father I knew when I was a child.

The house is quiet except for his playing. I sit on the stairs and listen to him gracefully play a song by Barry Manilow. The piano sounds better than I remember.

I notice how calm he seems. My heart aches for him. I watch him as I used to when I was small. I think back on the earlier years, before the drugs, the girls, the commotion. A time when he was my hero.

A distinct pain in the pit of my stomach tells me I will be sad for a very long time.

Twenty-One

At eighteen years old, I feel twelve or even younger.

I am in college in Washington, D.C., surrounded by perfect-looking women with sunny dispositions. Meeting nice, friendly students from average families is a grueling ordeal. Anything normal is uncomfortable. Being polite, making small talk, remembering names, and keeping to any kind of schedule are all exercises in futility.

The girls at college are a completely different breed. They're concerned with getting married, having kids, pleasing everyone, generally themselves. I never find myself wistful at the thought of the day when my dreams will be fulfilled.

I am consumed with my past, with the nightmares and outrage, the unanswered questions they inspire. It is a battle to fight the memories out of my head. Images stream behind my eyes, fast and incomprehensible like an MTV video. If I could only slow them down, decode them, maybe I could make sense of my life.

I move through campus scared stiff of people and banal conversation; the world is as soundless as my nightmares. All the details of life are like wasted colored confetti in a fog.

One day I am cornered by a posse of freshmen Southern belles in nearly identical culottes and knee-high boots. I want to run away from them, be spirited away to a dark bar where the whiskey's flowing and music blares from the jukebox.

The Cure blasts from my Sony Walkman headset, which I resentfully lift off my ears for a moment when a redheaded Tinker-bell asks if I know where group orientation is. I stare at her, wondering if I could ever be that lame. I try to answer, but my voice is scratchy from too many cigarettes and not enough sleep. She looks at me through a veil of health and sunny disposition as if I'm speaking a foreign language and she can't begin to understand me. It's not good. I walk away without another word, puffing heavily on a cigarette.

The daze follows me into the cafeteria. I try to lay out things in my mind, organize them and arrange them like homework assignments I can't quite make sense of. Suddenly, the room begins to expand and contract. I can't breathe. I need more space. This has happened before—this anxiety—and the lack of control terrifies me. It comes from nowhere and overwhelms my body. I feel dizzy and nauseated and the room spins. It's like being drunk on disgustingly cheap alcohol and needing air. Cliques of girls whisper among themselves at every table. Pure attitude.

At night, when most are asleep, I routinely meet a fellow student in dark corners of the college, paying her to complete all my term papers. I end up putting in an extra hundred for stolen answers to the exams.

The following spring, dogwoods bloom bright and pink on campus. Some have white blossoms, easily bruised by the sun and humidity. My eyes stay hidden behind dark sunglasses, squinting because they still have not adjusted to the bright surrealism of this normal place.

I go to get my hair done. My hairdresser, Ashley, lives in Dupont Circle, the hub of D.C.'s gay capital. He is my closest friend. At forty, he is still at the center of the underground club scene, which is where I am most comfortable.

I move through quaint streets with wrought-iron lampposts and outdoor cafés. Enigma wafts from open windows, the music mixing with the scent of Nag Champa incense. The streets intersect at a gigantic cement Gothic-style fountain. Men and women stand around it, posing in Ray-Bans with bowl haircuts, wearing plastic Jelly shoes.

Ashley has pushed a pink headband over his thinning hair and wears blue Spandex shorts and a bright yellow tank top. He wears full makeup, his eyes catlike, circled with black eyeliner. He never knows when an impromptu cocktail party will descend on him. Beautiful throws with gold and black stitching adorn his comfy couch and chairs. Sandalwood and orange-spice scented candles rest in blue glass holders. Bright green spider plants sit in baskets, which hang from the ceiling. His shelves are stocked with Campbell's soup and his refrigerator is full. On his wall there is a huge poster of Madonna striking a pose. Fashion magazines, hair products, and makeup are piled in corners and spill from tables onto the floor.

Ashley grabs both my arms and kisses me on the cheek. I feel very at home here. He and I are survivors who share stories and cling to each other like life support.

We sing along to the Pet Shop Boys as he dyes my hair a temporary black, piling it high on my head with loads of mousse and gel. He lends me Madonna-style lace gloves and a white Spandex top. The final touch is blue eye shadow and purple lipstick.

We will slide coolly into the D.C. clubs, envied and careless.

And so the college years pass. Though I am constantly surrounded by other people, I feel apart from them. I quickly learn that I was never taught the basics of how to get along. I have to reexamine every thought I have for sensibility. There are days when I can't imagine how I'll survive.

A few friends I meet invite me over for family dinners on Sundays. Hesitant at first, I am curious how parents outside Beverly Hills interact. By now I am used to them having to prep their parents on their "L.A. friend who comes from a fucked-up family." I can tell by the way their parents embrace me with that sad look in their eyes as I walk through their front door. They open their home to me, treating me as a second daughter. I am parented for the first time by parents who are concerned with a life not based on appearances, parties, drugs, and hot girls whose names I will never remember in the morning.

I am no longer that girl glimpsing into windows around my neighborhood, getting an idea of the kind of family I've always wanted. There are suddenly names to the faces. There are mothers baking fresh chicken and vegetables in the kitchen; brothers and sisters who are generous and loving; fathers who are stable and truly available to their children's needs, providing them support and advice. I learn a lot from these parents. I often cry when I leave their homes because I know I'll never have parents like them.

As graduation nears, the visits to my friends' parents' homes become less frequent. I am sad because no matter how much they include me, I will never be a part of their family—no matter how hard I try. It was all a facade that showed me what I was missing, what I will always be missing. All I ever wanted were parents I could rely on, who were consistent and loved me. Parents who would help me find my way in the world.

I drive off acutely aware that I have been on my own for a very long time.

Two weeks before I graduate, two men in dark suits claiming to be FBI agents come to visit my dorm room. They tell me they are friends of my father's and are here to help, that they are investigating Vicki and her ex-boyfriend Marco Santiago, the infamous Colombian drug lord. They ask me what I know about Vicki storing drugs underneath my father's house.

"You'd have to ask him," I say calmly, unresponsive, and clearly indifferent. I walk them to the door and let them out without another word. I spend the rest of the afternoon lying on my bed, staring up at the ceiling.

I may never know the answers to all my questions.

Twenty-Two

After college graduation, I move back to L.A. with a new set of eyes. I find myself in a vacuum where no sound of comfort or sense of peace can penetrate. I float in darkness, vaguely aware of a light at a distance. I know that is where the others are. My mother, who chooses to keep herself so distant from me, and my father's life, which is so self-involved that he cannot hear me from inside his cocoon no matter how loudly I scream. I suffer a void of aloneness and abandonment. I have been imprisoned here since I was a child, suspended in this solitary, embryonic state.

I am a girl still witnessing, barely controlling her uncontrollable fury at the unfathomable neglect by the two people she needed most to guide and protect her in life. No one acknowledges the reasons behind my wrath, only that I am angry.

I will be compelled forever by my formative years and the roles I developed as a child. The loss and profound emptiness resulting from my childhood will eat away at me for years. It is as though someone is chewing away at my stomach until there is nothing left but raw flesh and eventually I fade away.

I struggle to get along with my mother, wondering if our relationship will ever deepen beyond the surface. I attempt to have real conversations with my father but he is trapped in a bubble that no one can puncture, not even his own father. I want nothing more than to reconnect with my sister but she is too wrapped up in her own life. Nothing works. So I give up trying to live by the straight and narrow, trying to forget, to live and let live. Because frankly it is bullshit.

It is disgusting how the world has to lie to us.

Today I wake up in my own bed, in my own life, with my own choices.

It is only by being on my own, purged of any emotional or financial help from my parents, that I am able to see myself and my past as it truly was. So many things had been taken from me—my confidence, my self-esteem, my trust, and survival skills. It was a poor exchange for the material luxuries I was given.

By the millennium, I had moved into an apartment in Hollywood and began hosting high-stakes poker games in upscale private cigar bars in Beverly Hills. I filled my life with the company of old-school Beverly Hills high rollers, those who partied with Frank Sinatra and Sammy Davis Jr. in their heyday, and with younger celebrities like Ben Affleck, Matt Damon, Leonardo DiCaprio, and Tobey McGuire. I had met some of the men at local home games, some through my father, and others at Mansion parties. I enjoyed being around them, laughing with them about the women in their lives as they offhandedly gamble away mountains of chips.

At night, I ventured into nightclubs and after-hours spots,

where I found the voices of other lost souls trying to escape memories of their own past.

It is then that I began to write.

These bars are a combination of emergency room and performance-art stage. To me, they felt like home. I was surrounded by fabulous superstars in short shorts and Spandex, grungy guys in ski caps, and skinny girls sporting tinted big-framed sunglasses and colored fur scarves. They inhaled whip-its while jumping up and down to remixes of Depeche Mode. The sweat of the recklessness was provocative and biting.

No one can touch us, even if they tried.

Time passes and I find myself frequenting the Mansion again, looking for something to ease the emptiness that has become my constant companion. The Mansion is still a fable of sorts, an enchanting kingdom where I can escape and become lost in adventures.

Hef and my father are out on the town frequenting all the hot spots. They show up for all my birthday bashes, making rowdy entrances with an entourage of blond beauties. Hef's house parties for young, hip Hollywood are still the talk of the town. It seems a whole new generation of celebrities have come out to play.

My thirtieth birthday approaches and I decide to spice it up and celebrate at Stray, a trendy hipster/bisexual bar in Hollywood. I invite my parents, my sister, and Hef, as well as a hundred of my closest friends.

My mother stands stiffly beautiful in the corner, sipping a glass of champagne, overwhelmed by the clubgoers and appalled by their lax attitude on undefined sexuality. I appreciate her appearance, considering her feelings on club scene decadence and promiscuity. Mom finds the whole atmosphere so socially embarrassing that she eventually starts pretending it never occurred.

After college, when I told my parents I was bisexual, my father shrugged while my mother dropped me off at a post-trauma center for rehabilitation. Though it will be voiced as disapproval, her guilt for not saving her daughter will live inside her forever.

On the dance floor, my friends and I dance and sip martinis, listening to Eminem as Savannah runs up to me.

"You're not going to believe this, Jennifer."

"What?"

"The idiot dyke bouncer won't let Hef in. She has no idea who he is. He and Dad have been waiting outside for twenty minutes!"

"Oh my God," I laugh.

I quickly run downstairs and yell at the fat chick bouncer with a bad boy's haircut, and apologize to Dad and Hef. They are both smiling, as amused at the situation as I am.

In the confusion of the moment, I don't take note that my father is wearing a huge orange Afro wig. Hef's in his silk pajamas as usual.

Dad smiles. "We're off to a costume party after this."

They enter the bar, followed by Hef's entourage: fifteen eye-catching girls in micro-miniskirts and high heels, mostly blondes, all sexy, and most important, all here for my birthday.

A family again.

Along with Hef's usual group comes the Court Jester. The Jester follows Hef around with a notepad. He approaches attractive girls, gets their phone numbers, and encourages them to send a head shot to the Mansion. If they pass round one of the inspections, the girls are invited to attend every Sunday's Fun in the Sun party, where they'll be casually screened for Playmate potential and/or poolside decor.

As the larger Mansion parties roll around, hundreds of girls send in photographs with hopes of being invited. They are so concerned about getting in that some of the girls send in shots of themselves in various positions, making out with other girls, with sex toys—anything to catch Hef's eye.

"What some people will do to get into a party," Hef will chuckle as my father hands him more pornographic pictures of random girls he met in strip joints no one's heard of.

Mom's face cringes as the Playmates surround her. There's an assortment of air kisses and communal laughter.

My parents are now standing on either side of Hef as everything in my life converges in this one moment.

"I think it's time for me to go," says Mom.

"Are you sure you don't want to stay for a bunny lap dance?" I joke.

"I do enough charity work, honey. Feel free to send any of them to one of my treatment centers." Mom smiles. We hug good night and again I find myself never wanting to let go. Nothing will make up for the years we lost, and despite all the time that has passed, I yearn for the love that only a mother can give, as if I were still a child.

Dad, Hef, and his girls leave shortly thereafter. I pass on meeting them at the costume party. Instead, my high school friends and I close the bar down and then head over to Amber's parents' house in the Canyon for after-hours.

Hef 's huge birthday bash at the Mansion rolls around, and for the first time in my life I miss it because I am out of town. When I get back, I stop by Bar Fly, an old-school Hollywood bar, as the week of his birthday festivities continues. I bring Tyler, my new twenty-four-year-old bisexual girlfriend whom I met while she was having lunch at the Polo Lounge with her family. She unlocks a hunger, a desire I never thought I could feel again. Our heated intensity reminds me of the passionate affair and lasting seduction I experienced as a teenager with Kendall more than a decade ago. Tyler seems to trigger all the unfulfilled craving and broken love I never received as a child.

The place is packed as Hef and his entourage make a grandiose entrance with ten bodyguards and an assortment of Playmates he chose to bring for the night. They are quickly ushered behind a roped-off section. Cameras are flashing as out-of-towners and star-fuckers ooh and ahh over Hef and his girls, asking him for autographs and pictures while security holds them back.

The security guards lift the velvet rope as Tyler and I walk up to Hef to wish him a happy birthday and give him a gift. My father is nowhere to be found. Guys and girls are hitting on us, trying to gain entrance, offering us money to get closer to Hef. Tyler turns to me and asks where my father is.

"I don't know," I tell her.

The Jester comes in with his own entourage of young beauties trailing behind. "Hey, Jennifer, where's Doc?" he asks.

"I talked to him earlier and he said he was going to a party in the Hills and then he would come by. But, you know, he's never on time." I see Hef looking at his watch and overhear the Jester calling my father on his cell.

"We're all here. Hurry your ass up," the Jester says.

An hour later, there is still no sign of my father. Hef leaves with a disappointed look on his face as he makes a grand exit to his limo waiting out front.

Five minutes later, guess who walks in, scattered, with some dumb brunette hooker.

"Look who finally arrived," I say. "You just missed Hef."

"Oh shit," my father says as he gets on his cell. "I need to get a hold of him. I have his birthday present right next to me." He gives both my girlfriend and me a kiss hello as he introduces us to Hef's birthday present.

"What do you think of her?" he asks as I shrug, clearly unimpressed by his choice of girls these days.

"Not much. Does she speak English?" The girl half smiles at me as if I didn't just insult her.

"Are those real?" my father asks, staring at Tyler's perfectly shaped breasts. She ignores him and proceeds to ask if she can hunt for eggs at Hef's Easter party the next day.

"Only if you wear your hair in pigtails," he responds. She ignores him again as she can feel he is clearly flirting.

"I have to leave. I have to go to the Mansion to drop off his gift," Dad tells us.

"So soon? You just got here," Tyler responds politely.

"Sweetie, call me when you're done with Jennifer," he says. "You won't need to be on any list if you're with me. Oh, and don't forget to wear your pigtails tomorrow." I roll my eyes. Some things will never change.

The next day, Tyler and I spend Easter Sunday at Hef's. As we're driving past the back gate to the Mansion, two people jump out of their parked car, waving us down. They're holding plastic cups in their hands as they approach my car asking for directions to the Mansion. I quickly realize it is my father with his ex-girlfriend, who at one point had a restraining order against him. They are slurring their words, scratching, unable to stand up straight, or focus on anything. They're giggling like children and appear extremely loaded. I don't know what they are on but it is definitely not just alcohol.

"Hi, Dad. What are you doing?"

"We can't find the Mansion," he says, using his cell phone to call Hef.

"Dad, you've been coming here thirty years and you still don't know where the Mansion is?"

"If you don't have the information I need then move on," he orders, directing us with his hand as he presses redial on his cell phone to figure out where the hell he is. We drive off twenty feet to the front gate, laughing as we approach the entrance.

"There are like a hundred things wrong with that picture," I say to Tyler, too embarrassed to express what I am really thinking or feeling. "Please excuse my father," I say, not wanting to get into it.

We pull up to the front gate as a voice coming from the Rock welcomes us.

"Morning, Jennifer," one of the security guards says through the microphone. "Just bringing one friend up with you today?"

"Yes, sweetie."

"By the way have you seen your father? Hef is wondering where he is," the voice asks.

"I think he's lost," I tell him as the gates open. Tour buses pass by as we head up the driveway that is covered with colorful Easter decor.

We arrive at the front door and are greeted by Tommy Lee and Pamela Anderson, a former Playmate, who are standing with their two little sons holding Easter baskets.

"Hey, guys. How's it going?" Tommy asks.

"Why are you leaving so soon?"

"We've been here for hours. The kids are tired," Pamela answers. We kiss them good-bye and go through the front door, passing Fred Durst along the way. We walk inside and instantly, it's like I'm a kid again. There's a sense of timelessness. It's like a divorced child's Christmas for that one special morning a year when everything is warm and inviting.

Tyler and I head to the backyard and our eyes light up. A huge carnival is going on. Billy goats and other farm animals are in pens. Balloons, trolleys of popcorn, and ice cream are everywhere. Kids jump up and down on a very large trampoline. We watch as Hef autographs a brand-new toy car for the winner of the Easter-egg hunt.

Strolling past the buffet area, we notice James Caan, Smokey Robinson, Jeff Goldblum, and Bill Maher, surrounded by tons of Playmates. We fill our plates with hamburgers and French fries. Then we sit on a lounge chair in front of the roped-off section watching flamingos walk by.

Looking around at all the memorable faces I feel myself begin to relax like I haven't in years. What I was hearing and seeing around me was so absolutely familiar, so real, so much of what I know, that it was like breathing fresh air again. I felt like I had come home and many of the women I had known since the eighties were like sisters. As I overhear them talk about different parties and people they know, it was like listening to my own story.

Old-school Playmates, butlers, security guards, and Mansion regulars ask where I've been, why I don't come up as often anymore.

"I've reduced my Mansion drop bys to only the big parties," I tell them. But then I stop to think about why I don't frequent the Mansion as much, and the truth is there is a difference between now and the wide-eyed delight I experienced as a child.

I look around at all the tan skinny girls who are still in their early twenties and I begin to feel the wrinkles underneath my eyes, the stresses that go along with everyday responsibilities.

Sometimes it's hard to believe that my two very different teenage lives were part of one lifetime. I cannot allow myself to become lost in never-never land again, to escape reality to such a degree that I can no longer differentiate between the two worlds.

Yet I continue to gravitate toward it because it was once my home, a place where I felt most comfortable and complete.

I notice Hef sitting alone behind the roped-off secured section next to the pool. There is a security guard standing in front of the velvet rope. Hef is waiting for my father to begin playing backgammon. Tyler and I walk up to say Happy Easter to Hef as the security guard asks me if I know where my father is. I finally tell them he is outside the back gate with one of his ex-girlfriends. I overhear security guards on walkie-talkies communicating with each other as they search for my father.

"I think he's lost." I overhear security guards on walkie-talkies, communicating with each other as they search for my father.

"Jennifer says he may be off the grounds, near the back gate." There is silence as another security guard responds.

"Is the Doc off the property? Copy?"

"Jennifer says he is by the back gate. Mr. Hefner is looking for him to begin playing backgammon. Please find him immediately." The security guards "Roger" and "Over and out" each other.

We reach Hef, who is sitting underneath a yellow umbrella. He taps the backgammon table, eager to play, as Tyler says, "Jennifer has taught me how to play backgammon and now I'm hooked," she says, shaking me out of my thoughts.

"Well, I guess if you're going to be hooked, it's better to be hooked on backgammon," Hef says as my father runs through the backyard half dressed.

"There's Doc," we overhear security guards say through walkie-talkies.

He appears so dazed that all the security guards are laughing. His shirt is off and his belt buckle is hanging undone. He races toward us. "I'm not hired help!" he yells at me as if I have something to do with his erriatic behavior.

"Sorry, Hef, a girl was in dire need," Dad says as he stares Tyler up and down. "Nice tits," he mumbles under his breath. "What can I say? She wanted me," he tells Hef (regarding the girl in need).

"She must've been confused," Hef says. My father grabs a Cuban cigar in a long silver container out of his duffle bag, which is filled with bottles of prescription pills. "Here, batteries aren't included," he says, handing it to me. Tyler looks at the cigar, confused.

"Do you care to inspect it yourself, little girl?" my father asks Tyler and she turns away, embarrassed. We get up and walk back down the cobblestone pathway to the bar.

One of the security guards whispers to me, "You're father is a crackup. He comes into the pantry every day looking for deodorant, telling us he forgot to put it on." He shakes his head. "You should take a picture of him and send it to him on Father's Day saying, 'Thanks for embarrassing me.'" The security guard chuckles and his laughter echoes through me.

"Your father reminds me of Ozzy Osbourne," Tyler says,

laughing. We laugh, but inside I am very sad. A fog surrounds him now. He has become a shell of the man who in many ways is a true genius.

He graduated Phi Beta Kappa from Dartmouth, my grandfather continues to remind me to this day. He can diagnose anyone, discover problems that other doctors often overlook. He has an instinct about people and their illnesses. It separates him from everyone else. He is respected and rewarded not only for his knowledge but also for saving lives. People turn their cheek and ignore his behavior because of his charm and quick wit. No one knows what to say about it, so they don't say anything. They simply acknowledge he is Hef's right-hand man, a medical genius who enjoys himself a little too much, and they leave it at that.

It was as if I was now seeing him clearly, not only through my eyes but also through the eyes of others, and the image was not pretty.

My deep sorrow for him and who he has become affects me in ways I cannot explain. It's painful to watch the downfall of your hero. In the eyes of my youth, he could do no wrong. As a child, I recall standing next to my father, watching him with reverent eyes. He was able to walk between worlds, calmly cross lines that most people never dreamed of crossing.

I cannot reach my father now. We have grown apart. Though he loves me, our language is a distant dialogue filled with years of forgotten moments. I doubt if he recalls the tremors I still feel from the past. I want him to admit how he brainwashed me to view the world with an untrusting eye. I want him to take responsibility for his behavior, the damaging words he fed me like a daily poison, but that day never comes.

I am haunted every night by the unresolved horrors; the unanswered questions are calling out to me and I cannot unscramble them. I cannot face them. My heart races and nothing will slow it down. Thoughts spin out of control as voices from the past begin to resurface. Fear and anxiety are such a part of my life now. They are my permanent escort, my eternal consolation prize.

I'm having a mid-thirties breakdown.

It is impossible to miss the message of my childhood: emptiness inside stemming from irreconcilable parental neglect. My parents thought it was over once I became of age, once they were free from responsibility. But they can never erase their unfortunate mistake. I wonder if I will ever swim free from the anxiety that binds me to my childhood.

That's when things get pharmaceutical. Once a youth medicated for survival, now I self-medicate to ease the mental noise that never ceases, never eases up on me. I seek solace in the chemical courage of forbidden pleasures, trying to comfort the demons that reared up and threaten to envelop me. I'm on a diet of antidepressants and anti-anxiety meds. I have succumbed to prayer and massive doses of Klonopin. I'm on the fast track to nowhere. The wonderful thing about anti-anxiety pills is that I can be at the epicenter of my own personal tragedy and I don't even know it.

I leave the Easter party and stop by my pharmacist's house, a few blocks from the Mansion, to pick up the bottle of Zoloft he left waiting for me outside his door.

After a falling-out with Michael Jackson's plastic surgeon in the late nineties, Dad relocated his office and now shares office space in Beverly Hills with the newest and hottest plastic surgeon of the millennium.

I stop by for a botox injection. The reception area is high-tech with flat-screen television monitors covering every wall. Samples of various types of silicone implants are on display for women to touch. Video monitors run footage of before and after pictures of topless women.

I recognize ex-Playmates and many well-known actresses on

their cell phones. Out of nowhere, a blonde screams "Jennifer!" as I'm signing in at the front desk. At first I have no idea who she is until she says, "I'm a friend of your father's. Do you remember me? Your father and I had dinner at the Ivy a few weeks ago." I vaguely recall running into my father and a soap opera actress while they were having dinner with a few friends. He was obsessing over some dumb Russian nineteen-year-old.

"I'm on the phone with your father right now! He's yelling at me because he's running an hour late and expects me to wait!" the actress laughs, and I attempt to fake a smile.

Two seconds later, the reception door opens and three cute young girls rush into Dad's waiting room giggling, asking to see Dr. Feel Good. They are told to leave their head shots and naked pictures of themselves at the front desk.

On their way out, I overhear them say, "I pray to be invited to the Halloween party. I heard the list was closed days ago."

The other girl says he's "known around town as the guy to get you in at the last minute."

Dad finally arrives at his office and he gives the actress a wet kiss on the lips.

"You're next to see the Doc, Ms. Dunkin Donut."

"Last night somebody told me you were dead," the actress tells my father.

"And you still kept your appointment?" he asks.

"Hi, Dad, remember me?"

"Have we met?" he looks at me through beady eyes.

"Very funny, ha, ha. What about all the other people waiting?" I ask.

"Those aren't people, those are models," he tells me as we go into his office.

I immediately pour myself a cup of coffee as strong as heroin as his secretary's voice comes in over the intercom, announcing that Hef is on line two. Dad picks up the phone.

"What? I'm extremely busy and important," he says with a

smile. "Okay, fine, send me an embarrassingly large limo with a driver and a hooker, and I'll be there in ten minutes," he chuckles and hangs up. "Call me shallow," he shrugs as he quickly examines the actress. "You're fine," he tells her. "Lose ten pounds and make an appointment in two weeks," he says as he quickly gathers all his scattered papers and throws more bottles of prescription pills into a duffel bag.

"You can't leave. Don't you have to work? I ask.

"I am working. What's wrong with you? I'm being paid to treat and undress ten gorgeous Playmates at the Mansion. Which would you choose?" he says sternly, exiting his office in a mad dash through the side door with his stethoscope dangling around his neck.

I grab a bottle of Valium and run after him.

It's Halloween at the Mansion. As I walk along the property, I feeling that magical pull into the familiar world of lingerie and glitter. The ultimate playground for consulting adults.

A secret society.

A game with no rules; a place where everyone avoids the truth yet continues to search for it in places where they will never find it; diluted versions of what is real.

I am back where I started.

On the front lawn are stone tombstones covering the grounds. A fog machine pumps billows of white smoke, casting a dreamy haze in the air. It's an eerie feeling as the names of Hef's ex-girlfriends become apparent on the tombstones. On the outside of the castle, the words "House of Hefenstein" are projected onto an enormous screen with white spotlights with lightning bolts reflecting off the sides.

Oversize monsters pop out from behind bales of hay and scare everyone. Huge tents have been erected and turned into haunted houses. The atmosphere is festive, campy, and over the top. It feels like an amusement park.

Television monitors line the stage and dance floor, playing old black-and-white horror movies. The DJ spins hip-hop and trance over the speckled dance floor. It's another raging party and I'm rolling on ecstasy in a SWAT team vest, fishnets, Versace heels, and a toy Uzi strapped across my waist.

Someone in a gorilla suit asks me where the buffet table is. We make some small talk and I point him in the right direction. Later, I see him eating finger sandwiches, his mask removed: it's Mick Jagger.

I wave to Ben Affleck as he and Jared Leto, Justin Timberlake, Leonardo DiCaprio, and Tobey McGuire dash by in baseball jerseys, white pants with kneepads, and black makeup underneath their eyes. Batgirl, Tarzan, vampires, and women dressed as young schoolgirls prowl around the property exuding openness and sexual freedom.

I look around at all the familiar faces.

I smile when I see Hef. His spirit and enthusiasm still amaze me. I make sure to walk over to thank him and kiss him hello.

Hours later, I'm in the game room with Tori Spelling and Stephen Dorff. I play a quick game of Foosball with Thora Birch and then waltz into the blue room, where I find girls snorting coke off some guy's bare chest. I am speechless for a moment because their high-pitched squealing noises are beyond annoying.

Out of nowhere, someone pounds on the door. "Security," a deep voice announces. I hide out of habit. One of the girls stops sniffing long enough to open the door while I duck behind the curtain.

"We have to keep the door unlocked. We've had some complaints of rape," the security guard informs us, leaving the door wide open as he leaves. This place has become so strict over the years.

These days, background checks are done on all guests attending the parties. Mansion regulars and old-time Playmates with plastic smiles are shuttled in from a nearby parking lot where check-in tables are stationed with alphabetized names. A mandatory photo ID is required before one receives a Playboy wristband. Security guards check for wristbands before, during, and after the five-minute shuttle ride to the Mansion. Fire marshals, paramedics, and security guards with walkie-talkies line the perimeter of the property. I constantly feel like I'm being watched. Unlike in the seventies and eighties, drugs are not seen in public, so people sneak into bathrooms to indulge discreetly in their addiction of choice. Though safety measures and precautions are taken, the Mansion is still the most free-spirited, sexually liberated environment around.

The familiar faces beg me to get water. It seems our drymouth has taken full affect. I grab handfuls of water bottles from the mini refrigerator in the game room and say hello to Owen Wilson, who is lounging on the couch.

I return to the X-Zone (the blue room), where the three girls are now naked under the sheets. They are kissing one another as one of the girls pulls out an eighteen-inch strap-on vibrator and starts fucking the other girl from behind.

"This must be your lucky night," I say to the guy who is fingering the other two girls at the same time.

People are walking in and out of the room as if it's no big deal.

One of the girls rubs against me and I pull away feeling claustrophobic. "What's wrong with you? I thought you love this shit," one of the girls I vaguely recognize says to me.

"That was before I was legal. But I hear orgies are back," I say, slipping off the bed as my discomfort level peaks.

"You're boring. Go away," some naked Asian skank on the floor says to me, like I'm the asshole who's ruining their little pussy party.

"I may not speak Chinese, but I'm pretty sure the words for 'gay porn' are universal," I say, kicking her in the shin on my way out.

I'm too old for this shit. I close the door on the live entertainment.

I then meet up with my sister, who is wearing a Trashy lingerie police officer uniform, short black skirt and five-inch Manolo Blahniks.

"Do I look fat?" she asks.

"No. You look beautiful," I tell her, knowing nothing I say will ever make the mantra in our heads go away.

I will become sickened by my parents' obsession with weight and the dichotomy they represent: my father helps people starve themselves while my mother counsels those who are starving.

One daughter will eat to fill the void, while the other one won't eat at all, hoping love may come along and save her.

It will be years before I can acknowledge my emotional transaction: not of love but of rage: my rage over never receiving the kind of emotional support, love, and guidance I needed so desperately to survive. The effects of my childhood warfare are so powerful I disguise myself behind a mask, a wall so thick I learn to keep everyone at a distance.

I'm on a desperate search for drama. Our feet sink into oversize pillows as we waltz around the tented backyard. I kiss the twin glam Playmates hello.

"How do you know them?" my sister asks as we make our way to the outdoor bar passing Cameron Diaz, Britney Spears, and the "hot" Paris Hilton along the way.

We make loops around the maze of celebrities. Sarah Jessica Parker and Mini Me are surrounded by tall naked women in body paint. I hug and kiss a few Playmates and throw air kisses to Tony Curtis, who whizzes by. Anthony Robbins has two blondes, one on each arm. When he kisses them his entire mouth envelops their face. I tell him I have all his tapes but he doesn't seem too interested.

A compilation of Dr. Dre and Eminem blares through the speakers as Savannah and I stare at video monitors running footage from previous Mansion parties. We watch ourselves in a few blurbs, faced with the uniqueness of our childhood.

I overhear my sister talking to one of the Playmates.

"Ask Jennifer, she's Dad's daughter. I'm my mother's."

I pull Savannah aside, more annoyed than hurt.

"Why do you continue putting us into separate categories? It's like you revel in my mistakes from the past," I tell her.

"You are so insecure, it's criminal. Maybe that's why you fit in so well," she snickers, looking around at the Hollywood scene she has grown to despise.

"You're fine so long as Mom favors you. The moment you detect her and me getting close you move in and scapegoat me as the outcast of the family."

"The consummate victim. You dwell on it. I'm leaving. I don't even know why I came." Savannah takes off in a huff.

I look away, knowing we are still playing out the split in our family. We both know things will never be as they once were. One moment we are sisters, laughing and playing, the next moment we are two women standing on opposite sides of the fence.

I think of when we were kids, trying to figure out the day she became a woman instead of a child. She is a stranger to me now. I look over at the waterfall and remember us as kids taking turns jumping off. I think back on a time when we enjoyed the simple things in life like hopscotch, water puddles, sharing an ice cream cone.

A time when we were happy.

I hear Limp Bizkit scream, "Do you know where you are?" Where am I? I think to myself. My palms are wet. I tell myself everything would be okay if I could just separate the present from the past. Maybe my thoughts are creating my reality.

I go after my sister and find her in the valet line. I look down, profoundly saddened by the loss of not having grown up with her.

"Here I am your older sister and I don't feel like I've been there for you as much as I should've been. Sometimes it's like we're not even sisters," I tell her through a well of guilt.

"We're sisters." She puts her arm through mine.

"Sisters are supposed to have a mom and dad, but you have a mom and I have a dad."

"It's weird, there will always be a part of me that wants to fit into Dad's world," she says, looking up at the gray stone castle. "But it's not who I am. I don't know why I keep trying," Savannah confesses.

"I know what you mean. I still feel on the outside of Mom's world. I guess we both lost out on a parent."

We look at each other. Two very different sisters.

"I want us to be close again, like we once were, when we were little," I say, sincerely.

"It's never going to be like that. We were kids then." Tears fill my eyes when she says this. They are always just under the surface when it comes to my sister.

Savannah leaves and things are never the same between us.

I rejoin the party, bumping into Tommy, a Mansion regular, who puts his arm around Hef and boasts, "Hef, do you know who this is? This is Jennifer Saginor!" he shouts and I am amused only because I know Tommy is wasted.

Hef looks at Tommy and then at me.

"Of course I know Jennifer. She grew up here," Hef replies confidently and a huge sense of relief overcomes me.

Hef's acknowledgment of my childhood is strangely meaningful.

As I stand there, I realize that Hef's the one person who never wronged me, never hurt me, and never treated me with anything less than absolute care. He allowed me to be a child in his midst.

These thoughts are interrupted by some slut who slurs, "What ever happened to Dr. Feel Good? I used to get all my shit from your father back in the eighties, and now he won't prescribe shit."

I shrug, moving past her.

Someone cracks open a bottle of Cristal as a size-zero naked blonde drenched in body paint passes a tray of Absolut Jell-O shots. I down a few, peering around as the Jester jots down a hot girl's phone number on Hef's notepad. I laugh to myself, asking Hef who all these new girls are.

"I have no idea." He smiles warmly and then asks if I've seen the crazy doctor.

And then I do.

A man dressed in a red devil suit, complete with tail and pitchfork, reaches out to hug me. It's him. He's wearing one of his outrageous trademark hats. This one resembles Dr. Seuss' because it's three feet tall with red and white stripes.

"What's with the hat?" I ask my father.

Dad shrugs. "It's Halloween. I can do what I want."

"As if Halloween makes a difference."

"That's true," he says, looking around at all the gorgeous tan beauties, "Life is great if you're like Hef and me."

"It's paradise . . . ," Hef says, singing along to a classic tune.

"We're like Peter Pan," Dad confirms, "We never get old!"

Hef chuckles as a young blond pulls him away. He sings "Lollipop, lollipop . . ."

"What's her name?" I ask.

"I don't know any of their names," Hef smiles, being whisked off.

"Names are irrelevant," my father chimes in. "All you need to know is that the hotter they are, the more expensive they are."

Unless one really understood the pattern of everyday life, it is difficult for people outside the inner circle to comprehend it.

I adjust my father's hat, which leans to the side, and smile at him because I know he loves me and I love him. We've had some crazy times. Times I'll never forget.

I feel a kind of an odd understanding for my father, something I have not felt before. I am beginning to see the face of a much sadder man.

A man who sacrificed his identity to live in the shadow of another.

"It's all a distraction," he says as conflicting emotions run through me.

"Pretty girls were always your downfall."

"What matters, what's always mattered, is that you are taken care of, Jennifer. If I had to do it again, I'd make sure you knew that," Dad says humbly. We stand there for a long time saying nothing, just silent, comfortable with each other as a father and daughter should be.

So much has been said between my parents and me over the years, but it doesn't matter. In the end, the ways in which we betrayed each other aren't relevant anymore. My parents may never be who I want them to be. I may never be loved the way I want to be. My scars may never go away. My parents may never live outside their realm of self-involvement. But I will always long for a time when we can be close again. It's a secret type of longing, like an old lover you can't get out of your head. My parents' spirit will always be with me. Like a dream I will always have. Maybe one day it will be our time again. And when that day comes, I will feel at last that they forgive me, as I do them.

Perhaps my freedom will finally come when I stop hoping for a different childhood, different parents.